Pricing the Priceless Child

PRICING THE PRICELESS CHILD

The Changing Social Value of Children

Viviana A. Zelizer

Basic Books, Inc., Publishers   New York

Chapter 4 appeared in a slightly different form in "The Price and Value of Children: The Case of Children's Insurance," *American Journal of Sociology* 86 (March 1981): 1036–56. University of Chicago Press. Copyright © 1981 University of Chicago.

Library of Congress Cataloging in Publication Data

Zelizer, Viviana A. Rotman.
   Pricing the priceless child.

   Bibliography: p. 229
   Includes index.
   1. Children—Economic aspects—United States—History.
2. Child rearing—United States—Costs. 3. Children—
Employment—United States. 4. Children—United States—
Public opinion—History. 5. Public opinion—United States
—History. 6. Social values. I. Title. II. Social
value of children.
HQ792.U5Z45 1985   305.2'0973   84–45302
ISBN 0–465–06325–X (cloth)
ISBN 0–465–06326–8 (paper)

To Bernard Barber,

my teacher and friend

CONTENTS

ACKNOWLEDGMENTS

ONE of the pleasures of finishing a book is finally being able to translate private feelings of gratitude and affection into a public statement of acknowledgment. I thank Bernard Barber, to whom this book is dedicated, for helping me so much with invaluable advice and inspiring me with the excellence of his own scholarship. Other friends and colleagues provided encouragement and important ideas. Although I did not always follow their suggestions, I always benefited from their comments. I am grateful to Harry C. Bredemeier, Jonathan Cole, Sigmund Diamond, Glen H. Elder, Jr., Irving Louis Horowitz, Jacob Mincer, and David J. Rothman. Barbara Laslett gave intelligent and incisive criticism, which allowed me to interpret my materials better. Michael B. Katz offered many important insights and Sarane Spence Boocock showed me new ways of thinking about childhood and research on children. Martin Kessler, my editor, contributed his expert guidance and valuable ideas. I am indebted to my research assistant, Mark Momjian, who was a great help even during his busy first year in law school.

Research for this book was generously supported by Barnard College and a Rockefeller Foundation Humanities Fellowship. I am also grateful to the National Endowment for the Humanities for a 1983 summer stipend for another project, *Money and Social Value*, whose theme partly overlaps with this book and its research.

This book would never have been written without the love and unique friendship of my mother. I also thank my husband, Jerry, and my son, Julian, for understanding and sharing so well the fun and trials of writing this project. Julian was a patient instructor of word processing. Elizabeth McGregor helped us with affection.

Pricing the Priceless Child

Introduction

THIS BOOK is about the profound transformation in the economic and sentimental value of children—fourteen years of age or younger—between the 1870s and the 1930s. The emergence of this economically "worthless" but emotionally "priceless" child has created an essential condition of contemporary childhood.

For in strict economic terms, children today are worthless to their parents. They are also expensive. The total cost of raising a child—combining both direct maintenance costs and indirect opportunity costs—was estimated in 1980 to average between $100,000 and $140,000. In return for such expenses a child is expected to provide love, smiles, and emotional satisfaction, but no money or labor. One 1976 comprehensive time-budget study of 1,300 white, two-parent families in Syracuse, New York, found that children between the ages of six and eleven contributed on the average three and a half hours a week to household tasks, while their mothers spent some fifty hours doing housework.[1] Even the few chores that children perform are more often justified as an educational experience for their own benefit than an expected contribution to the household division of labor. Asked by researchers, "Why do you ask your children to work?," three-quarters of the parents in a study of 790 families from Nebraska explained children's domestic chores as character building. Only twenty-two parents responded, "I need the help."[2] Money-making children, such as child actors or models, are considered an uncomfortable exception in our society; their parents are often suspected of callousness or greed.

Yet, children expect a regular income. While some "earn" their allowance by helping out around the house, many children, as *Parents Magazine* explains, receive it simply "in recognition of the fact that they are full members of the family."[3] After all, children must learn to spend their parents' money long before they begin to earn their own. Advertisers know it. As one prominent market-research firm points out, "there are 37 million children in the six to fourteen group [who] consume billions of dollars worth of goods and services every year."[4] Parents cannot even expect significant public support to raise these expensive young consumers. While in all other major industrial countries a system of family allowances grants children at least partial monetary value, in America income-transfer programs remain notoriously inadequate and mostly restricted to female-headed, single-parent households below a certain income level. Tax exemptions for children, on the other hand, benefit primarily high-income families.[5]

In a recent book, *Costs of Children,* the economist Lawrence Olson concludes, "That so many young couples still decide to have children attests to the nonmonetary benefits they expect to derive from their progeny." After all, as he points out, "in purely monetary terms, couples would be better off putting their money in a bank as a way of saving for their old age."[6] A national survey of the psychological motivations for having children confirms their predominantly sentimental value. Asked about "the advantages or good things about having children," the most common response was the desire for love and affection and the feeling of being a family.[7] A child is simply not expected to be useful. Significantly, in the many studies and articles written about the unequal distribution of household work, the roles of husbands and wives are examined, while the role of children is usually ignored.

In sharp contrast to contemporary views, the birth of a child in eighteenth-century rural America was welcomed as the arrival of a future laborer and as security for parents later in life. The economic value of children for agricultural families has been well documented by anthropologists. In many cultures, between the ages of five and seven, children assume a variety of work responsibilities—caring for younger children, helping with household work, or tending animals. In rural China today, for instance, researchers found children as young as five or six helping to feed the family fowl, clean the house, and prepare meals.[8]

By the mid-nineteenth century, the construction of the economically worthless child had been in large part accomplished among the American urban middle class. Concern shifted to children's education as the determinant of future marketplace worth. Far from relying on his child as old-age "insurance," the middle-class father began insuring his own life and setting up other financial arrangements such as trusts and endowments, to protect the unproductive child. As one well-to-do father explained in *Harper's Weekly,* in 1904, "We work for our children, plan for them, spend money on them, buy life insurance for their protection, and some of us even *save* money for them. This last tribute is the most affecting of all . . . saving, for our children's start in life . . . is evidence of serious self-denial. Profound must be the depths of affection that will induce a man to save money for others to spend. . . ."[9]

However, the economic value of the working-class child increased, rather than decreased in the nineteenth century. Rapid industrialization after the 1860s introduced new occupations for poor children, and according to the 1870 census about one out of every eight children was employed. Working-class urban families in the late nineteenth century depended on the wages of older children and the household assistance of younger ones. Child labor laws and compulsory education, however, gradually destroyed the class lag. By the 1930s, lower-class children joined their middle-class counterparts in a new nonproductive world of childhood, a world in which the sanctity and emotional value of a child made child labor taboo. To make profit out of children, declared Felix Adler in 1905, was to "touch profanely a sacred thing."[10] To be sure, child labor did not magically and totally vanish. In the 1920s and 1930s, some children under fourteen still worked in rural areas and in street trades. Moreover, the Great Depression temporarily restored the need for a useful child even in some middle-class households. But the overall trend was unmistakable. In the first three decades of the twentieth century, the economically useful child became both numerically and culturally an exception. Although during this period the most dramatic changes took place among the working class, the sentimentalization of child life intensified even among the already "useless" middle-class children.

How did the social valuation of children change so dramatically within a relatively short period of time? Why did the sentimental value of children's lives increase just when their contributions to the household disappeared? And what accounts for the curious paradox that the market price of an economically useless child far surpassed the money value of nineteenth-century useful child? By the 1930s, for example, childless couples were paying large sums of money to purchase a black market baby. In cases of accidental death, courts began to award increasingly large sums to compensate parents for the loss of their child.

The Price and Value of Children:
A Sociological Approach

Although the shift in children's value from "object of utility" to object of sentiment is indisputable, historian Joseph F. Kett notes that a "precise characterization of this change has remained elusive."[11] The sociological impact has never been systematically explored. Indeed, since the 1930s, the study of children has been predominantly psychological in orientation. The sociology of childhood remains a surprisingly undeveloped specialty. Significantly, the latest edition of the *International Encyclopedia of the Social Sciences* has only two listings under child: child development and child psychiatry. Research on the value of children has been dominated by psychologists, economists, and demographers, all similarly concerned with parental motivation for childbearing and its relation to fertility patterns and population policy. For example, the recently completed cross-national Value of Children project interviewed national samples of married women under forty and their husbands in seven countries in order to identify the perceived psychological satisfactions and costs of having children. According to one participating researcher, the investigation "is seen as important for predicting changes in fertility patterns and for affecting the motivation for fertility."[12] But, although these studies contribute to the understanding of children's value, they remain limited by a primarily individualistic and utilitarian framework and by an ahistorical perspective. They produce organized lists of children's costs and benefits, but largely ignore the cultural and social determinants of such international inventories.[13]

Microeconomic theories of fertility also focus on decision making by rational, utility-maximizing parents. From this perspective, the demand for children is essentially dictated by their relative price and by income. Accordingly, as soon as children ceased to be profitable as economic investments, fertility declined and children became expensive consumption goods; their changing price determined their new value. The perceived utility of educated children outweighed the immediate benefits of their contribution to the family income. Thus, in the economic model, what matters are the choices made by individuals on the basis of their own assessment of the costs and benefits involved in the various alternatives. As with psychological theories, changes in the cultural and social context, which shape individual choice, are not examined.

American historians, for the most part, seem to be more intrigued with the social creation of adolescence than the changing status of younger pre-adolescent children. Existing historical interpretations of childhood are psychologically oriented or else focus mostly on the impact of structural change, in particular, changes in the economic system. From this perspective, the productive value of children disappeared with the success of industrial capitalism at the turn of the century, which required a skilled, educated labor force.[14]

Changes in the family are also linked with the shift in children's value. In his pioneer study, *Centuries of Childhood*, Philippe Ariès argues that the "discovery" of childhood as a separate stage of life in the sixteenth and seventeenth centuries in Europe, was a measure of the growing importance of family life: "The concept of the family . . . is inseparable from the concept of childhood. The interest taken in childhood . . . is only one form, one particular expression of this more general concept—that of the family."[15] In nineteenth-century America, the increasing differentiation between economic production and the home transformed the basis of family cohesion. As instrumental ties weakened, the emotional value of all family members—including children—gained new saliency.[16] In particular, the sentimentalization of childhood was intimately tied to the changing world of their mothers. The increasing domestication of middle-class women in the nineteenth century, as Carl Degler points out in *At Odds*, "went hand in hand with the new conception of children as precious." The changing value of children, argues Degler, served women's interests: "Exalting the child went hand in hand with exalting the domestic role of woman; each reinforced the other while together they raised domesticity within the family to a new and higher level of respectability."[17] The specialization of women into expert full-time motherhood intensified at the turn of the century, spreading (in ideal if not always in practice) to the working class. The creation of the family wage—a salary which would support a male wage earner and his dependent family—in the early twentieth century, was partly intended to implement the "cult of true womanhood" and "true" childhood among the working class. Feminist analysis suggests the collaboration of capitalism with patriarchy in this process:

Capitalism needed a healthy, well-disciplined, and well-trained current and future labor force. Men in individual families needed to decrease competition with the large numbers of women and children working in the market (in the late nineteenth century); they also needed to have someone to take care of their household needs, especially children. The family wage helped ensure that it would be women who continued to perform these tasks.[18]

The precise nature of the relationship between changes in the economic roles of women and children, however, remains unclear and largely undocumented. One historian, for instance, suggests that the decline in child labor pushed mothers into the labor force between 1920 and 1940: "It is possible that wives and mothers moved into the labor force in unconscious response to the withdrawal of children."[19] Thus, rather than a new shared domesticity, there was a substitution of secondary wage earners in many working-class and lower middle-class families. Mothers took over children's work responsibilities, without, however, relinquishing their former household duties.

Historian Christopher Lasch presents a very different, and more polemical interpretation of changes in family and child life. He sees the removal of children from the labor market as part of a general effort by Progressive reformers to remove children from family influence, especially the immigrant family. Public policy contributed not to the sentimentalization of domestic ties, but to their deterioration, specifically through the appropriation of parental functions by new "agencies of socialized reproduction,"—educators, psychiatrists, social workers, penologists. Reformers, claims Lasch, "sought to re-move children from the influence of their families, which they also blamed for exploiting child labor, and to place the young under the benign influence of state and school."[20] The sacrali-zation of children, was in fact, their alienation from the home. It marked the beginning of the end of the family as a "haven in a heartless world."

Demographic theories, on the other hand, contend that the new emotional value of children is best explained by falling birth and mortality rates in the twentieth century. Philippe Ariès and Lawrence Stone, in a landmark study of the English family, suggest that in periods of high mortality parents protect themselves against the emotional pain of a child's death by remaining affectively aloof. From this perspective, it is "folly to invest too much emotional capital in such ephemeral be-ings."[21] The decline in early mortality, therefore, can be seen as an independent variable that encouraged "the deepening of emotional bonds" between parents and children.[22] A similar cost-benefit accounting explains why falling birthrates and smaller family size augment the emotional value of each individual child. Between the mid-nineteenth century and 1915, for instance, the annual birthrate for native whites dropped nearly 40 percent, from 42.8 to 26.2 per thousand. Fewer children made each child more precious. But the economic equation of longevity or scarcity with value remains highly speculative, as will be shown in Chapter 1. For instance, Demos submits that in seventeenth-century Plymouth a high death rate may have encouraged a special concern for and tenderness toward infants.[23]

This book focuses on one sociological dimension that has received little attention in the literature: the independent effect of cultural factors redefining the value of children in the United States.[24] I will argue that the expulsion of children from the "cash nexus" at the turn of the past century, although clearly shaped by profound changes in the economic, occupational, and family structures, was also part of a cultural process of "sacralization" of children's lives. The term sacralization is used in the sense of objects being invested with sentimental or religious meaning. While in the nineteenth century, the market value of children was culturally acceptable, later the new normative ideal of the child as an exclusively emotional and affective asset precluded instrumental or fiscal considerations. In an increasingly commercialized world, children were reserved a separate noncommercial place, *extra-commercium*. The economic and sentimental value of children were thereby declared to be radically incompatible. Only mercenary or insensitive parents violated the boundary by accepting the wages or labor contributions of a useful child. Properly loved children, regardless of social class, belonged in a domesticated, nonproductive world of lessons, games, and token money. It was not a simple process. At every step, working-class and middle-class advocates of a useful childhood battled the social construction of the economically useless child.

The first three chapters examine this dramatic change in the economic and sentimental value of children. Chapter 1 looks at changing attitudes toward the death of a child as one measure of the new sacred value of child life. At the turn of the century, as the protection of children's life and health emerged as a national priority, child death became a national disgrace. In particular, I look at public response to the accidental death of young children killed by streetcars and automobiles in the early decades of the twentieth century. Why did child death evoke different, more intense and organized reactions than similar adult deaths? How did children's life change as a result of the many efforts to save and protect them? What was the relationship between the collective magnification of child mourning and the new exaltation of children's sentimental worth?

Excluding sacred children from the world of work was a particularly difficult and controversial process. Chapter 2 turns to the extended struggle over child labor legislation between the 1870s and 1930s. What was the controversy about? Why was the useful child defended so vehemently? Redefining children's economic roles became an intricate task. Even the staunchest supporters of child labor legislation were unwilling to declare all forms of child work illegal or morally illegitimate. Chapter 3 examines the gradual differentiation between unacceptable forms of child labor and "good" child work. Why were certain kinds of occupations, such as newspaper delivery, exempted from child labor legislation? In particular, what accounts for the surprising paradox that many leading opponents of child labor became enthusiastic supporters of child actors? Besides attending school, what did formerly useful children do after they stopped working? As the occupational world of children changed, so did their relationship to money. Children stopped working just as the rise in consumerism and mass advertising created tantalizing new opportunities for spending. Parents, whether they could afford it or not, were expected to train children as expert consumers. A series of issues were raised: Should children receive an allowance? Should they "earn" it by helping out with housework or were they entitled to a free unearned income? Should parents regulate their children's finances?

Chapters 4, 5, and 6 look at three major institutions directly involved with the economic and sentimental valuation of child life: children's insurance; compensation for the wrongful death of children; and adoption and the sale of children. In the early twentieth century there were other new major institutions with profound influence in the life of children, such as the juvenile court system, but my focus is exclusively in the changing interaction between the price of a child and its sentimental value.[25] In this context, the term price, which has a variety of different technical and lay meanings, represents economic worth, as distinct from noneconomic determinants of value. Based on legal, commercial, or social welfare criteria, each of the institutions selected here attaches a price tag to a child's life or death. At the turn of the century, all three of these ledgers were revolutionized by the cultural redefinition of a child's place. How was a "priceless" child priced?

Chapter 4 investigates the issue of children's life insurance. Policies for children became a great commercial success in the late nineteenth century among the urban working class. Yet child-savers and their many supporters led more than eighty nationwide attempts to declare child insurance illegal. The controversy had little to do with issues of finance. It was a moral dispute created by the changing relationship between the price and value of children. If the new child was economically worthless but emotionally priceless, how could insurance companies determine his or her life-value? Its opponents condemned insurance as a mercenary extension of child labor; but its supporters hailed it as a sacred expense. What was the relationship between the sentimentalization of children and insuring child life? How did the insurance industry successfully market its controversial product?

Chapter 5 examines the changing criteria used by American courts to compensate parents for the accidental death of a child. Nineteenth-century civil courts relied on pragmatic monetary equations, irrespective of age or sex. In the case of children, the measure of damage was the lost value of their services less the cost of support. As children lost economic value, their death created a legal quandary: How could value be assigned if price were absent? The clash between economic legal principles and the sentimentalized view of childhood caused confusion in the courts and public outrage. Pricing the "priceless" child emerged as a unique form of emotional bookkeeping.

Chapter 6 studies the transformation in the "exchange" value of children. In the nineteenth-century boarding-out system, foster parents exchanged childcare for child labor. How did the creation of a "priceless" child affect substitute care arrangements? Older boys, for instance, were in great demand by nineteenth-century foster homes, but after the 1920s, adoptive parents were only interested in (and willing to wait several years for) a blue-eyed baby or a cute two-year-old curly-haired girl. What created the booming twentieth-century black market in babies? Why, for instance, were nineteenth-century mothers forced to pay to get rid of a baby but, by the 1930s, unwanted babies were selling for $1,000 or more?

The book will argue that the changing relationship between

the economic and sentimental value of children resulted in a unique pattern of valuation of child life in the United States. While in the nineteenth century economic criteria determined both the "surrender" value of children at death and their "exchange" value, the price of the twentieth-century child had to be set exclusively by its sentimental worth. Children's moral "pricelessness" shaped their economic price. Child-insurance policies, compensation awards, and the sale price of an adoptive child became unusual types of markets, regulated by noneconomic criteria. I will show how this exclusively emotional valuation had a profoundly paradoxical and poignant consequence: the increasing monetization and commercialization of children's lives. Today, bereaved parents receive cash compensation for the loss of their child's love and companionship; adoptive parents are willing to pay as much as $40,000 to buy an infant's smiles and tenderness. Thus, dollar values are routinely assigned to affection and pain, extending the market into supposedly unquantifiable sentiments. Yet this monetization of sentiment is never an ordinary business transaction. Its unusual characteristics, which this book explores, prove the uniqueness of pricing the priceless child.

Testing the Limits of the Market: The Case of Children

A broader sociological question this study addresses is, what is the general nature of the relationship between economic and noneconomic factors in social life, between price and value? How does the market deal with those aspects of society that are regulated by sentiment and value, not price? The dialogue between economists and sociologists on this issue has been limited and overpowered by a dominant economic ideology that is largely indifferent to the importance of noneconomic variables in determining how individuals or groups behave. In the nineteenth century, rational utility-maximization models presupposed a society regulated by the isolated pursuit of individual self-interest. Marxist historical materialism identified economic forces as key causal agents of all social change. At the turn of the century, two sociologists, Emile Durkheim and Max Weber, pioneered an intellectual revolution by empirically disputing market determinism. In his *Protestant Ethic*, Weber traced the independent impact of religious ideas, values, and attitudes on economic activities. Durkheim's writings demonstrated that the market could not be conceptualized as simple self-interest, but involved the "institution" of the contract. This "non-contractual element" regulated types of socially approved contracts as well as the expected behavior of the contracting parties, independent from their self-interest. Reacting against the prevalent economic ideology, Durkheim and Weber stressed the role of nonutilitarian, nonmaterial social forces. Theirs was an important attempt to integrate the economic and noneconomic dimensions of social life.

But, as two later pioneers of sociological thought, Talcott Parsons and Neil Smelser, recognized half a century later in *Economy and Society*, the potential synthesis of economic and sociological approaches never materialized. Instead, with improved techniques and different theoretical models, economic thought conquered contemporary research. This "absolutization of the market," as Bernard Barber calls it, is maintained first, by the continued reluctance of most economists to systematically consider the interdependence of the market with the noneconomic features of society; and second, by their unwillingness to revise established behavioral assumptions.[26] Kenneth Boulding, an economist, admits that "one of the most interesting of the unasked questions of intellectual history is how the science of economics . . . [has] become an abstract discipline void almost of any cultural context." In *Dangerous Currents,* his harsh critique of conventional economic theory, Lester Thurow considers "absurd" the notion that "economic events never have social consequences and that social events never have economic implications." For Thurow, economists' unmovable allegiance to the view of individuals as rational utility-maximizers is a form of intellectual blindness: "Contrary behavioral evidence has had little impact on economics because having a theory of how the world 'ought' to act, economists can reject all manner of evidence showing that individuals are not rational utility-maximizers. Actions that are not rational maximizations exist, but they are labeled 'market imperfections' that 'ought' to be eliminated."[27]

Yet, despite such criticism, the economic paradigm persists and only in a few exceptions, as with Karl Polanyi's *The Great Transformation,* have the economic "insiders" tested the boundaries of their paradigm. Instead, economic boundaries have expanded to include traditional sociological domains. Since the late 1950s, a group of micro-economists have developed a novel field of sociological economics that suggests a different approach to the problems of fertility, crime and punishment, education, health, marriage and divorce.[28] Unfortunately, this new possibility for interdisciplinary rapprochement has been largely squandered. Economists practice an intellectual imperialism of sorts, force-testing the analytical scope of their paradigm with new territorial conquests. Sociologists, however, are not blameless intellectual victims. As one sociologist has perceptively noted: "Sociologists . . . generally have no clearer notion of economics than economists have of sociology; they assume that the two disciplines are engaged in a zero-sum game and that, if economic arguments are valid, they are *ipso facto* out of business."[29] Ironically, while some dismiss economic models, other sociologists (as well as a group of psychologists, political scientists, and anthropologists), have further bolstered the dominance of a market model by often adopting economic analytical tools for their own research.

Where do noneconomic factors fit in the new economic paradigm? Gary Becker, the most brilliant and eloquent exponent of sociological economics, explains that the "heart" of his approach lies in a concise analytic trio: The assumptions of 1) individual utility-maximizing behavior; 2) market equilibrium —that is, the existence of markets as principal coordinators of individual or collective behavior; 3) stability of preferences. These key concepts predict responses to both market and nonmarket goods, serving equally well to explain the supply–demand for eggs or for children. In this context, values and norms, "preferences," are assumed "not to change substantially over time, nor to be very different between wealthy and poor persons, or even between persons in different societies and cultures."[30] Although Becker concedes that noneconomic factors will influence human behavior, sociological economics never answers, (or asks) precisely how.

This book provides a counterpoint to the economic paradigm by focusing on the *interrelation* between economic and noneconomic factors, specifically between the market or price (as defined earlier), and personal or moral values. Attention is also given to how social structural factors, such as class and family structure, interact with both price and value. While many economists and sociologists concerned with an apparently limitless expansion of the market in the modern world have been intrigued by this problem, few have examined it with empirical data. Three underlying assumptions shape most observations about the nature of the relationship between the market and nonmarketable personal values. First, price and value are seen as entirely dichotomous categories; second, economic concerns are constantly and inevitably enlarging; and third, the power of price to transform (usually corrupt) values is unquestioned, while the reciprocal transformation of price by value is seldom conceptualized.

The single, most profound and extensive analysis of this issue is found in Georg Simmel's *Philosophy of Money,* published in 1900, where he traces the historical dissociation between money and personal values. Simmel, one of sociology's most creative theorists, attributes this polarization to a radical transformation of both the value of a person and the value of money. While an earlier, relativist concept of human life made its quantification legitimate, Christianity sacralized human existence, setting life above any financial consideration. Paradoxically, the growing inadequacy of money was also a consequence of its increasing significance. While primitive money was reserved only for special, often sacred purposes, modern money became the "colourless and indifferent" equivalent of everything and anything. Money's successful conversion of all items into a quantifiable cash equivalent clashes with the modern belief in the uniqueness of human values.

Thus, Simmel suggests a radical contradiction and necessary tension between a monetary economy and personal values, which initially obstructs the expansion of the market into certain areas of exchange. But this "protection" of human values is precarious and is continually threatened by an invasion of the cash nexus: "The more money dominates interests and sets people and things into motion, the more objects are produced for the sake of money and are valued in terms of money, the less can the value of distinction be realized in men and in objects. . . ." Inevitably, says Simmel, pricing will "trivialize" or destroy value: "Whenever genuine personal values have to be offered for money . . . one finds that a loosening, almost a loss of substance in individual life takes place." For instance, in prostitution, marriage for money, or bribery, when price and value most directly intersect, monetization leads to a "terrible degradation of personal value." The sale of nonmarketable commodities is thus the ultimate conquest of the market in the modern world.[31]

Marx expressed similar concerns over the dehumanizing effects of a greedy "cash nexus." A corrupt "fraternization of impossibilities," was created in bourgeois society when personal values became purchasable: "Since money, as the existing and active concept of value, confounds and exchanges all things it is . . . the confounding and compounding of all natural and human qualities."[32] More recent discussions of the relation between price and value follow the general perspectives set by Marx and Simmel. For example, in his *Social Limits to Growth*, British economist Fred Hirsch describes the social threat posed by the "commodity bias" of both capitalist and socialist markets. More specifically, Hirsch identifies a "commercialization effect," which diminishes the quality of a product or activity by supplying it commercially. Prostitution is the prime example of a value (sexual relationship-emotional concern) negated by price. Similarly, sociologist Peter Blau, despite a predominantly "market" model of social behavior, maintains that pricing inevitably erodes intangible values, "by supplying goods that moral standards define as invaluable for a price in the market, individuals prostitute themselves and destroy the central value of what they have to offer."[33]

Even firm believers in the value of altruism seem to resign themselves to the powerful laws of the marketplace. Richard Titmuss' *The Gift Relationship*, an imaginative cross-national comparison of voluntary and commercial systems of providing human blood for transfusions, presents a unique empirical document. Titmuss was greatly concerned with the social consequences of marketing those "processes, relationships or things," which have no exchange value. His study concludes that commercialized blood markets are not only inefficient in economic terms but, more importantly, ethically and socially corrosive. Transform blood into a commercial commodity, argues Titmuss, and soon it will become "morally acceptable for a myriad of other human activities and relationships to exchange for dollars and pounds." Once more, pricing necessarily destroys value; the unlimited reach of the market is accepted even by its severest critics.[34]

A link is missing. The "commercialization effect" has its precise counterpart—a reciprocal "sacralization" process by which value shapes price, investing it with social, religious, or sentimental meaning. How is the market shaped by these cultural and social factors? The social construction of the economically "useless" but emotionally "priceless" child at the turn of the past century provides a unique setting to test the historical relationship of price to value, their independence and interdependence. The power of the market has been overestimated. This book is an attempt to document, with empirical evidence, some of its limits.[35]

CHAPTER 1

From Mobs to Memorials: The Sacralization of Child Life

What is more sacred than the life of a child?

Felix Adler, 1908

Jack and Jill went up the hill
to get some milk for mother
with good advice to each of them
to take good care of the other

"Let's run across the street" cried Jack
"Honk, honk," the bus replied
Too late they heed its warning note
Jack in the roadway lies.

From *Safety Education: A Plan Book for the Elementary School*, 1923

ON JULY 22, 1903, Mary Miner, five years old, was playing with some friends across from her father's restaurant in the Bowery when she was struck and killed by a Third Avenue electric car. The motorman "had a narrow escape from violence at the hands of a mob estimated by the police . . . to have been 3,000 strong." Press accounts describe the girl's father as "so frenzied with grief that he had to be forced to give up a frantic attempt on the motorman's life." Twenty years later, on May Day, 1926—a nationally declared "No Accident Day" for children—memorial services were held at the unveiling of two monuments in New York City. The crowd solemnly honored the memory of the 7,000 boys and girls killed in traffic accidents during the previous year.[1]

In the first decades of the twentieth century, the accidental death of children killed by streetcars and automobiles emerged as a new and alarming social problem. Public response to child victims was more intense and organized than to similar adult deaths. At first, neighborhood mobs spontaneously demonstrated their solidarity with the grief of bereaved parents by fiercely attacking the killers of children. By the mid-1920s, collective feeling had been formalized into official acts of public mourning. A national safety campaign was also launched to protect young children's lives.

Why did child victims elicit such expressions of group concern? What created the need for special memorials dedicated to children? This chapter will argue that the magnification of child mourning in the twentieth century is a measure of the transformation in the cultural meaning of childhood—specifically, the new exaltation of children's sentimental worth. If child life was sacred, child death became an intolerable sacrilege, provoking not only parental sorrow but social bereavement as well. The response to accidental death was only one manifestation of a broader surge of public concern with child life that began in the late nineteenth century. The "waste of child life," particularly among the impoverished urban working class, because of disease or malnutrition, became a visible and embarrassing anachronism to a society newly committed to the welfare of its children.[2] Therefore, the reduction of infant and child mortality rates quickly emerged as a national priority.

From the establishment of pediatrics as a separate medical specialty in the 1880s, to the passage of the federal Sheppard-Towner Act in 1921, which provided federal funds to protect the health of infants and mothers, the campaign for the conservation of child life engaged a broad range of individuals and organizations. As one leading reformer explained, "Health is no longer a purely individual matter; it has become the concern of the community. Preventable infant mortality is a social crime."[3]

When automobiles began killing large numbers of children playing in city streets, Americans were confronted with a different kind of child death. The analysis of the response to children's accidental death serves as a measure of the "sacralization" of child life.

The Death of a Child: From Resignation to Indignation

Until the eighteenth century in England and in Europe, the death of an infant or a young child was a minor event, met with a mixture of indifference and resignation. As Montaigne remarked, "I have lost two or three children in infancy, not without regret, but without great sorrow." Lawrence Stone, in his investigation of the English family, found no evidence of the purchase of symbols of mourning, not even an armband, when a very young child died in the sixteenth, seventeenth, and early eighteenth centuries. Parents seldom attended their child's funeral.[4] In some sections of France, according to Philippe Ariès, the child who died "too soon," was probably buried in the backyard, as a cat or dog is buried today. At death, even the children of the rich were treated as paupers, their bodies "sewn into shrouds made of cheap sacking and thrown into big, common graves." Between the fifteenth and seventeenth centuries, when the European upper classes chose to be buried in the church, the cemetery was reserved for the very poor and the very young, regardless of "whether their noble, bourgeois, or petit bourgeois parents had chosen the church for themselves and their families."[5]

Social historians suggest that while parents in colonial America were never indifferent to the death of their children, they maintained a degree of aloofness and detachment from the child. Many eighteenth-century parents, for instance, referred to their newborn infants as "it" or the "little stranger." Young death, especially of infants, was lamented but passively accepted; mourning rituals for children were sober and restrained. As one man put it in 1776, "[T]o lose a Child when first brought into Life is very hard but it is a Tax we must pay."[6] Another child replaced the lost one; significantly, it was a common practice to name newborns after a sibling who had recently died.

But by the nineteenth century, a dramatic revolution in mourning children had taken place. Among upper- and middle-class families in England, Europe, and the United States, the death of a young child became the most painful and least tolerable of all deaths. In her perceptive analysis of American culture, Ann Douglas describes a "magnification of mourning," between 1820 and 1875; more specifically, the surge of concern among the middle class with a child's untimely death. Traditional parental restraint gave way to unabashed outpourings of sorrow. The emotional pain of the bereaved father and mother became the dominant subject of a new popular literary genre—consolation literature. Mourners' manuals instructed parents how to cope with the tragedy of a "vacant cradle," while countless stories and poems described with great detail the "all-absorbing" grief of losing one's child. After Reverend Theodore Cuyler, a well-known New York clergymen, published *The Empty Crib,* as a literary memorial for his dead child Georgie, he received thousands of sympathetic letters from similarly bereaved parents. Ann Douglas quotes one of them: "My dear Sir, If it ever falls in your way to visit Allegheny Cemetery, you will see there 'a flower' on three 'little graves,' Anna, aged 7 yrs; Sadie, aged 5 yrs; Lillie, aged 3 yrs; all died within six days, and all of scarlet fever! It sometimes may reconcile us to our affliction to hear of one still greater elsewhere . . . ." By the mid-1850s, special coffins were designed for these "small household saints," with soft linings and a nameplate inside the box. A lock and a key replaced the "remorseless screws and screwdrivers."[7]

The new sensitivity toward child loss was part of a broader transformation in the cultural response to death. Philippe Ariès refers to a nineteenth-century "revolution in feeling," by which the "death of the other," particularly the death of a close family member was defined as an overwhelming tragedy: "The death which is feared is no longer so much the death of the self as the death of another. . . ."[8] The death of a young child was the worst loss of all. Lawrence Stone notes that in nineteenth-century England, as in the United States, "extreme grief at the death of a child . . . was now both a social convention and a psychological reality."[9] In the large urban cemeteries of Italy, France, and America, the small child quickly became the favorite subject of funerary art. French parents eulogized their children by commissioning elaborate portrait statues for their tombs. Ariès comments, "When we look at them today, as when we read the American consolation literature of the same period, we realize how painful the death of the young had become. These long-neglected little creatures were treated like famous personages. . . ."[10]

By the late nineteenth century, the revolution in child mourning expanded. Social historians concur that by then, as lower-class families in England and Europe adopted middle-class patterns of parenting, their response to child death was similarly sentimentalized. But the change was even more profound and more radical. The domestic grief of all parents for their dead child was gradually defined as a public concern. Elaborate private mourning for individual children was not enough; the death of all children—rich and poor—emerged as an intolerable social loss. While Victorian sentimentalists eulogized children, turn-of-the-century American activists were determined to avoid their death. As one reformer explained it, "The child has a right to a fair chance in life. If parents are delinquent in furnishing their children with this opportunity, it is the clear duty of the state to interfere ... Earth holds no greater tragedy than the ruthless destruction of a sturdy human life not even conscious of its own existence. ..."[11] The romantic cult of the dead child was therefore transformed into a public campaign for the preservation of child life.

Saving Child Life

The movement to reduce infant and child mortality began in the latter part of the nineteenth century. A new medical field and specialized institutions were created to treat childhood diseases and preserve the health of children. In 1881, Dr. Abraham Jacobi organized the Pediatric Section of the American Medical Society. Six years later, the American Pediatric Society was formed, for "the advancement of the Physiology, Pathology and Therapeutics of Infancy and Childhood." By the mid-1890s, most large cities had at least one children's hospital. After physicians uncovered the connection between bad milk and the health of children, a safe milk campaign was launched by philanthropic individuals and some municipalities. Milk stations and depots were established where poor mothers could buy at cost, and sometimes obtain without charge, pasteurized milk for their babies. They also received lessons in childcare and hygiene from the attendant trained nurses.[12]

In the 1890s, the psychological health of children also became the focus of much scientific interest. G. Stanley Hall, a psychologist at Clark University, pioneered the field of child study, which changed prevalent views of childhood. Hall's studies influenced established principles of childrearing by demonstrating different stages of child development. Children's problems were not only distinct from those of adults but changed within childhood, by age. Special parental skills were required to cope with this newly discovered psychic complexity of childhood.[13]

Proper mothering was considered a key element in the conservation of child life and health. While lower-class mothers were being instructed in proper childcare, middle-class mothers joined organizations devoted to the health and welfare of all children. The National Congress of Mothers, a network of Mothers Clubs, organized in 1897 by 2,000 delegates, assumed the task of educating the nation, and women in particular, "to recognize the supreme importance of the child." In its goal of educating women for motherhood, the association advocated courses in domestic science and sought to establish university chairs in the field of child study. By 1920, the Congress had attracted 190,000 women from thirty-six states.[14]

Public commitment to child welfare expanded in the twentieth century, when the Progressives' agenda established the preservation of child life as a national priority. Infant and child mortality rates became a critical gauge to judge the success of the reformers' programs. Settlement workers actively lobbied for the creation of separate municipal agencies to deal with the problems of child health. In 1908, the world's first public bureau devoted exclusively to child health was established in New York City. Public health nurses ran community baby health stations—a combination of milk depots and training schools in child hygiene for tenement mothers. By 1919, sixty baby health stations were in operation. By 1926, forty-seven states had a bureau for child hygiene or its equivalent. The number of public health nurses in the United States also grew; from 900 in 1907, to an estimated 11,500 in 1927. After the 1890s, the school health movement, which had made some inroads in the 1870s, actively joined the infant welfare campaign. School physicians and nurses were appointed for the medical examination of young students.[15]

The establishment of the United States Children's Bureau in 1912 officially certified the conservation of child life as a national concern. For two years, the study of infant mortality monopolized the Bureau's meager funds and limited staff. National Baby Weeks and "better babies" contests were sponsored to highlight infants' health needs. Reformers achieved a major victory in 1921, when the Sheppard-Towner Bill was passed by large congressional majorities. Some seven million dollars were provided by the federal government to the states in a pioneer grants-in-aid program to promote infant and maternal health and welfare. The organization of the American Child Health Association further contributed to the child health movement.[16]

The results were encouraging. During the 1890s, deaths among children under the age of five had averaged about 40 percent of all deaths. By the 1920s, the number dropped to 21.7 percent. Between 1915 and 1921, infant mortality decreased by 24 percent. By 1925, according to a report from the

Bureau of Child Hygiene, the major communicable diseases had been almost eliminated among New York schoolchildren, in large part as a result of mass inoculation for diphtheria and smallpox vaccination.[17]

What explains the surge of private and public concern with child life and child death? What inspired the nineteenth-century cult of child mourning and the twentieth-century campaign for child life? Based on a "rational investment" hypothesis, some historians suggest that demography regulates sentiment. According to this view, traditional indifference or resignation to child death was a logical psychological response to high mortality rates. David Stannard estimates that in seventeenth- and early eighteenth-century New England, a young married couple could anticipate the probable death of two or three of their children before they reached the age of ten. He suggests that the emotional restraint of Puritan parents may have been "an intuitive response to this possibility, a means of insulating themselves . . . against the shock that the death of a child might bring"[18] From this perspective, children were mourned more deeply only after they became safer emotional investments by living longer. As Stone explains, "For a child-oriented society to develop . . . it is essential that children should be less liable to sudden and early death. . . ."[19]

Yet, the link between children's high mortality rates and low parental affect remains questionable. In the United States, mortality rates for infants and young children decreased only by the latter part of the nineteenth century, following, and not preceding, the Victorian cult of mourning. In fact, one major study by Yasukichi Yasuba argues that death rates actually increased in the decades before the Civil War, particularly among urban children under ten years of age. Mid-nineteenth-century concern for child death could not, therefore, be the product of reduced mortality. Similarly, Ariès points out that an early surge of sensitivity toward the value of children's lives in Europe, preceded by more than a century any reduction in mortality. The first portraits of dead children proving "that the child was no longer . . . considered as an inevitable loss," appeared as early as the sixteenth century, a period of "demographic wastage."[20]

In *The Making of the Modern Family,* Edward Shorter offers an alternative to the "rational investment" hypothesis. After showing that the "surge of sentiment" for children in Europe preceded any reduction in mortality rates, he argues that the shift from traditional indifference to greater concern for children was itself responsible for improving longevity. According to this "better love" hypothesis, maternal concern for child life and death actively shaped demographic patterns. Traditional mothers, argues Shorter, "did not *care,* and that is why their children vanished in the ghastly slaughter of the innocent that was traditional child-rearing."[21] As soon as mothers learned to love properly, child mortality plunged.

Shorter's assumptions do not work well for the American case. There is ample evidence that colonial parents were never indifferent to their children. As David Stannard remarks, "a deep-seated parental affection for children was the most common, normal, and expected attitude," among Puritans. And yet their sorrow was restrained when a child died. Peter Gregg Slater, in a study of changing attitudes toward child death in New England from the mid-seventeenth to the mid-nineteenth centuries, suggests that although Puritans "were warmly loving of their children," perhaps nineteenth-century New Englanders "loved their offspring with greater intensity so that the loss of a child was more psychologically devastating to the parent."[22]

The individualistic and psychological focus of both the "rational investment" and "better love" arguments is misguided. The nineteenth-century revolution in child mourning as well as the twentieth-century campaign for child life are less significant as measures of changes in private sentiment, that is, an improvement in mother-love, than as dramatic indicators of a broader cultural transformation in children's value. As children, regardless of their social class, were defined as emotionally priceless assets, their death became not only a painful domestic misfortune but a sign of collective failure. Individual and group responses were therefore shaped by a cultural context that upheld child life as uniquely sacred and child death as singularly tragic.[23] The case of children's accidental death provides empirical evidence of the new meanings of child life in twentieth-century America.

The Case of Accidental Death

On November 1, 1908, 500 New York City children marched on Eleventh Avenue, better known as "Death Avenue." They were demonstrating against the New York Central Railroad and seeking the removal of train tracks from their neighborhood. As the *New York Times* reported, the pathetic marchers had often seen "their companions killed under freight cars and . . . lost brothers and sisters in that way."[24] At the head of the procession came little Gerald Garish bearing the lid of a child's coffin as a symbolic emblem.

The demonstrators showed unexpected foresight. By 1910, accidents had become the leading cause of death for children ages five to fourteen. It was a sad irony. Just when the campaign for the conservation of child life was making significant progress, a different death threat appeared. Railroads, streetcars, and automobiles emerged as fiercer killers of children than communicable diseases, which were being rapidly controlled by medical research and improved public health. While other vehicular accidents decreased after 1911, automobile fatalities sharply rose for all age groups.[25] In the early period, however, its chief victims were children.

It was a contest for space. As a commentator on traffic problems recognized, "The city street is the playground of many children, both from necessity and from choice. It is the only open place under the sky in many parts, and . . . the social center and gathering place of playmates."[26] An Englishwoman visiting New York in 1905 was shocked by the number of "nicely dressed children from good homes playing about in the streets even after dark." In Chicago, in 1912, the Juvenile Protective Association estimated that in any given afternoon, almost 6,000 children could be found playing within eighteen or nineteen blocks. It was most common in overcrowded tenements, where the only available "child space" was outdoors, in the street. As a writer in *Outlook* explained, "The family mansion . . . is an apartment occupying one-fourth of one floor of a four or five storied tenement-house. It consists, in most cases of three rooms . . . the larger about the dimensions of a moderate-sized rug—ten by twelve feet. Place within this restricted area the beds, stove, washtub and other furniture necessary for a family of half a dozen or more, with perhaps a boarder or two thrown in, and what room is left for an active and restless child?"[27] Playgrounds were usually inaccessible, too far from children's homes. As a Russell Sage Foundation study in 1914 of a West Side neighborhood in New York City discovered, "not only will a boy not go far afield for his games, but he cannot. He is often needed at home after school hours to run errands and make himself generally useful."[28]

The street held multiple attractions for children, "Now a funeral, now a fire; 'craps' on the sidewalk; a stolen ride on one of Death Avenue's freight trains; a raid on a fruit stall; a fight, and accident, a game of 'cat'—always a fresh incident and excitement. . . ." Spring was the season for playing marbles, bonfires the rage of fall days; snowballs the preferred winter sport. Boys also joined adult men in baseball games, or pigeon flying from tenement roofs. Street fighting and boxing matches were another favorite neighborhood pastime. The Russell Sage report noted the frequent street bouts between youngsters of seven or eight being watched by a crowd of young men, "who encourage the combatants by cheering every successful blow."[29] The street was not only a playground but a workplace as well. Children, boys in particular, peddled goods, ran errands or bootblacked, and sold newspapers or ice. Younger children engaged in scavenging, the business of gathering and selling usable trash.

The presence of children in city streets was not new. In the 1850s, as their numbers increased with the influx of German and Irish immigrants to New York City, local authorities became alarmed. Indeed, one recent study suggests that mid-nineteenth-century reformers considered the presence of poor children in New York's streets as a key element of the problem of urban poverty. Children's street life was held as irrefutable evidence of parental neglect and a pathological lower-class family environment that initiated children into lives of misery and crime.[30] At the turn of the century, child-savers launched a new national campaign to offer a supervised, educational alternative to the moral hazards of street life. By 1910, under the auspices of the Playground Association of America, founded in 1906, thousands of city playgrounds provided organized play activities for urban children. That year, New York City alone spent $121, 606 for playground maintenance, and employed almost 1,000 workers at some 250 playgrounds.[31]

As in the 1850s, some of the concern for child welfare may

have been a response to the increasing number of immigrants in American cities. Playgrounds, like other Progressive institutions for children, were part of an Americanization program for foreigners' children. Yet despite the vitality and progress of the playground movement, working-class and immigrant children did not surrender their street games easily.[32] The eviction of children finally came about when automobiles transformed city streets into deathly playgrounds. Reformers had found an unlikely ally.

The eviction of children was harsh. Between 1910 and 1913, over 40 percent of New York traffic victims were under fifteen years of age. In 1914, the rate jumped to 60 percent. As late as 1927, an insurance bulletin reported with alarm that "nearly 40 percent of the automobile fatalities are those of children under fifteen, and the mortality is particularly heavy between the ages of five and ten."[33] That year, 558 boys and girls were killed and 15,623 injured in New York State alone. In the five to fourteen age group, accidents caused nearly three times as many deaths as any single disease. Most accidents took place within a block or two of the child's home, while the child played or ran an errand for his or her parents. Being a child, concluded one observer, had become "the most dangerous job in the world."[34]

But by 1930, a startling shift had occurred. While the general automobile fatality showed a consistent increase (30,200 persons were killed in 1930), the rate for school-age children suddenly dropped. In 1922, 477 children died in New York City streets; but only 250 in 1933.[35] The trend began approximately at mid-decade; between 1927 and 1929, adult vehicle fatalities increased over 25 percent while fatalities to children of school age decreased by 10 percent. Pedestrian deaths, characteristic of children, showed a similar age differential; between 1925 and 1936 rates declined 37 percent for boys and

25 percent for girls, while adult rates (ages fifteen to sixty-four) jumped 77 percent for males and 18 percent for females.[36] The relative reduction in child fatalities was promptly hailed as "the sole instance in which the automobile hazard has been brought under control." Thus, in the span of a few years, child accidents passed from being an ominous threat to becoming the "most gratifying fact," in traffic mortality trends.[37]

What explains this curious chronology? How did Americans respond to the sudden and brutal invasion of child space by streetcars and automobiles? More specifically, how did the public react to the violent death of children in city streets in the early decades of the twentieth century?

Child Victims: The Special Affront

Between 1900 and 1913, wagons, streetcars, and automobiles began to invade city streets where young children played. As early as 1901, a writer in *Outlook* commented, "One who reads the newspapers gets the impression that hardly a day passes without the killing of a child. . . ."[38] It was a violent, often gruesome event. Unlike death on a sickbed, death in a crowded street was also highly visible.[39] Public reaction was "vendetta-style," immediate, indignant, and violent. Onlookers awaited no trial to adjudicate blame. As a *New York Times* editorial noted, "[Child death] is a tragedy which appeals to the sympathies of the quickly assembled crowd so powerfully that if the motorman under whose car it happens is not protected by the police he is likely to be mobbed."[40] When sixteen-month-old Bernard Winegold was run over by a horse on May 1911, a large crowd assembled almost instantly. As many others, details of this particular incident made front-page news: "Kill him. He killed a child! . . . Women's shrill voices

sounded high above those of men, urging them to take ven-
geance." After a bloody struggle between the driver, armed
with a whip, and several men from the crowd, a policeman
arrived. The horsecar had been completely wrecked by the
mob.[41]

By the 1920s, social response to the accidental death of
children had changed dramatically. A child killed by an automobile was more than an isolated neighborhood tragedy or a
catchy news-item; children's accidental death emerged as a
"serious, fundamental national problem."[42]

The first two alarming newspaper stories on child death
appeared in 1904. Recognizing that "with disquieting fre-
quency children are ground up under street cars . . . ," a *New
York Times* editorial recommended separate legal standards to
judge the culpability of motormen, drivers, and chauffeurs
involved in the accidental killing of a child.[43] Yet, even if
sympathetic, the press in this early period pinned most of the
blame on parents. Insisting that modern life "cannot be re-
tarded to enable heedless children to get out of the way,"
parents were regularly chided for not supervising their children
properly. Letters to the editor echoed this sentiment: "Parents
should realize that they are responsible for the child's life, and
if they turn it out to play in a crowded street and it is run over
they are . . . to blame."[44] There were some suggestions to
control children directly, by reporting the names of those "who
run into the streets on the approach of an automobile and
throw their hats beneath the wheels or hit the car with sticks
as it passes, or standing in front and wave their arms until the
car is almost upon them."[45] Children, dramatically warned
Henry S. Curtis, secretary of the Playground Association of
America, "are putting themselves, their parents, shopmen, and
all motormen, drivers, and chauffeurs under a nervous strain
. . . which will surely be recorded in drink and dissipation, in

lessened capacity for work, in lessened enjoyment of life, in nervous breakdowns, and, in the next generation, in degeneracy."[46]

Indeed, many regulations were passed to transform children's street games into criminal offenses. The 1914 Russell Sage study of a New York neighborhood observed that "everything [a boy] does seems to be against the law. If he plays ball, he is endangering property by 'playing with a hard ball in a public place.' If he plays marbles or pitches pennies, he is 'obstructing the sidewalk,' . . . Street fighting is 'assault,' and a boy guilty of none of these things may perforce be 'loitering.'" In just one summer month that same year, 415 New York children were arrested and taken to court for playing ball or other games, and for shouting or making a noise in the street."[47] In the District of Columbia, under the act for the preservation of the public peace and the protection of property, 655 children were arrested as "criminals" between July 1, 1914 and June 30, 1915, for playing games in the street. These youthful law-breakers learned to conceal their illegal acts. When a policeman "stalks majestically into a street which has been unlawfully converted into a playground . . . Instantly the youthful ball-players scatter; the games of cat, of tag . . . cease abruptly; the high pitched childish voices become quiet."[48]

The number of vehicle fatalities kept climbing inexorably. Average yearly rates of 6,700 for 1913 to 1917 rose to 12,500 for 1918 to 1922. For children five to fourteen, the corresponding increase was from 1,600 to 3,100, making this age group the most vulnerable. The *New York Times* remarked that traffic victims were drawn from "the immature, the unprotected . . . just those classes of society which civilization boasts that it most protects."[49] A growing sense of alarm over the "ceaseless slaughter," was occasionally conveyed by readers' comments, "I must . . . relieve my feelings by expressing through your columns something of the horror I feel at the destruction of children's lives that is daily going on . . ."[50]

Yet, the anger of the early mobs was not immediately matched by active public and official response. A speaker at the 1913 International Congress on Industrial School Hygiene called child accidents "the most neglected phase of the modern problem of conservation of human life and health." In that meeting, only two out of over forty presentations addressed the accident situation. The second spokesman criticized schools for spending "time, money and brains," in children's health while overlooking "the fearful ravages" of preventable accidents.[51] Indeed, child welfare organizations, deeply involved with improving children's physical welfare, focused more attention on death by disease than by accident. Organized safety efforts were also heavily engaged in the control of industrial accidents and occupational diseases. The American Museum of Safety, organized in New York in 1907, sponsored exhibitions and published extensive reports on industrial safety. It did not become involved with street accidents until 1913. Similarly, it took the National Safety Council six years from its inception in 1913, to combat actively public accidents.[52] As late as 1925, the Metropolitan Life Insurance Company still urged the safety movement to direct its attention to automobile accidents, "just as vigorously as it does to the control of occupational accidents." Industrial injuries to young children also captured special attention. Although numerically less significant than street deaths, children killed on the job provided powerful symbolic ammunition to the struggle against child labor.[53]

The first safety efforts against street accidents were promoted and financed by street railway companies. In 1913, the Brooklyn Transit Company launched a "Children's Safety Crusade." Safety lectures were organized in Brooklyn public schools; their message further publicized by the distribution of 600,000 safety leaflets and 300,000 badges among the students. The following year, a similar campaign was conducted in the Boston area schools by the local railway company. Among other strategies, a contest was held for the best verses written by students on "Caution in the Streets."[54] A full-fledged "Safety First" movement took shape in major cities across the nation between 1913 and 1920. Its outstanding characteristic was an intensive and almost exclusive concern with school children. The movement was supposedly triggered by "the horror men have felt over [the] slaughter of children."[55]

Safety lectures soon expanded into widely publicized Safety Days, Safety Sundays, and Safety Weeks. Gradually movement leaders persuaded reluctant school boards to infiltrate the entire curriculum with safety concerns. Nursery rhymes were re-written to dramatize the danger of accidents ("Little Miss Muffet/ instead of a tuffet/Sat on the curb one day/ Along came an auto/ and soon she got caught/ Her feet having got in the way"). Art and drama classes were newly inspired with safety plots and even a "new" arithmetic was contrived, "The number of children killed last year was what percent of the number of children who attend your school? If the number seriously injured were twenty-four times the number killed, how many were injured?"[56]

By 1919, the National Safety Council joined the bandwagon, convinced that "the most effective step . . . toward the elimination of the yearly toll of . . . accidental deaths . . . is the systematic instruction of every child in the schools."[57] A nationwide campaign was launched to secure the adoption of a syllabus on "Education on Accident Prevention" by all public and parochial schools.

On October 9, 1922, 15,000 New York children paraded up Fifth Avenue. Their march ended on the large meadow in

Central Park where a Child Memorial—a monument to child victims of accidents—had been erected. This officially designated "Children's Day" parade became the emotional focus of the city's Safety Week. According to press reports, "all eyes were turned," to a special division of 1,054 boys representing an equal number of children accidentally killed during 1921 and to the fifty "white-star" mothers marching behind, who had lost their children. Prefaced by clergymen's prayers, the city's Health Commissioner spoke of the singularly tragic quality of child death: "We dedicate monuments to our hero dead, and to our great men in art and science, but we are met today to perform a unique service. We are here to dedicate a monument to the martyrs of civilization—to the helpless little ones who have met death through the agencies of modern life."[58]

Organized group mourning symbolized a new dimension of public response to the accidental killing of a child. The statistical magnitude of the problem, well-publicized by safety groups, now became compounded by the social "discovery" of its moral significance. New ritual labels were affixed to the safety movement: "Let us hope that they [the children] shall not have died in vain . . . May the memory of these children move us to devise methods to save their companions and others who will bless us in the days to come."[59] The quasi-theological challenge of controlling fatal child accidents was brought up by the chairman of the newly-formed Educational Section of the National Safety Council in 1919:

Of all the riddles of a difficult world nothing is more inscrutable than an accident. What powers or processes in heaven or earth . . . are furthered by the crushing out of the life of an innocent, happy child? What manner of bargain is this in . . . which a parent's love and pride are bartered for bleeding flesh and ruined hopes? . . . It is past understanding. There is only one thing I see . . . to make the world over into a place where such damnable things shall not happen . . .

New monuments were dedicated to child victims in 1926. Weekly records of child deaths were posted on the stones and memorial services held each Saturday by Boy Scouts and Girl Scouts.[60]

Secular and instrumental safety programs collaborated with the new symbolic testimony of concern for child death. In the 1920s, "Save the Children's Lives" committees multiplied; the police initiated safety training for school teachers and children were organized into junior safety councils. Rallies were held in 700 New York City public schools, "to curb the killing and injuring of children in the streets."[61] Mothers were reminded not to "shirk the fact that the most pitiful havoc among their children by accidents is from vehicles, and if these little ones are to be saved, it is the mothers . . . that must save them."[62]

Insurance companies and the automobile industry became eager financial donors to the safety cause, subsidizing programs and publications. In 1926, the National Society for the Study of Education officially endorsed safety education. On the basis of a national survey of 1,862 school systems, the 1932 White House Conference on Child Health and Protection reported that 86 percent of elementary schools included safety concerns in their curriculum. The safety movement even produced its own media hero; in 1920 "Uncle Robert" began a popular series of radio broadcasts on child safety.[63]

Public response to the accidental killing of a child had taken different shapes and new moods—from the violent grief of early twentieth-century mobs, through the sober didactic approach of safety organizations, to the Child Memorials of the 1920s. In the process, a child's accidental death became not only an isolated, personal tragedy, but increasingly a matter of public concern. The construction of special monuments for child victims cannot be dismissed as an architectural whim. The need to create separate "sacred" space was linked to the new value of child life and the deepening moral offensiveness of killing children. Although child memorials had an utilitarian purpose ("so that the tragedies of reckless driving would be dramatized and 'brought home' to automobilists")[64] their essential function was to symbolize collective feeling. In a study of war memorials, Bernard Barber has shown how spatial localization of the memorial symbol is necessary to express, "those attitudes and values of a community towards those persons and deeds that are memorialized."[65] In the case of children killed by automobiles, private mourning and parental sorrow alone were inadequate. Group mourning at the site of child memorials served to express collective grief.

Child Life: A Moral Priority

When Cotton Mather's daughter burned herself seriously with fire, he blamed her misfortune on his sins. Such a deterministic view of accidental death as divine punishment persisted well into the nineteenth century. In 1855, after a tragic railroad accident in New Jersey, "God's Providence in Accidents" was interpreted by the clergyman's funeral sermon, "We may no more exempt one class of deaths from God's control, than another. The sword, the poison, the accident, are as much His instruments as the paralysis or the fever . . . all have a common place in the great scheme of Providence."[66]

Traditional attitudes faltered in the latter part of the nineteenth century, as both death and disease became increasingly perceived as postponable or remediable consequences of inadequate sanitation or other technical deficiencies controllable by men. After the death of eight high-school students in a 1903 trolley collision, Newark's Episcopal rector reassured his congregants that "the will of God is not shown in the death of these children, for God did not take these children out of the world. They were thrown out of it by those responsible for the crime."[67] Accidents were less the will of God than the will of a trolley company president or, in the case of industrial injuries, the bad will of the employer. From this perspective, the child safety movement represented an enthusiastic expression of the emerging activist mood. Its leaders pledged to "make the world a place that shall be animated by a purpose and not by soulless chance." Mothers were urged to "take the burden of death off the shoulders of the Lord," by accepting that their children's accidents had preventable causes.[68]

Why, however, did early public safety efforts concentrate so heavily on children? Why did children constitute the "saddest of records," evoking much more intense public response than similar adult deaths?[69] To some extent, it was a matter of quantity. Young children were killed in relatively higher numbers than older people, making child death more visible. Greater numbers and visibility, however, do not necessarily transform an issue into a social problem. Public perceptions of the accidental death of children were shaped by a mixture of economic, social, and cultural factors.

One look at the list of its major sponsors—trolley companies, insurance organizations, and the automobile industry—reveals the underlying economic motive in child safety programs. It was soon recognized that such institutions "have a stake in making the streets safe from a humanitarian and a business point of view."[70] Indeed, as damage suits multiplied, accidental killing became increasingly unprofitable. In 1905 alone, the trolley companies of Greater New York paid out over

$2,000,000 in damages plus an additional million for legal expenses. Accidents were also being identified as a worrisome financial drain for insurance companies. Claim payments on account of accidental death by the Metropolitan Life Insurance Company totaled over $8,000,000 in 1927. Three years later, company disbursements reached $16,500,000 as accidents ranked second in importance to heart disease as a cause of mortality. Although precise age breakdowns in death claims are not available, children undoubtedly constituted a significant percentage of industrial policyholders accidentally killed. Metropolitan Life Insurance Company figures for 1924 to 1925 show that 55 percent of 1,600 policyholders killed as pedestrians were children.[71] Yet, the child safety movement can hardly be dismissed as merely a product of the selfish interest of insurance and transit companies. After all, damage claims and death payments for adult breadwinners were, in the early decades of the twentieth century, considerably higher than similar payments for children.

Insurance spokesmen raised an additional economic rationale for saving children, by defining early death not as a company loss, but as a financial disservice to the general community. Addressing the American Child Health Association in 1927, Louis Dublin, an insurance statistician, calculated that neglect of child life cost the United States about two and a half billion dollars each year. While acknowledging that economic balance sheets for child life constituted a "direct challenge to our moral sense," Dublin proceeded to show why, "if we were moved only by the crudest and coldest calculations of dollars and cents, we could not afford to neglect our children."[72]

Public reaction to a child's accidental death was also shaped by the social class of young victims. The death of a poor child elicited a different type of social response than the death of a middle-class child. Organized response to children's accidental death did not begin until 1913, becoming fully effective only in the 1920s. Before 1913, group protest was restricted to the mobs of immediate witnesses. Yet poor children were already being killed by railroads, wagons, and streetcars. An Interstate Commerce Commission report for 1901 to 1910 estimated that 13,000 children under fourteen had been killed or injured by trains. In 1908 alone, 346 children died in streetcar accidents and 469 were killed by wagons.[73]

Noting that "every child so killed has been of poor parents," an 1893 *New York Times* editorial suggested that indifference to "child-slaughter" by the city's trolley cars derived from class prejudice: "If it were practicable to confine the loss to the families of stockholders in the highly profitable trolley companies it would . . . be a terribly cruel measure, but it might bring home to the Directors their own heartlessness . . ." Similarly, apathy to railroad fatalities was attributed by one vocal critic to the widespread conviction that victims were all "hoboes" or tramps.[74] Child victims of railroad and traffic accidents were indeed the children of the working class and the urban poor. Many were young immigrants confused by the novelty of city traffic, as illustrated in the case of Ettie Pressman. In 1893, Ettie, seven years old, was killed by a team of horses as she crossed Ludlow street in the lower East Side of New York with her sister Dora, nine years old. When the case came to court in 1896, Dora described their predicament: "I am in America now going on four years . . . My sister was not born in America. . . . The day the accident happened we had been living in New York two weeks. I cannot say how wide Ludlow Street is. I don't know how long it would take to run across; it don't take a minute."[75]

Insurance data confirm the particular vulnerability of lower-class children. A 1919 bulletin from the Metropolitan Life Insurance Company noted with alarm that among their industrial policyholders, over 50 percent of automobile fatalities occurred with children under fifteen, a much higher rate than the 28 percent among children in the general population.[76] Accidental killing of these children was characteristically attributed to irresponsible lower-class behavior. The press rebuked tenement children who "congregate in swarms about the [trolley] car tracks and torment the motormen and conductors as recreation." Bereaved parents were also at fault. As late as 1922, *Collier's* denounced the carelessness of tenement mothers: "It is one of the awful facts of this whole sad business that women so often neglect or refuse their obvious duty . . . until a limp crushed body has been put into their arms."[77]

The social class of child victims explains some of the anger of mobs in poor neighborhoods. "Devil wagons," as automobiles were dubbed, were generally the suspect and resented property of the wealthy. To some extent, the death of a child symbolized mechanical invasion and destruction. Yet demonstrators attacked with equal vehemence the nonaristocratic drivers of milk wagons and trolleys, if a child was killed.

As the automobile became an established presence, its danger reached to more neighborhoods. Gradually, death in the streets came to be perceived as a threat to the middle-class child as well; it was no longer the exclusive problem of "hoodlum urchins who infest the sidewalks."[78] The occasional killing of a child in a "good" neighborhood provoked strong public outrage and public response. At 8 P.M. on March 27, 1909, Ingward Tremble, the thirteen-year-old son of a prominent Kentucky lawyer who was visiting New York, was killed by a car as he played in the street with a group of children. His death quickly became a cause célèbre. The press called it murder: "While the deliberate intent to kill was doubtless absent, the man in the car . . . sacrificed the boy's life . . ." William Darragh, a hired chauffeur, was arrested and charged for murder in the first degree, a sentence without local or national precedent. Finally convicted of manslaughter, Darragh complained of harsh treatment only, "because I accidentally killed the son of a rich man."[79]

It is uncertain whether the growing fear that the automobile was an equal threat to all children was justified. A 1927 "murder map" issued by the City Club of New York showed that the highest percentages of children killed were still from lower-class immigrant neighborhoods. On the other hand, 1929 accident statistics indicate that collision with other motor vehicles was the single type of accident involving school children which was increasing. Upper-income groups were particularly vulnerable to this type of accident.[80]

Warranted or not, middle-class fears triggered a greater response to children's accidental deaths. Unlike the poor, affluent parents had knowledge of, and access to, official channels of protest. For instance, in 1912, after an automobile killed ten-year-old Patrick Fay in an exclusive upper west-side neighborhood, a flurry of residents' complaints led to increased police supervision. The incident provoked a much publicized dispute among the police, the magistrates, and the district attorneys of Manhattan, each side trying to shirk its responsibility and shift the blame.[81]

A child's accidental death, however, was more than a threat to middle-class parents or an economic debit for transit and insurance companies. Public sentiment was strongly aroused by twentieth-century conceptions of the uniquely sacred value of child life, which transcended class distinctions. This age-specific collective sensitivity was apparent in other areas. Public reaction to the kidnapping of children, for instance, was also remarkably intense. A study of ransom kidnapping in the United States between 1874 and 1974, found that child victims increasingly elicited the strongest and most emotional public response. It did not matter whether the victim was the son of an Italian pushcart merchant, as in the 1921 New York kidnapping case of five-year-old Giuseppi Verotta; or the child of a wealthy Norristown, Pennsylvania family, as in the abduction of thirteen-month-old Blakely Coughlin in 1920. Community concern for the victimized child was independent of his or her parents' social class.[82]

Killing a child, even without deliberate intent, emerged as a singularly obnoxious and almost sacrilegious crime. In a society that prided itself for spectacular improvements in children's health, their accidental deaths stood as an uncomfortable anachronism. The special symbolism of child death intensified even as accident rates began to decline. Asserting that "the importance of children to the nation is so primary that such matters as traffic are subsidiary," a 1931 editorial in *Commonweal* advocated stricter standards of culpability for causing the death of a child. It also proposed a series of speeches and articles on "What It Means To Kill a Child," designed to convey the unique tragedy of child fatalities. Recognizing the "more marked sentimental" public response to child accidents, the Journal of the American Medical Association recommended the collection of better statistics for this age group, as a strategy to obtain public support for general safety programs.[83]

From the Streets to the Playroom: Domesticating the "Sacred" Child

By 1930, the problem of children's accidental death was paradoxically transformed into the moral pride of safety experts. While automobile fatalities rose steadily, rates for children five to fourteen unexpectedly declined. There was no obvious demographic explanation, since the number of children in that age group had increased from 22,158 million in 1920 to 24,631 million in 1930. Children were spending more of their time safely indoors, in school. Yet larger school enrollments alone could not be responsible for the reduction in child mortality. Although almost a million more pupils were enrolled between 1922 and 1930, almost three million were added between 1918 and 1922, the period of the highest accidental mortality rates. The introduction of important new safety devices for automobiles in the 1920s and 30s is also an inadequate explanation, for it does not account for the age differentials in improved safety. Puzzled yet pleased, safety leaders congratulated themselves for the unique effectiveness of their safety education programs.[84]

The age reversal in accident rates extended to the home. In 1924, the death rate from domestic accidents for persons under fifteen was 14.4 per 100,000 compared to 11 for those over fifteen. By 1932, the rate shifted to 11.1 per 100,000 for the younger group and 15.5 for the older one. Rates for other childhood accidents (aside from home and motor-vehicle) decreased as well. The downswing was more dramatic, however, with automobile injuries, which had caused the largest number of deaths. Children, concluded one prominent safety educator, "are learning to meet the dangers of their surroundings better than adults."[85]

The preferential preservation of child life was accomplished by a dramatic reorganization of child space and child time, and by new risk socialization techniques. Most child accidents took place between 4 and 5 P.M. (5 P.M. was the deadliest hour), on nonschool days, and during summer months, when children played on the streets with minimum adult supervision. Safety programs restructured these high danger leisure time periods.

The playground movement, for instance, gained new impetus in the 1920s; by 1927, 790 cities reported 5,600 supervised playgrounds for children. These figures excluded an additional 5,000 recreation areas without leadership, plus newly designed play spaces set aside by realtors; such as block and roof playgrounds as well as "tot-lots" for the smaller children. Cities aided by increasing the number of ordinances against street games.[86] Parents were urged to provide adequate indoor playing space for their children, "Why not begin by converting the so-called parlor or front room into a playroom? Nothing could be more useless than the parlor. . . . During the week it is almost always locked, while the children play on the sidewalk." Parents were also advised against sending young children alone on errands: "If the child must cross the street it is best to go after him and escort him across."[87] Peer supervision increased as well, as older boys were instructed to protect younger students. Junior safety councils included the reporting of violations of safety conduct, such as crossing streets against traffic or playing ball on the street. Repeated offenders were penalized. Girls, initially organized into separate "careful clubs" responsible for home safety, were later included in coed traffic safety patrols.

Safety instruction socialized children to risk, making them "cautious and dependable . . . thoughtful of the consequences of [their] acts as possibly injurious to other people." It was not a subtle message. Safety posters and cartoons illustrated gruesome incidents of children killed by automobiles. Slogans reminded them that, "A boy in the playground is worth two in the hospital," or that "Better belated than mutilated." Streets were portrayed as deathtraps: "When a child leaves the curbstone of safety, he enters a lane of death."[88] The focus of safety programs on child socialization conveniently diverted public attention away from the automobile industry and from drivers.

It was easier to regulate children than adults and certainly cheaper to educate children than to buy or develop improved safety equipment. Children learned that "every street is a base-ball diamond; every trolley, every wagon, every automobile may be considered a player on the opposite team." The dramatic message was supplemented by the teaching of specific traffic rules. The list of don'ts was continually expanding: "Do not play in the street. Never chase a ball across the street. Do not coast. Don't 'hitch' on autos, streetcars or other vehicles. Never run between parked autos."[89] Good learners were re-warded; winners of safety essay contests received prizes and hero medals were awarded to any child who saved another child's life.

Saving child life meant changing the daily activities of city children, pushing them indoors into playrooms and school-rooms or designing special "child" public spaces, such as play-grounds. Streets were not only physically dangerous, but so-cially inadequate; the proper place for a "sacred" child was a protected environment, segregated from adult activities. The "domestication" program which sent children indoors, affected boys' lives more than girls, whose public activities were already limited. While girls stayed in to help their mothers, boys were much more likely to play outdoors, and therefore be the primary victims of fatal accidents. For example, of the 422 children killed in New York City in 1926, only 100 were girls. Insurance statistics show that between 1911 and 1930, death rates for children varied from 25.9 per 100,000 for boys to only 11.3 for girls. For all ages, automobile accidents among males were three times that for females. The differential success of safety efforts reflected the sex bias as well as a class differential; the greatest reduction in child fatalities occurred among the sons of working-class families.[90] Middle-class boys had already been partially domesticated.

Recent studies of human spatial behavior note the relative powerlessness of children in the distribution of indoor household space. As Mark Baldassare explains, dominant members of a family "can obtain the space they need for their activities ... by taking it from subordinate members ... Children cannot obtain space and can lose rights to what they have when others demand more, and so children suffer."[91] Similarly, the new twentieth-century rules for urban outdoor space, designed by adults for their convenience, constricted the public life of children. As one fourteen-year-old boy observed perceptively in 1921, ". . . a child doesn't make traffic rules, drive cars, etc. The child's main object is to keep out of the way of moving vehicles."[92] A recent study by Sarane S. Boocock of the daily lives of some 300 children between the ages of four and eight, from six different communities in the Northeast, confirms the continuing restriction of child space in urban environments. Asked, "How far away from home are you allowed to go without a grownup?" 39 percent of a high-income group, and over half of a low-income group of New York City children, said they were not allowed to go outside of their own building— almost none had yards. Only 12 percent of the low-income group was allowed to go farther away than their own block. When asked where they usually played, another sample of eleven- and twelve-year-olds from Oakland, California mentioned most often their own homes and yards or those of their friends.[93]

But if children lost the contest for public space, they staked in this period a new claim to indoor space; a separate domain for sleeping, playing, or studying. In 1931, the Subcommittee on Housing and Home Management of the White House Conference on Child Health and Protection strongly urged that housing be considered "more and more with reference to its effect upon the health, protection, and welfare of children."

In the ideal home, each child would have a room of its own, "in which at times he can be by himself. Children require a place, also, where they may carry on their own legitimate activities unhindered and unhampered . . . a place where they may play or work without interference from or conflict with the activities of the adult members of the family." If the family could not afford the extra room necessary for a playroom, "a corner of a bedroom, nursery, enclosed porch . . . may be used." The goal was to assure the child's physical space within the home. The Housing Committee recommended that even the household's adult domains, such as the living room, should contain separate child space, "at least one chair to fit each small child, and a few toys and suitable books on a low shelf." In the bathroom, a low towel rod and a hook for a washcloth would accommodate children's needs.[94] Although the Committee expected its housing standards to be implemented in all households regardless of social class, current data suggest that, even in the 1980s, class still regulated child space. Boocock's study found that only 21 percent of the low-income group of New York children had their own bedrooms, compared with 68 percent of the high-income group. As a result of the lack of space, the indoor behavior of the poorer children was found to be heavily regulated by their parents, that is, rules against running or making noise in the house, breaking windows or furniture, and jumping on the beds and sofas. Lower-class children therefore lost the streets without gaining significant new indoor space.[95]

The "sacralization" of children in the twentieth century led to an increased intolerance of child death, whether by illness or accident, and a great concern for protecting child life. Children of all social classes were not only vaccinated against disease and better nourished, but their lives were increasingly supervised and domesticated. In *The Policing of Families,*

Jacques Donzelot notes a similar "social retraction" particularly among lower-class French children in the early decades of the twentieth century. Children, observes Donzelot, were increasingly led to spaces, "where [they] could be more closely watched: the school or the family dwelling."[96]

But taking children off the streets and protecting their health was not enough. It was essential to take the sacred child out of work. As Rabbi Stephen S. Wise asserted at the Sixth Annual Conference on Child Labor, "The term child labor is a paradox, for when labor begins . . . the child ceases to be."[97] The next two chapters examine the controversial resolution of that paradox and the transformation of children's economic roles.

CHAPTER 2

From Useful to Useless:
Moral Conflict Over
Child Labor

> Where do we go from here—where?
> —We remnants of the throng that started with us
> Shall we keep on—
> Or drop off on the way, as they have done?
> They're earning money now, and make us feel
> But useless children in comparison.
> Why can't we, too, get into something real?
>
> from "Eighth Grade," by F.B.W., 1923

THE 1900 U.S. Census reported that one child out of every six between the ages of ten and fifteen was gainfully employed. It was an undercount: The total figure of 1,750,178 excluded many child laborers under ten as well as the children "helping out" their parents in sweatshops and on farms, before or after school hours. Ten years later, the official estimate of working children reached 1,990,225. But by 1930, the economic participation of children had dwindled dramatically. Census figures registered 667,118 laborers under fifteen years of age. The decline was particularly marked among younger children. Between 1900 and 1930, the number of children ten to thirteen years old in nonagricultural occupations alone decreased more than six fold, from 186,358 to under 30,000.[1]

The exclusion of children from the marketplace involved a difficult and prolonged battle lasting almost fifty years from the 1870s to the 1930s. It was partly an economic confrontation and partly a legal dispute, but it was also a profound "moral revolution."[2] Two groups with sharply conflicting views of childhood struggled to impose their definition of children's proper place in society. For child labor reformers, children's early labor was a violation of children's sentimental value. As one official of the National Child Labor Committee explained in 1914, a laboring child "is simply a producer, worth so much in dollars and cents, with no standard of value as a human being. . . . How do you calculate your standard of a child's value? . . . as something precious beyond all money standard."[3] On the other hand, opponents of child labor reform were just as vehement in their support of the productive child, "I say it is a tragic thing to contemplate if the Federal Government closes the doors of the factories and you send that little child back, empty-handed; that brave little boy that was looking forward to get money for his mother for something to eat."[4]

The child labor conflict is a key to understanding the profound transformation in the economic and sentimental value of children in the early twentieth century. The price of a useful wage-earning child was directly counterposed to the moral value of an economically useless but emotionally priceless child. In the process, a complex reassessment of children's economic roles took place. It was not just a matter of whether children should work or not. Even the most activist of child labor reformers were unwilling to condemn all types of child work, while their opponents were similarly reluctant to condone all child labor. Instead, their argument centered over conflicting and often ambiguous cultural definitions of what constituted acceptable work for children. New boundaries emerged, differentiating legitimate from illegitimate forms of economic participation by children.

It was not a simple process. As one perplexed contemporary observer noted: "To work or not to work—that is the question. But nobody agrees upon the answer. . . . Who among the controversialists is wrong? And just what is work anyway? When and where does it step across the dead line and become exploitation?"[5] Child work and child money were gradually redefined for the "sacred" twentieth-century child into primarily moral and instructional tools. While child labor laws regulated exclusively working-class children, the new rules for educational child work cut across classes, equally applicable to all "useless" children.

The Useful Child: From Family Asset to Social Problem

In recent studies, economists and historians have documented the vital significance of child labor for working-class families in the late nineteenth century. Using extensive national data from the 1880s and 1890s, Michael Haines concludes that child labor "appears to have been the main source of additional support for the late nineteenth-century urban family under economic stress."[6] In her analysis of U.S. Federal Population Census manuscripts for Philadelphia in 1880, Claudia Goldin found that Irish children contributed between 38 and 46 percent of the total family labor income in two-parent families; German children 33 to 35 percent, and the native-born 28 to 32 percent. Unlike the mid-twentieth century when married women entered the labor force, in the late nineteenth century a child, not a wife, was likely to become the family's secondary wage earner.

To use children as active participants in the household economy of the working class was not only economically indispensible but also a legitimate social practice. The middle class, with its own children in school, still wistfully admired the moral principle of early labor. As late as 1915, one observer recognized: "There is among us a reaction to be noted from the . . . overindulgence of our children and a realization that perhaps more work and responsibility would do them good. . . ."[7] Even children's books and magazines, aimed at an educated middle-class audience, "hymned the joys of usefulness," praising the virtues of work, duty, and discipline to their young readers. The standard villain in these stories was an idle child.[8]

Child labor as a morally righteous institution was not a nineteenth-century invention. American children had always worked. In his classic study of family life in Plymouth Colony, John Demos suggests that by the time children turned six or eight, they were expected to assume the role of "little adults," engaged in useful tasks in their own homes, or apprenticed elsewhere.[9] Laws governing the poor in the seventeenth and eighteenth centuries similarly reflected prevalent Puritan views on the virtue of work by providing employment for dependent children.

Industrial work created different job opportunities for young children in the late eighteenth century. Employers welcomed their nimble "little fingers" for the "gigantic automatons of labor saving machinery."[10] Indeed, the first workers in the American spinning mill set up in Rhode Island by Samuel Slater in 1790, were nine children between the ages of seven and twelve. By 1820, young boys and girls constituted 55 percent of the operatives employed in Rhode Island's textile mills.

An enthusiastic writer for *Nile's Register* eagerly anticipated the pecuniary payoffs of child labor for local economies: "If we suppose that before the establishment of these manufactories, there were two hundred children between seven and sixteen years of age, that contributed nothing towards their maintenance and that they are now employed, it makes an immediate difference of $13,500 a year to the value produced in the town!"[11]

Rapid industrialization multiplied job opportunities for children in the late nineteenth century. Official estimates show an increase of over a million child workers between 1870 and 1900. One-third of the work force in the newly developed southern textile mills, for instance, were children between the ages of ten and thirteen, and many even younger.[12] For working-class families, the employment of children was part of what historian John Modell calls a limited "defensive" mode of family cooperation, "an attempt to pool risks in what was experienced as a very uncertain world."[13] Particularly for nineteenth-century urban families dependent on daily wages, the unemployment, sickness, or death of the main family earner constituted a major threat. The middle-class father could afford to purchase financial protection from life insurance companies; as early as 1851, over $100 million of security was bought. Although cheaper industrial insurance became available to the working-class after the 1870s, it only provided limited burial coverage. Mutual aid groups and voluntary associations offered some institutional protection, yet Modell concludes that, for the working class, it was the "individual coresident family that, as budgetary unit, adapted in the face of uncertainty."[14]

The useful child, therefore, provided a unique economic buffer for the working-class family of the late nineteenth century. But by 1900, middle-class reformers began indicting chil-

dren's economic cooperation as unjustified parental exploitation, and child labor emerged for the first time as a major social
problem in the United States. The occasional attempts to
regulate the work of children earlier in the century had been
largely ineffective and unable to galvanize public opinion. Existing state laws were so lax and vague as to be unenforceable.
In fact, they were not even intended to put children out of
work. Instead, early child labor legislation was primarily concerned with assuring a minimum of education for working
children. The pioneering Massachusetts statute of 1836, for
instance, required three months' schooling for young factory
laborers. As late as 1905, a *New York Times* editorial contested
the "mistaken notion that the advocates for the restriction and
regulation of child labor insist that children under fourteen
everywhere shall not work at all and shall be compelled to
attend school practically all the time." The true aim of the
earlier movement was to determine "the amount of labor and
the amount of schooling that would be reasonable." In fact,
nineteenth-century child welfare organizations were more
concerned with idle and vagrant children than with child
laborers.[15]

Child labor only gradually achieved national visibility. In
1870, for the first time, the U.S. Census provided a separate
count of adult and child workers. Bureaus of Labor Statistics
were organized in ten states between 1869 and 1883, producing and distributing data on child workers. Child labor became
an issue in the press. Poole's Index to Periodical Literature lists
only four articles under child labor between 1897 and 1901.
Between 1905 and 1909, according to the *Readers' Guide to
Periodicals,* over 300 articles were published on child workers.
Child labor rapidly established itself as a priority item in the
political agenda of Progressive social reformers. Organizational

growth was impressive. The first Child Labor Committee was formed in 1901; by 1910 there were twenty-five state and local committees in existence. A National Child Labor Committee was established in 1904. These groups sponsored and indefatigably publicized exposés of child labor conditions. Child Labor committees were assisted by the National Consumer's League, the General Federation of Women's Clubs, and the American Federation of Labor. The emerging Socialist Party also directed much attention to the issue of child labor. For instance, in 1903, Mother Jones, the well-known union organizer, led a dramatic "March of the Mill Children," from the Philadelphia area, through New Jersey and into New York, in order to expose the evils of child labor. By 1907, an article in Hearst's influential *Cosmopolitan* assured its readers that child labor would soon take its place "with all the institutions of evil memory—with bull baiting, witch-burning, and all other execrated customs of the past."[16]

Why did twentieth-century child labor lose its nineteenth-century good reputation? What explains the sudden vehemence and urgency to remove all children from the labor market? Most historical interpretations focus on the effect of structural, economic, and technological changes on child labor trends between the 1870s and 1930s. The success of industrial capitalism is assigned primary responsibility for putting children out of work and into schools to satisfy the growing demand for a skilled, educated labor force. Rising real incomes, on the other hand, explains the reduced need for children's wages. As the standard of living steadily improved between the late nineteenth century and the 1920s, child labor declined simply because families could afford to keep their children in school. Particularly important was the institutionalization of the family wage in the first two decades of the twentieth

century, by which a male worker was expected to earn enough
to forgo the labor of his wife and children. Stricter and better
enforced compulsory education laws further accelerated the
unemployment of children.[17]

In his analysis of changes in the youth labor market, Paul
Osterman contends that children were "pushed out of industry" not only by the declining demand for unskilled labor but
also by a simultaneous increase in its supply. The tide of turn-
of-the-century immigrants were children's new competitors.
For Osterman, compulsory school legislation was the result,
not the cause, of a changing youth labor market: "Since firms
no longer required the labor of children and adolescents, those
pressing for longer compulsory schooling were able to suc-
ceed."[18] Joan Huber similarly points to a conflict of interest
between age groups created by the new economic system. In
an agrarian economy, as in the early stages of industrialization,
the labor of "little work people," was a welcome alternative
that freed men for agriculture. But by the turn of the century,
the cheap labor of children threatened to depress adult
wages.[19]

Demand for child laborers was further undermined by new
technology. For example, in late nineteenth-century department stores, such as Macy's and Marshall Field's, one-third of
the labor force was composed of cash girls or cash boys, young
children busily involved in transporting money and goods between sales clerks, the wrapping desk, and the cashier. By 1905,
the newly invented pneumatic tube and the adoption of cash
registers had usurped most children's jobs.[20]

The issue of child labor, however, cannot be reduced to neat
economic equations. If industrial technological developments
combined with the increased supply of immigrant unskilled
workers inevitably reduced the need for child laborers, why

then was their exclusion from the work place such a complex and controversial process?

The Child Labor Controversy

The history of American child labor legislation is a chronicle of obstacles and defeats. At every step of the battle that lasted some fifty years, the sustained efforts of child labor reformers were blocked by an equally determined, vocal, and highly effective opposition. Until 1938, every major attempt to pass national regulation of child labor was defeated. The two groups were divided by conflicting economic interests and also by opposing legal philosophies. Yet, the emotional vigor of their battle revealed an additional, profound cultural schism. Proponents and opponents of child labor legislation became entangled in a moral dispute over the definition of children's economic and sentimental value.

Child labor legislation was first resisted on a state level. Although by 1899 twenty-eight states had some kind of legal protection for child workers, regulations were vague and enforcement lax. The typical child labor law, which only protected children in manufacturing and mining, often contained enough exceptions and loopholes to make it ineffective. For instance, poverty permits allowed young children to work if their earnings were necessary for self-support or to assist their widowed mothers or disabled fathers. As late as 1929, six states retained such an exemption. Legislative progress in the early twentieth century was further undermined by a lack of uniformity in state standards. Progressive states became increasingly reluctant to enact protective legislation that put them at a competitive disadvantage with states where employment of a cheap juvenile force was legal or else minimally regulated.[21]

The struggle for national regulation of child labor began inauspiciously in 1906 with Indiana Senator Albert Beveridge's dramatic but unsuccessful attempt in the U.S. Senate to create a federal law to end what he termed "child slavery." The threat of federal regulation only served to consolidate the opposition. In 1916, when Congress finally passed the first federal law banning the products of child labor from interstate and foreign commerce, opponents promptly challenged the new law in court, and two years later the bill was declared unconstitutional. A second federal law was passed in 1919, only to be again dismissed three years later by the Supreme Court as an unconstitutional invasion of state power.

The toughest battle began in 1924 after Congress approved a constitutional amendment introduced by reformers that would authorize Congress to regulate child labor. The campaign against state ratification of the amendment was staggering: "The country was swept with propaganda. It appeared in newspapers and magazine articles, editorials, and advertisements, in enormous quantities of printed leaflets, and in speeches, at meetings, and over the radio. The proposed child labor amendment was one of the most discussed political issues of the year."[22] The opposition effort succeeded; by the summer of 1925, only four states had ratified the amendment and thirty-four had rejected it. Briefly revived in 1933, the amendment again failed to secure sufficient state support. Effective federal regulation of child labor was only obtained after the Depression, first with the National Industrial Recovery Act and in 1938 with the Fair Labor Standards Act, which included a section on child labor.

What accounts for this catalog of obstacles? Why weren't child labor reformers able to easily dazzle legislatures or swiftly persuade the public with the justness of their cause? In large part, resistance to legislation was engineered by powerful interest groups. After all, in 1920 over 1 million children between the ages of ten and fifteen were still at work. From the start, southern cotton mill owners refused to forgo the profitable labor of their many child employees.[23] Child labor reform was often depicted as a dangerous northern conspiracy to destroy the recently expanded southern industry. Mill owners were eventually joined by farmers and other employers of children. Not surprisingly, the National Association of Manufacturers and the American Farm Bureau Federation were two leading forces against the 1924 constitutional amendment. A different type of opposition was based on political and legal principle. In this case, the target was federal regulation. Conservative citizen organizations and even prominent individuals, including the presidents of Columbia University and Hunter College, actively crusaded against the federal child labor amendment because it challenged states' rights.[24]

It would be inaccurate, however, to caricature the child labor dispute simply as a struggle between humane reformers and greedy employers or to reduce it to a technical dispute over the relative merits of state versus federal regulation. The battle involved a much wider range of participants, from clergymen, educators, and journalists to involved citizens, and included as well the parents of child laborers. At issue was a profound cultural uncertainty and dissent over the proper economic roles for children.

In Defense of the Useful Child

In a letter to the editor of the *Chicago News,* a Reverend Dunne of the Guardian Angels' Italian Church bitterly criticized the 1903 Illinois child labor law as a "curse instead of a blessing to those compelled to earn their bread by the sweat of their brow." The priest ridiculed a law that transformed the noble assistance of a working child into an illegal act: "He must not attempt to work; he must not dare to earn his living honestly, because in his case . . . that is against the law."[25] From the early skirmishes in state legislatures to the organized campaign against the 1924 constitutional amendment, opponents of child labor legislation defended the pragmatic and moral legitimacy of a useful child. As a controversial article in the *Saturday Evening Post* asserted: "The work of the world has to be done; and these children have their share . . . why should we . . . place the emphasis on . . . prohibitions . . . We don't want to rear up a generation of nonworkers, what we want is workers and more workers."[26] From this perspective, regulatory legislation introduced an unwelcome and dangerous "work prohibition": "The discipline, sense of duty and responsibility, . . . which come to a boy and girl, in home, on the farm, in workshop, as the result of even hard work . . . is to be . . . prohibited."[27] The consequences would be dire: "If a child is not trained to useful work before the age of eighteen, we shall have a nation of paupers and thieves." Child labor, insisted its supporters, was safer than "child-idleness."[28]

Early labor was also nostalgically defended as the irreplaceable stepping stone in the life course of American self-made men. The president of the Virginia Farm Bureau, fondly recalling his early years as a child laborer, insisted on the need "to leave to posterity the same chance that I enjoyed under our splendid form of government."[29] Similarly upholding children's "privilege to work," a writer in the *Woman Citizen* speculated if "Lincoln's character could ever have been developed under a system that forced him to do nothing more of drudgery than is necessitated by playing on a ball team after school hours."[30] Overwork, concluded the article, was a preferable alternative to overcoddling. Child work was even occasionally defended with theological arguments: ". . . The Savior has said, 'My Father worketh hitherto, and I work . . . May not the child follow the footsteps of the Savior . . . ?" If labor redeemed, regulatory laws served the interests of Hell, by making of idle young people the devil's "best workshop."[31]

For working-class families, the usefulness of their children was supported by need and custom. When parents were questioned as to why their children left school early to get to work, it was often "perplexing" for the mother to assign a reason for such an "absolutely natural proceeding—he's of an age to work, why shouldn't he?'" As one mother who employed her young children in homework told an investigator: "Everybody does it. Other people's children help—why not ours?"[32] Studies of immigrant families, in particular, demonstrate that the child was an unquestioned member of the family economic unit. For example, in her study of Canadian workers in the Amoskeag Mills of Manchester, New Hampshire, Tamara Hareven found that the "entire family economy as well as the family's work ethic was built on the assumption that children would contribute to the family's income from the earliest possible age."[33] While generally older boys were more likely to become wage-earners, boys under fourteen and girls were still expected to actively assist the family with housework, childcare, and any income obtained from odd jobs.[34]

Government reports occasionally provide glimpses of the legitimacy of child labor: A mother boasting that her baby— a boy of seven—could "make more money than any of them picking shrimp"; or an older sister apologizing for her seven-year-old brother who was unable to work in a shrimp cannery "because he couldn't reach the car to shuck."[35] Work was a socializer; it kept children busy and out of mischief. As the father of two children who worked at home wiring rosary beads explained: "Keep a kid at home, save shoe leather, make better manners."[36]

Child labor legislation threatened the economic world of the working class. In 1924, one commentator in the *New Republic* predicted the potential disruption of traditional family relationships: "The immemorial right of the parent to train his child in useful tasks ... is destroyed. The obligation of the child to contribute ... is destroyed. Parents may still set their children at work; children may still make themselves useful, but it will no longer be by right and obligation, but by default of legislation. ... "[37] Many parents resented and resisted this intrusion. A 1909 investigation of cotton textile mills reported that "fathers and mothers vehemently declare that the State has no right to interfere if they wish to 'put their children to work,' and that it was only fair for the child to 'begin to pay back for its keep.' "[38] In New York canneries, Italian immigrants reportedly took a more aggressive stand. One study reports a quasi-riot against a canner who attempted to exclude young children from the sheds: "[He was] besieged by angry Italian women, one of whom bit his finger 'right through.' "[39] Parents routinely sabotaged regulatory legislation simply by lying about their child's age. It was an easy ploy, since until the 1920s many states required only a parental affidavit as proof of a child worker's age. For a small illegal fee, some notary publics were apparently quite willing to produce a false affidavit.[40]

Middle-class critics also opposed child labor legislation in the name of family autonomy. Prominent spokesmen such as Nicholas Murray Butler, president of Columbia University, warned that "No American mother would favor the adoption of a constitutional amendment which would empower Congress to invade the rights of parents and to shape family life to its liking."[41] An assemblyman from Nevada put it more suc-

cinctly: "They have taken our women away from us by constitutional amendments; they have taken our liquor from us; and
now they want to take our children."[42]

In Defense of the Useless Child

For reformers, the economic participation of children was an
illegitimate and inexcusable "commercialization of child
life."[43] As one New York City clergyman admonished his
parishioners in 1925: "A man who defends the child labor that
violates the personalities of children is not a Christian. . . ."[44]
The world of childhood had to become entirely removed from
the world of the market. Already in 1904, Dr. Felix Adler, first
chairman of the National Child Labor Committee, insisted
that ". . . whatever happens in the sacrifice of workers . . .
children shall not be touched . . . childhood shall be sacred
. . . commercialism shall not be allowed beyond this point."[45]
If the sacred child was "industrially taboo," child labor was a
profanation that reduced "the child of God [into] the chattel
of Mammon."[46]

The persistence of child labor was attributed in part to a
misguided economic system that put "prosperity above . . . the
life of sacred childhood."[47] Employers were denounced as
"greedy and brutal tyrants," for whom children were little
more than a "wage-earning unit," or a profitable dividend.[48]
Any professed support of child labor was dismissed as convenient rhetoric: "A prominent businessman who recently remarked that it is good for the children to work in industry is
a hypocrite unless he puts his own children there."[49]

Reformers sympathized with the financial hardships of the
working-class, yet, they rarely understood and seldom condoned working-class economic strategies. Instead, parents were

depicted as suspect collaborators in the exploitation of their own children. "If fathers and mothers of working children could have their own way, would they be with the child labor reformer or against him?" was a question asked in *The American Child*, a publication of the National Child Labor Committee.[50] Others were more forthright in their indictment: "Those who are fighting for the rights of the children, almost invariably, find their stoutest foes in the fathers and mothers, who coin shameful dollars from the bodies and souls of their own flesh and blood." A child's contribution to the family economy was redefined as the mercenary exploitation of parents "who are determined that their children shall add to the family income, regardless of health, law, or any other consideration."[51] As early as 1873, Jacob Riis had declared that ". . . it requires a character of more disinterestedness . . . than we usually find among the laboring class to be able to forego present profit for the future benefit of the little one."[52] At the root of this harsh indictment was the profound unease of a segment of the middle class with working-class family life. The instrumental orientation toward children was denied all legitimacy: " . . . to permit a parent . . . at his or her will to send a child out to work and repay himself for its maintenance from the earnings of its labor, or perhaps . . . make money out of it seems . . . nothing short of criminal."[53] Child labor, "by urging the duty of the child to its parents," obliterated the "far more binding and important obligation of the parent to the child."[54] This "defective" economic view of children was often attributed to the foreign values of immigrant parents, "who have no civilization, no decency, no anything but covetousness and who would with pleasure immolate their offspring on the shrine of the golden calf."[55] For such "vampire" progenitors, the child became an asset instead of remaining a "blessed incumbrance."[56]

Advocates of child labor legislation were determined to regulate not only factory hours but family feeling. They introduced a new cultural equation: If children were useful and produced money, they were not being properly loved. As a social worker visiting the canneries where Italian mothers worked alongside their children concluded: "Although they love their children, they do not love them in the right way."[57] A National Child Labor Committee leaflet warned that when family relations are materialistic, "It is rare to find a family governed by affection."[58] By excluding children from the "cash nexus," reformers promised to restore proper parental love among working-class families. "It is the new view of the child," wrote Edward T. Devine, editor of *Charities and the Commons,* a leading reform magazine, "that the child is worthy of the parent's sacrifice."[59]

Thus, the conflict over the propriety of child labor between 1870 and 1930 in the U.S. involved a profound cultural disagreement over the economic and sentimental value of young children. While opponents of child labor legislation hailed the economic usefulness of children, advocates of child labor legislation campaigned for their uselessness. For reformers, true parental love could only exist if the child was defined exclusively as an object of sentiment and not as an agent of production.

CHAPTER 3

From Child Labor to Child Work: Redefining the Economic World of Children

Ask a dozen persons "What is child labor?" and you will get a dozen answers, most of them in a rather startled and hesitant manner, and in language that may be violent but is likely also to be vague.

From "The Truth About Child Labor,"
Raymond Fuller, 1922

THE battle line between proponents and opponents of child labor legislation was confounded by imprecise and ambivalent cultural definitions of child labor. For instance, it was often unclear what specific occupations transformed a child into an exploited laborer, or what determined the legitimacy of some forms of child work. In the early part of the twentieth century this ambiguity frustrated government attempts to reach a precise national accounting of the number of child laborers: "Is a girl at work who merely helps her mother in keeping the house? When a child helps its parents, irregularly, about a little store or a fruit stand, is it working? What of the children who are kept out of school to 'tote dinners' . . . ?"[1] Opponents of legislation insisted on children's right to work, yet often categorized certain occupations as illegitimate forms of employment. Reformers' passionate advocacy of the useless child was similarly qualified. Accused of giving work a "black eye," they defensively retorted that the anti-child labor movement was also pro-work. Raymond Fuller, at one time Director of Research at the National Child Labor Committee and one of the most vocal spokesmen for child labor reform, protested that "Nothing could be farther from the truth than the . . . widespread notion that child labor reform is predicated on the assumption that children should have no work."[2] As the child labor dispute evolved, the relationship of children to work was increasingly examined and reappraised. Gradually, the nineteenth-century utilitarian criteria of labor and wages appropriate for the useful child, were replaced by a noneconomic, educational concept of child work and child money better suited to the twentieth-century useless child.

Illegitimate Child Labor or "Good Work"?
The Search for New Boundaries

Investigation of why children quit school early suggested that work appealed to them: "The 'call' is one which involves the use of energy in creative work—in accomplishing something useful in the work-a-day world."[3] Yet, where could the useless child find useful outlets? Reformers acknowledged the quandary: "The dilemma for the city child seems to be either painful exhaustion and demoralizing work on the one hand, or futile idleness . . . on the other."[4] One observer only half-jokingly proposed the creation of a Society for the Promotion of Useful Work for Children.[5] Raymond Fuller identified the essential difficulty:

The category of child labor tends to become . . . too broad or too narrow. Some of us are so sure of the badness of child labor that we call bad nearly every activity that takes the aspect of work; and some of . . . us are so sure that work is a good thing for children that we leave out of the category of child labor much that belongs there.[6]

The solution was to devise criteria that would differentiate more clearly between legitimate and illegitimate economic roles for children. Child labor reform would not simply be an absolutist anti-child labor campaign, but instead a pro "good" child work movement. "To establish children's work," asserted Fuller, "is quite as important as to . . . abolish child labor."[7]

It was a difficult task. As Fuller himself admitted: "There is a dividing line between . . . ordinary, not too numerous, not too heavy tasks, and the tasks that represent an abuse of labor power of children; but it is not a clear, sharp dividing line."[8] At what age, for instance, was the line crossed? By nineteenth-century standards, the employment of a nine- or ten-year-old had been legitimate and for the most part legal. In fact, age was not considered a very important criterion of legitimacy until after the 1860s. Before then, only four states limited the age of employment of children. Nineteenth-century child labor legislation focused primarily on reducing the hours of work and providing some education for child laborers rather than establishing age limits. In 1899, there were still twenty-four states and the District of Columbia without a minimum age requirement for children employed in manufacturing. Child labor reformers met with formidable resistance as they struggled to institute age as a central boundary distinguishing child work

from child labor. Critics objected to a legal requirement keeping children useless until twelve and protested even more force-
fully against a fourteen-year age limit. Often, parental and legal
conceptions of a proper age limit clashed. Enforcement officials complained that many immigrant parents were unable to
calculate age in American terms: "I ask a mother the age of her
daughter. After the fashion of her particular [Jewish] race, she
will shrug her shoulders or turn her head, signifying that she
does not know. I insist upon an answer, and she will say 'Tues-
day' or 'four o'clock.' "9 Gradually, age became an accepted
measure of legitimacy. Between 1879 and 1909, the number
of states with age limit provisions (for any occupation except
dangerous employments and mining) increased from seven to
forty-four. The legal age limit was first raised from ten to twelve
and then to fourteen. After the 1920s, child labor organizations
fought to raise the age limit from fourteen to sixteen.10

If it was difficult to establish a proper age boundary, it
became even more complex to differentiate between types of
jobs. Industrial child labor was the most obvious category of
illegitimate employment. As one of the most passionate opponents of early labor explained: "Work is what children need.
. . . But the bondage and drudgery of these mill-children and
factory children and mine-children are not work, but servi-
tude."11 Accordingly, the earliest child labor laws were almost
exclusively designed to regulate the manufacturing and mining
industries. Yet, even this area of work found its committed
supporters. A 1912 book, *The Child That Toileth Not*, provoked a heated debate in the press by asserting that government reports had misled the public by censoring information
about the beneficial aspects of child labor in cotton mills. The
author, who had investigated child labor conditions in the
southern textile industry concluded: "If I were a Carnegie or
a Rockefeller seeking to improve the conditions of our poor

mountain people, I would build them a cotton mill. I would gather their children in just as they are big enough to doff and spin. . . ."[12]

If defending factory work was unusual, farm labor on the other hand was almost blindly and romantically categorized as "good" work. Even though by 1900, 60 percent of all gainfully employed children (ten to fifteen years old) were agricultural workers, their labor was not defined as a social problem. In his pioneering and dramatic exposé of child labor before Congress in 1906, Senator Beveridge of Indiana deliberately excluded agricultural labor: "I do not for a moment pretend that working children on the farm is bad for them . . . there can be no better training."[13] The legitimacy of farm work was reflected in its legal status. Even as the number of rural child laborers continued to increase, most state laws and the two federal child labor bills focused on industrial child labor, and consistently exempted agriculture from regulation. To be sure, this indemnity was carefully preserved by the powerful farming interests; yet, it was also the result of an equally influential cultural consensus. As an officer of the National Child Labor Committee remarked in 1924, "Everybody is against [child labor but] work on farms . . . is not held to be child labor. The presumption that everything is well with the child in agriculture runs so strong that any inquiry . . . is held by some not only useless but almost improper."[14] As late as 1932, the White House Conference on Child Health and Protection still noted that " . . . the attitude of a large part of the public is not opposed to the employment of children in agriculture. . . . "[15]

The idealization of farm work by child labor reformers wavered as investigations in the 1920s began to uncover some of the hardships experienced by young agricultural laborers. A survey of 845 children in North Dakota, conducted by the U.S. Children's Bureau, found boys and girls under age seventeen engaged in a wide variety of farm work. Seventy-one percent of the children were under fourteen. Aside from field work, herding cattle was their most common task. Boys and girls, often as young as six years old, were "out on the prairie alone on foot or on horseback for long hours in the heat of the summer without shelter or drink . . . in danger of being thrown from horseback . . . or trampled on by the cattle." Others were involved in the construction of barbed-wire fences, digging or drilling holes for posts as well as assisting with butchering jobs, cleaning seed for the spring planting, and even taking care of farm machinery. Out of the 845 children, almost 750 were also responsible for routine chores and housework. One nine-year-old boy, for instance "built the fires in the morning, swept the floors of a two-room house, and brought in fuel and water; in addition, before he made a two-mile trip to school, he helped feed stock (5 horse and 12 cows) and chopped wood; in the evening he did the chores and washed dishes."

In the North Dakota study, 20 percent of the children had worked away from home during the preceding year, either for wages or for their board; the majority were under fourteen years of age and had assisted with harvesting chores or as general farm helpers. The Children's Bureau study showed that farm and homework took children away from their school work. For instance, an examination of the school records of 3,465 children in six rural areas in North Dakota revealed that 42 percent of the 2,776 children under fourteen years of age, and 59 percent of those between ages ten and fourteen had been kept home for work in defiance of child labor regulations.[16] An earlier investigation of rural children in several North Carolina counties found a similar situation. In a typical mountain county, for instance, a father of eight was asked why he did not buy a corn planter. He responded: "I already have eight." The family's workday often began at six or seven in the morning and ended at sundown, with an hour off for dinner. The report concluded that "although early training in habits of industry is desirable, and . . . a reasonable amount of farm work would scarcely injure a healthy child of sufficient size and strength, children's work on the farm . . . as is described in this report . . . [puts] undue strain upon the strength of the child, the interruption of his schooling . . . the ill effects upon his health."[17]

But the solution was not a wholesale condemnation of farm labor; instead, reformers sought to differentiate better between "good" farm work and exploitative farm labor. As one writer in the *American Review of Reviews* explained in 1924: "Work on the farm performed by children under parents' direction and without interference with school attendance is not child labor. Work performed by children away from home, for wages, at long hours and under conditions which endanger the child's health, education and morals is child labor."[18] Thus, commercialized agriculture joined the ranks of illegitimate occupations, while the legitimacy of work on the home farm was idyllically preserved.

Between the extremes of industrial child labor and farm work, there was a variety of other occupations for children of a much more uncertain status and with different claims to legitimacy. Fred Hall, executive secretary of the National Child Labor Committee identified such occupations as "the borderland or frontier of the child labor program—an area in which the public often assumes that children's work is a valuable preparation for future usefulness."[19] Working as a Senate page, for instance, was a prestigious occupation for children. Working as a cash-girl or cash-boy in a department store also promised an attractive and legitimate entry into business life.[20]

Street work and particularly newsboys presented child welfare workers with a unique dilemma. As Raymond Fuller explained in his book *Child Labor and the Constitution:* "Many of us . . . are rather strongly prejudiced in favor of it, finding ourselves obliged to overcome serious difficulties in order to recognize it as child labor."[21] Legislatures similarly hesitated to challenge the legitimacy of street work. While other occupations gradually established fourteen as a minimum age limit, children in street work could legally start work at ten or twelve, and many began as young as six or seven. The White House Conference report of 1932 still considered the regulation of street work as "one of the most difficult problems in the whole field of child labor law."[22] Why, wondered an observer, did people condemn child labor in the factories, yet "tolerate it and even approve of it in the street?" Why did factory work transform a child into a slave, yet street work somehow qualified him as a respectable "little merchant"?[23] As one social worker complained in 1905: "It seems the part of the iconoclast to controvert the public conception of the newsboy."[24]

The legitimacy of newspaper sellers, as well as many child peddlers and bootblacks, was initially determined by nineteenth-century utilitarian values. Unlike factory workers or children in mercantile establishments, street traders were not employees but independent merchants, working for profits and not for wages. It was a glamorous form of entrepreneurship. J. G. Brown, a painter who specialized in nineteenth-century street boys, described them to a reporter: "My boys lived in the open. There wasn't a danger of the streets that they didn't face some time or other during the day. They would take a chance, any time, of being run down by a wagon or a streetcar for the sake of selling a paper or selling a 'shine' . . . they were alert, strong, healthy little chaps."[25] Even twentieth-century reformers were reluctant to put such children out of work. Pioneers in child welfare such as Jacob Riis admiringly referred to the "sturdy independence, love of freedom and absolute self-reli-

ance" of street boys.[26] In 1912, a major study of child labor
in the streets marveled at the persistent "widespread delusion
that . . . these little 'merchants' of the street are receiving
valuable training in business methods and will later develop
into leaders in the affairs of men."[27]

As with farm labor, exposés of children working in the streets
gradually punctured prevailing myths. A study conducted by
the Children's Bureau found children often as young as six and
seven selling papers in city streets. As one eleven-year-old newsboy complained, "My little brother sells more . . . because
people think he is cute."[28] Newsboys worked late hours, 10
P.M. or sometimes until midnight, especially on Saturday
nights, selling the Sunday papers to the theater and restaurant
crowds. Street work was found unfit for children, distracting
them from school and introducing them into a life of vice and
"unnatural desires." After all, if children's games were being
pushed off the street, certainly children's street work could not
survive much longer. As one expert in the field explained, street
work was considerably more hazardous than child play:

. . . there is a well-known difference in the physical and moral
influences surrounding street trading in the downtown district with
all the freedom from external control either on the part of city or
parent, as compared with . . . street play within the neighborhood
. . . where the restrictions of home and friends are able to influence
. . . [the child's] conduct.[29]

Once again, the boundaries of legitimacy shifted as reformers distinguished more closely between types of street work.
Earlier economic criteria (that is, the distinction between
wages and profits) were inadequate: "The effect on the child
of work is in no wise determined by the form in which his
earnings are calculated."[30] While most street occupations, including the sale of newspapers, were declared to be unfit forms

of child labor, the neighborhood carrier who delivered newspapers to the homes of subscribers was gradually singled out for legitimacy. The criteria for "good work," however, were dramatically reversed, converting the previously admired independent role of a newsboy into a liability. Why was the delivery of newspapers acceptable? Precisely because "the delivery boy is in no sense an independent merchant or dealer. He neither buys nor sells . . . and he assumes no responsibility except for his own work. He is an employee."[31] Carrying newspapers, concluded the Children's Bureau investigation "puts no temptations in the boy's way to stay out of school, nor does it bring him in contact with such influences as many of the street sellers meet." Unlike the newsboy, the carriers' hours were "unobjectionable"; boys delivering evening papers were finished usually before 6 P.M., "their work did not keep them on the streets after dark . . . nor interfere with their family life." It was a perfect occupation for the domesticated child, not real work but a "schoolboy's job."[32] The day messenger service was another form of legitimate street work for young boys. The night messenger service, on the other hand, was harshly condemned for allegedly employing youngsters to deliver telegrams but in fact using them to carry notes, food, liquor, and drugs to prostitutes, pimps, and gamblers.

Child labor in the home raised even more complex and confusing definitional problems. It also involved a different population; while selling newspapers or bootblacking was a boy's job, home occupations were largely, although not exclusively, a girl's domain. Studies suggest that young girls probably constituted from one half to three fourths of the children involved with homework, while of the 17,669 children ten to fourteen years of age working as newsboys in 1920, only 168 were girls. Unlike a factory, or a street, or a store, the home was sanctioned by reformers as a proper workplace: ". . . every child needs to be taught to work; but he needs to be taught not in the factory but in the home . . ."[33] Officially, domestic activities were not even considered "real" work. Instructions to census enumerators specified that "children who work for their parents at home merely on general household work, on chores, or at odd times on other work, should be reported as having no occupation."[34]

But what about industrial homework, that is factory work done at home mostly by mothers with their young children? It usually involved immigrant families or other unskilled low-paid groups living in the tenement districts of large cities. Industrial homework included a wide range of activities, chiefly finishing men's clothing, embroidering, making artificial flowers, and stringing tags. Children helped with the simpler tasks and often delivered the work from the home to the factory. By the late nineteenth century, homework had become one of the most prevalent forms of child labor. Yet many employers claimed that since the "little helpers" worked with their mothers, they were not really employed.[35] Parents themselves praised an occupation that kept their children busy and safely off the streets. Investigators discovered that "In certain streets home work was almost a universal occupation, and when a new family moved into the district the children would take up the work either in imitation of their playmates or at the suggestion of their parents. . . ."[36] Homework did not necessarily interfere with school work; children usually worked after school hours, Saturdays, and on vacation days.

The industrialized home forced reformers to reassess the meaning of domestic child labor. Tenement homework was condemned as a "peculiarly vicious" form of child labor.[37] After all, it polluted the one traditionally legitimate workplace.

As one critic regretfully remarked: "Truly a noteworthy change from the time when children got a large part . . . of their education in domestic industries to the time when domestic industries must be abolished in order to save the children from exploitation in them!"[38] Yet what distinguished tenement homework from legitimate housework? At what point did work for a parent become exploitation? Parents themselves were considered unreliable judges: "It is obvious many parents know little of the nature of work needed by, or suited to, their children. It is still work because there is work to be done, not because certain selected work is educational."[39] George Hall, secretary of the New York Child Labor Committee contended that " 'Helping mother' with house-work is all right, for the amount of work to be done is limited and there is little temptation to exploit the child; but 'helping mother' with paid work is another thing. The amount of work is unlimited, and ignorant and selfish parents sacrifice their children."[40]

The solution was not to remove all child work from the home, but to discriminate more intelligently among types of domestic employment. Taking factory work out of the home was only the first step. Equally important was to determine appropriate household tasks for children. As an article, significantly entitled "Ideal Child Labor in the Home," suggested: "The home will understand the educational necessity of work . . . and will allow each child . . . to contribute to the welfare of his family as a group and provide for his best development through the performance of a desirable amount of daily constructive work."[41] Fuller, for example, harshly criticized extreme parental dependence on children to do their housework. Yet, he maintained with equal conviction that "Work can be . . . a good thing for children. Little girls helping their mothers with housework . . . sewing and cooking; boys raking leaves . . . these and many other kinds of home occupations are a delight to behold."[42] One progressive Birmingham school even introduced a parents' report card in order "to help the child by recognizing industry and excellence in home occupations."[43] Parents were asked to grade as satisfactory, excellent, fairly good, unsatisfactory, ordinary, or very poor a wide range of domestic activities performed by their children, such as garden work, care of household tools, care of furnace, making fires, care of horse or cow, sweeping and dusting, making beds, and general cooking.

On the Boundaries of Legitimacy:
The Case of Child Actors

On January 4, 1910, the Supreme Court of Massachusetts ruled in the landmark case of *Commonwealth v. Griffith* that acting was work. It dismissed the defendant's claims that the word "work" should be given a narrow meaning and limited "to such as is done in a factory, workshop or mercantile establishment." Consequently, the defendant, a theater manager, was found guilty of violating the child labor law by employing a nine-year-old boy and a thirteen-year-old girl for a play at the Majestic Theater in Boston.[44]

Child actors triggered one of the most highly publicized and controversial definitional battles in the child labor controversy. Benjamin B. Lindsey, the noted juvenile court judge and an active supporter of stage work for young children, characterized the issue as, "the only question concerning child labor that has threatened any division of opinion among the best known of those in this country who have been foremost in the fight against child labor."[45] Indeed, in a bizarre turnabout, prominent child labor reformers were suddenly the leading advocates of child labor on the stage. *The Christian Advocate* also noted with dismay a similar inconsistency in the press and the general public:

[They] have been cordially sympathetic with the agitation of the National Child Labor Committee in its efforts to protect the child workers in the coal breakers, the glass factories and the cotton mills . . . but when . . . the same committee set itself against . . . using young children in stage plays, the editors . . . become critical and join with the play-going public in denouncing such activity as meddlesome interference.[46]

It was a dispute that lasted from the 1870s through the 1920s. It began in 1876 when Elbridge T. Gerry, president of the New York Society for the Prevention of Cruelty to Children, sponsored one of the first laws designed to regulate the employment of children in public exhibitions. Aimed primarily against street performances and dangerous acrobatic acts, the law became controversial when Gerry attempted to enforce it against the then very popular juvenile operettas. Theater managers accused him of a "monstrous discrimination against singing by children."[47] In 1881, when the well-known ten-year-old singer Corinne was stopped from appearing at New York's Metropolitan Casino, the *Nation* condemned the decision, reminding its readers that "as long as the theater continues to exist, some children will be fitted for theatrical life."[48] In 1887, eight-year-old Elsie Leslie "took playgoers by storm," in "Editha's Burglar," at the Lyceum Theater.[49] Her next success, in "Little Lord Fauntleroy," triggered a national "public craze" with child stars: "Little Lord Fauntleroys sprang up on every side, and every new play produced had its child interest. Some of the old plays were revised, and juvenile parts were written in."[50] Consequently, annoyance with existing restrictions of child actors intensified. An 1892 amendment to the New York law, which made the mayor responsible for licensing stage children, thus indirectly reducing Gerry's discretionary power, was hailed by the *New York Times* as "one of the few things for which the present Legislature may fairly claim some credit."[51] Support for child actors was formalized by the incorporation in 1893 of the Association for the Protection of Stage Children. Child actors themselves organized an "Anti-Gerry Society," which actively lobbied their cause. As one commentator observed some years later: "To infantile applicants the Gerry Society is a great ogre, lurking in wait to pounce upon and devour them. . . . If any one told them that this society was meant to do them good, they would think he was a lunatic."[52]

In 1910, the conflict over child actors escalated. Theater managers along with their many illustrious sympathizers mounted a national and highly visible campaign to exempt acting from child labor legislation. The National Alliance for the Protection of Stage Children, presided over by the noted playwright Auguste Thomas, had an impressive membership list ranging from John Alexander, a well-known painter, Percy S. Grant and Thomas R. Slicer, two prominent New York city clergymen also involved in civic affairs, to William Lyon Phelps, a famous professor of English literature at Yale. The alliance also included active child welfare workers as well as prominent actors, actresses, novelists, and producers. In 1911, the organization published and widely distributed "Stage Children of America," a booklet urging the public to recognize the legitimacy of acting for young children and warning against legislation based on "the radical theories of the uninformed . . . rather than upon the actual interest of the child himself."[53]

As demands to legally exempt child actors multiplied, the National and State Child Labor Committees rallied their supporters to counter what they perceived to be an unacceptable and dangerous challenge to child labor legislation. Between 1910 and 1912, the conflict drew the attention of the public and the press; stage children became the controversial theme of newspaper editorials and magazine articles.

The main legislative battles were waged in Massachusetts, Illinois, and Louisiana, the three most restrictive states for child labor on the stage. Theater advocates won their case in Louisiana, when the 1911 session of the legislature approved an amendment to the child labor law, authorizing children of all ages to work in the theater. Hailed by the victors, it was denounced by the secretary of the National Child Labor Committee as the "first backward step in child labor legislation in any state in eight years."[54] The Massachusetts and Illinois legislatures were less accommodating. Despite extensive lobbying, the almost universal support of the press, and the endorsement of prominent figures such as Merritt Pinckney, the noted Chicago juvenile court judge, and even an overseas telegram from Sarah Bernhardt, exemptions for child actors were rejected by both states. Yet, the theater interests were not easily discouraged. A national survey of stage children conducted in 1923 noted their continued efforts to modify child labor laws: "Bills are introduced in legislatures; attorney-generals, departments of labor, judges and juries have been appealed to, often successfully, on the interpretation of the law." By 1932, only seventeen out of forty-eight states, and the District of Columbia required a minimum age limit of fourteen or sixteen for the appearance of children in theatrical performances. In its report on stage children, the *White House Conference* of 1932 remarked that, "diverse as are the child labor laws of the various states, regulations applying to the appearance of children in public exhibitions are even more unstandardized."[55]

The intensity of the controversy surprised and dismayed many contemporary observers. After all, numerically, child actors were an insignificant sideline of the child labor problem. Reformers were criticized for this apparently unwarranted diversion from "child laborers who are really oppressed."[56] Yet, if the intensity of the efforts against child acting seemed misguided, the enthusiasm of theater sympathizers was no less mystifying. What explained the increasing appeal and legitimacy of child actors precisely at a time when other children were being put out of work? Why, as one theater expert remarked, "In no country has the child of tender years been permitted to hold so important a place on the stage as in the United States"?[57] The persecution of child actors by some as well as their absolution by others, reflected more than any other facet of child labor, the changing interaction between the economic and sentimental value of children in twentieth-century America.

Child Acting as Illegitimate Child Labor

For its opponents, a child actor was no different from any other child worker. When the press accused Elbridge T. Gerry of preventing children from "earning an honest living," he responded that "no parent has any right to profit pecuniarily by the exhibition of a child. . . . It was to protect children . . . that the law was passed, just as it forbids their use in begging, peddling, or in factories." In fact, theater work compounded the evil of economic exploitation with the risk of moral perversion: " . . . the associations are bad for the children . . . they are constantly brought into contact with persons about whose morality . . . the less said the better . . . the girls soon lose all modesty and become bold . . . they . . . usually end in low dance-houses, concert-saloons, and the early grave. . . . The boys . . . end by becoming thieves or tramps."

Children, contended Gerry, were put on the stage for the same mercenary reasons that they were sent to work in a factory or a department store, "to put money in the pockets of somebody," generally their parents.[58] As early as 1868, it was the "shrewd and business like" stage mother who took the brunt of the criticism:

> ... they make the bargains for the hire of the children and in all cases take their money. ... While their cherubs are swinging in mid-air as items of a "Vision of Beauty," the mothers are home chatting ... and should a neighbor drop in to announce an accident at the theater ... they would rush to the establishment distracted between an appropriate motherly alarm and the consideration of the proper sum to be demanded in damages of the management.[59]

In the 1910 Massachusetts legislative debates, opponents of child labor on the stage similarly raised the specter of profiteer mothers, "hawking their children as commercial assets at stage doors." Proponents of child acting also had to contend with religious and moral prejudice against the theater generally and not just against children on stage. As one proponent of child acting in Massachusetts remarked: "[I] ... wish a bill could be framed ... to keep all religious sentiment away from the matter. The labor end is bad enough, but the two together are seemingly fatal."[60]

Children on the stage were a topic of discussion in many meetings and publications of the National Child Labor Committee. Committee officials accused theater advocates of repeating the same arguments used by other employers of children. The defense of acting, claimed reformers, was based on outdated and inappropriate utilitarian criteria. The higher salary of some child actors, for instance, was an irrelevant consideration: "It has never been assumed that young children should be burdened with the problem of self-support and it can make no special difference . . . whether the employed child earns little or much."[61]

The necessity of an early apprenticeship was particularly controversial. While supporters of stage work produced long lists of ex-child actors—such as Julia Marlowe, Mrs. Fiske, Maude Adams, Francis Wilson, Annie Russell, Eddie Foy—who later became prominent adult stars, opponents of child acting claimed that only a few successful adult actors had begun their career as children. Everett W. Lord, secretary for New England of the National Child Labor Committee, noted that, according to the *Who's Who on the Stage in America*, only eighty-eight of almost 500 prominent actors and actresses of the time began their stage career under fourteen years of age. Ethel Barrymore, Sarah Bernhardt, and Eleanor Robeson were among those who began working after fifteen while Blanche Bates, Lily Langtry, John Mason, and many others made their first professional appearance after they were eighteen. Insistence that an early apprenticeship in the theater was an indispensable prerequisite was also disparaged on moral grounds: "[it] is the same argument used in the other industries that many successful men began to work early and it is now a thoroughly discredited reason for child employment." Future usefulness could no longer exonerate child labor of any kind.[62]

During a public debate about child actors in 1911, Owen R. Lovejoy, secretary of the National Child Labor Committee, rejected claims that "the American public has demanded the army of babies that are clamoring . . . for [theater] permits."[63] Instead, he attributed the success of child actors in the first decade of the twentieth century simply to the business skills of theater managers who exploited a cheap and vulnerable labor force. Allowing this "industry for children on the stage," concluded a speaker at the seventh annual conference on child labor that same year, was a "social abomination."[64]

Child Acting as Legitimate Child Work

Supporters of stage work refused to categorize the child actor as a child worker. Francis Wilson, a leading actor of the period and a vocal spokesman for theater advocates, insisted that "By some mistake of wording, the factory laws . . . have been made to include the stage-child. To place this royally paid child of the stage, with his few moments of mental effort, on the same level with the underpaid overburdened child of the factory is flagrantly unjust."[65] Unlike ordinary child laborers, the child actor or actress loved to work. But opponents responded this was a misguided and dangerous infatuation. As Gerry had explained in 1890, "Of course they cry when not permitted to perform. Children proverbially cry when deprived of what is hurtful to them. They enjoy the performance on account of the excitement . . . their brilliant tinsel costumes, and the applause of the audience, which flatters their vanity."[66]

The theater interests carefully delineated their boundary of legitimacy, for support of theater work did not extend to other forms of child labor. Accused by Bishop William Lawrence of Massachusetts of undermining factory laws by requesting exemptions for child actors, Francis Wilson responded: ". . . not a man or woman who stood up in defense of the stage child but is as firmly opposed to child labor in the mill, the sweatshop and the factory as the good bishop himself."[67] In a letter to the *New York Times,* the chairman of the Sweatshop Committee conveyed a similar distinction: "As a strong opponent of child labor of any kind, I yet feel dramatic work is quite different . . . I have never been able to see why children, (even little ones) . . . should not be allowed to develop the theatrical instinct."[68]

An 1868 report described the typical career sequence of a stage child: "From his wages of $1 as a 'squalling babe,' in a few years the toddling boy will earn $3 a week, and so he goes on, filling the successive roles of 'street urchin,' 'Babe of the Wood,' . . . for sums that enable his family to keep him in clothes and food, at least."[69] In its early stages, the defense of child acting relied heavily on such economic arguments; acting was not ordinary labor but lucrative work for children. A *New York Herald* journalist observed in 1892, that "very many children in this big city . . . work much harder and get much less for their pains than the children on the stage." The reporter contrasted the "rosy cheeked, happy" child actresses, who "work at play," for five dollars a week to cash girls or a shop girl: "Without overcoat or rubbers she hurried on. The little face was pinched and thin, and her bony fingers clutched the $1.75 she had just drawn after the hardest week's work in a year."[70]

Economic claims to legitimacy were still periodically invoked between the 1910 and 1912 stages of the controversy. In a newspaper interview, actress Ellen Terry explained that "stage children were cared for and looked after because they are wage-earners for the family and their health and well-being determine their value."[71] Yet, the defense of acting gradually shifted grounds; it was more often justified as education than as elite work: "The stage, with its lessons of history, costume, and custom . . . is a liberal education . . . in going to the stage [the child] is going to school."[72] As playwright Auguste Thomas put it, acting was "as valuable for a child as a scholarship for Oxford is for a young man."[73] Inflexible laws, warned Francis Wilson, arbitrarily deprived children of their singular "medium of expression": "Who would advocate a law prohibiting children with musical gifts from playing the piano? . . . Who . . . would deny the Chicago child scientist, or the Harvard child student?"[74] Even the alleged mercenary qualities of stage mothers disappeared in the sympathetic portrayals of theater supporters: ". . . They are more tender and painstaking with their stage children than the average mother."[75]

Opponents of stage work distinguished between commercial acting and educational drama. Jane Addams, for instance, encouraged an amateur children's theater in her own Hull House, explaining "The children of course are not paid for their services. . . . Any money that they make is spent for their summer outings."[76] The 1876 New York law sponsored by Gerry to regulate the employment of children in public exhibitions had similarly exempted children's vocational or philanthropical participation as singers or musicians in a church, school, or academy. Thus, acting was legitimate work as long as it did not become "real" wage labor. Theater advocates, however, insisted that even commercial stage work provided an artistic education. Payment was beside the point. Instead, supporters of stage work differentiated between types of dramatic experience: "Take the child out of the moving picture shows and the low burlesque companies. . . . By this means the merely commercial child of the stage is banished forever and the dramatic child genius given its opportunity to expand."[77] Thus, while admitting that child gymnasts, dancers, and singers were unfortunate laborers, theater enthusiasts upheld the stage child as a privileged exception.

The conflict over child acting could be characterized as another economic struggle: one between theater managers eager to increase box-office returns and reformers committed to prevent child labor. Yet, the evidence shows that allegiances did not follow these predictable patterns; interest in child welfare did not necessarily mean opposition to child labor on the stage. Both the enthusiasm and the consternation over child actors were tied to the cultural redefinition of the economic and sentimental roles of children. Children on the stage created a curious paradox; they were child laborers paid to represent the new, sentimentalized view of children. They worked to portray the useless child. The Little Lord Fauntleroys captivated by provoking "emotional havoc" in theater audiences largely composed of women. Already in the mid-nineteenth century, the cult of child mourning reached the stage; popular plays often dwelt on the sorrows of a young child's untimely death. The *New York Times* noted in 1868 that the sentimental dramas of the day "worked to their highest pitch by the introduction of a tender infant, or a docile child."[78] In the early twentieth century, theater enthusiasts raved about the "child-value" in plays, "the emanation of the spirit of childhood; an emanation that only a little child can convincingly give forth . . ."[79] The effect of children, observed a writer in the *New England Magazine,* "is puryfing . . . hardened faces relax and all sit back in sweet peace, for except as you are a little child, you shall not enter the kingdom of happiness."[80] In this celebration of the sentimental value of children, the work role of child actors was ironically camouflaged by their fictional roles. They succeeded as popular symbols of the new "sacred" child. Recognizing that "the charm of the child on the stage is its childishness," theater managers took every precaution to guard and publicize the ingenuous qualities of their young employees. Reporters certified that "a moment's talk with these little folk of the theater assures you that they belong as much to the land of dolls and tin soldiers as to the realm of limelight and rouge. . . ."[81] The specific appeal of childhood also meant that, unlike other forms of labor, child acting did not replace adult work. Significantly,

while most labor unions opposed child labor, the Theatrical
Stage Employees supported child acting.

The very sentimentalization of childhood on stage that se-
duced theater advocates infuriated its opponents. Ridiculing
"the comfortable belief that these little inhabitants of Stage-
land know only the silks and laces of existence," they refused
to confuse fiction with reality, the stage role with the child
laborer, "who lives in a disagreeable quarter of the city, with
a father or mother whom she supports and who is only interested in the money she can bring home."[82] Critics spent so
much time and energy against this apparently benign form of
child labor precisely because acting transformed the essence of
childhood into a commercial asset:

[T]here are some gifts of which no man has a right to make a capital.
It would ill become one to whom a talent of friendship has been given
to trade upon his powers of sympathy or a saint upon his devotional
capacities; and in like manner the idea of a professional child—a child
in whose case simple childhood is the sole stock in trade . . . is touched
with sacrilege.[83]

In other forms of child labor, monetary value was assigned to
the performance of specific tasks, but in acting, the "appeal of
childhood is the commodity actually offered for sale to a sentimental and unthinking public."[84]

The dispute over child labor on the stage was fueled by the
cultural redefinition of a child's worth. Acting was condemned
as illegitimate labor by those who defined it as a profane capi-
talization of the new "sacred" child. Yet, ironically, at a time
when most other children lost their jobs, the economic value
of child actors rose precisely because they symbolized on stage
the new economically worthless, but emotionally priceless
child.

House Chores and a Weekly Allowance:
The Economic World of the Useless Child

By 1930, most children under fourteen were out of the labor market and into schools. Yet, significantly, federal regulation of child labor contained some exceptions. The most influential statute in the field of child labor, the Fair Labor Standards Act of 1938, allowed children under fourteen to work in newspaper distribution and in motion pictures and the theater. Except for manufacturing and mining, a child also remained legally entitled to work for her or his parents. Agricultural labor, which still employed the largest number of children, was only semiregulated as children were permitted to work outside of school hours. Similar exceptions were contained in the National Industrial Recovery Act industrial codes passed in 1933 but declared unconstitutional in 1935. The defeat of the Child Labor Amendment in the 1920s and again in the 1930s was partly the result of its failure to recognize any differentiation between children's occupations. By empowering Congress to "limit, regulate, and prohibit the labor of persons under eighteen years of age," the amendment presumably left no room even for legitimate child work.[85]

To be sure, the cultural and legal immunity of certain occupations was partly dictated by the market, in particular, the powerful farming, newspaper, and entertainment industries that had much to lose by a child work prohibition. But it was also based on a radically revised concept of child work. As twentieth-century American children became defined by their sentimental, noneconomic value, child work could no longer remain "real" work; it was only justifiable as a form of education or as a sort of game. The useful labor of the nineteenth-century child was replaced by educational work for the useless child. While child labor had served the household economy, child work would benefit primarily the child: "We are interested . . . in work for the sake of the child, and are seeking to find kinds of work best suited to develop his body, mind and character."[86] The legal and cultural differentiation between legitimate and illegitimate occupations for children was thus guided by an entirely new set of criteria suitable for the unemployed "sacred" child. Labor on the home farm, for instance, was condoned "for the unselfishness and the sense of family solidarity it develops." Newspaper work was a legitimate "character-building" occupation. The Children's Bureau investigation in the 1920s found that parents of carriers were "emphatic in their approval of the work . . . because they believed that it provides training in the formation of good habits. . . . It was not the financial reason that stood out in their expressions of approval." Job advertisements for young carriers in the *Ladies' Home Journal* explained that the magazine had solved a problem for "thousands of the brightest boys in America," by providing them with an enjoyable pastime: "They get a lot of fun out of it, earn their own spending money, and get a moral and business training of inestimable value."[87] Acting, claimed its advocates, was not work at all but a liberal education and above all, a joyful child's game. "Work?" queried the *New York Dramatic Mirror,* "most child actors consider it play, and so it is practically that, except that their little minds are being unconsciously developed in a way which would be impossible elsewhere."[88]

As child work shifted from instrumental to instructional, special consideration was given to domestic chores. When an article appearing in *Home Progress* advised parents, "Let your children work," the work referred to "some little household task," not too difficult of course, "for their tender bodies."[89]

Already in 1894, popular magazines alerted their middle- and upper-class readers about their children's "eagerness to seize opportunities for sharing the work as well as the play of the home.... Shelling peas on Monday because the cook is washing is to him as enchanting as counting pearls on a string. ..."[90] As working-class children left the labor force for the classroom, their mothers were likewise instructed to keep them busy at home: "It is pitiful ... for a woman to believe that she is 'bettering' her children by ... allowing them to think that it is degrading for them to help in the housework...."[91]

Yet, the point was not to assist the mother, but to educate the child. In 1931, the Subcommittee on Housing and Home Management of the White House Conference on Child Health and Protection strongly recommended that "less emphasis ... be placed on the amount of assistance rendered and more on the educational values [to the child] of the responsibilities involved in the performance of household tasks."[92] It was not always an easy task. As Dr. Amey E. Watson, an expert in household work, acknowledged: "For a busy mother ... it is far easier to do the job herself than to stop to teach a child to do it; but if she has the long-range point of view and is thinking of the character development of the child, the work should be planned so that ... the mother ... can have enough leisure to stop and teach the child...."[93]

House chores were therefore not intended to be "real" work, but lessons in helpfulness, order, and unselfishness. Parents were warned to "take great care not to overburden the child with responsibility ... lest the weight of it should crush him instead of develop a greater strength."[94] Above all, warned *Parents Magazine*, one should "never give ... children cause to suspect us of making use of them to save ourselves work."[95] It was not easy to find such an ideal domestic job. As William Ogburn remarked in 1930, "The household duties are less, and hence the child loses the training and responsibilities that go with these duties. . . ."[96] A survey of junior high school students by the 1930 White House Conference noted that urban children performed about three-fourths as many household tasks as did the rural child.[97] The "servant-keeping" class was particularly limited in this respect. One well-meaning parent, reported the *Journal of Home Economics*, had tried to teach her young child the "dignity of labor," but the only available job was flower arrangement. In another family, the son simply tipped the butler to do the boy's chores. The problem of unoccupied middle-class children was not new. As Mary Beth Norton notes in a study of eighteenth-century women, "City daughters from well-to-do homes were the only eighteenth-century American women who can accurately be described as leisured."[98] Yet, even they did an extensive amount of sewing for their families. The new rules and problems of child work cut across classes, equally applicable to all unemployed children. For instance, in 1915, one observer had noted the extent to which parents of former child laborers were "entirely unprepared to cope with the situation, having little means of home employment for their children." The expanding school system attempted to incorporate "good" work into their curricula. As Edward T. Devine explained, "work which we deny . . . in the factory, for profit, may be demanded in school . . . for education and training."[99]

As children's involvement with work changed, so did their relationship to money. The wages of a working child had been considered legitimate family property. Thomas Dublin's analysis of the mid-nineteenth-century records of the Hamilton Manufacturing Company, a major textile mill in Lowell, Massachusetts, suggests that fathers signed for, and probably picked up their children's pay envelopes. As Dublin explains, "parents thought of their children's earnings as part of the family income." This financial collaboration survived into the twentieth century. In the Amoskeag Mills in Manchester, New Hampshire, Tamara Hareven found that "the custom for working children to contribute most of their wages to their families was an unwritten law."[100] A 1909 Senate investigation of the cotton textile industry showed that children's pay envelopes were "turned over to the parent unopened. There is no question as to this—it is taken as a matter of course." Similarly, studies of New York's West Side, conducted in 1914, noted that a "broken envelope violates the social standard." While an outsider might pity the child "who must hand over the bulk of his meager earnings," the investigators remarked that the "moral sentiment of the neighborhood insists upon this duty . . . for the rearing of children is indeed no easy matter here . . . and the slight help that the child can contribute . . . is the father's or mother's due."[101]

Yet, children often regained a small portion of their wages in the form of a spending allowance. For instance, a 1909 survey of 622 working children from several cities found that over half of them received a regular weekly allowance (usually between twenty-five and fifty cents), while others had more irregular arrangements. The 1914 studies of New York's West Side remarked that "some allowance from [the working child's] earnings is his by right." It was also noted that children's contributions were usually "standardized. How much they keep for themselves, how much they give in, is made a matter of rule and custom."[102] Yet, the rules for children's money depended more on parental attitudes than any economic logic. For instance, the 1909 Senate report discovered that some of the children earning the highest wages received no allowance while some children earning small amounts, received allowances of fifty cents or more. Immigrant parents were less apt than the native-born to give their children spending money.

Girls were more likely to contribute all their wages to the family, less likely to receive an allowance or, if they did, their stipends were smaller than boys'.[103] Tips were apparently considered a child's property. The 1914 West Side study noted that it was "a mark of high virtue to surrender them. A woman will tell with pride, 'He knew I was hard up and he gave me his tips.' "[104]

Even after being shut off from factories and stores, young working-class children sought alternative ways of raising some spending money. When an investigator asked a sample of over one thousand Chicago children between the third and eighth grades: "How do you get the money you have to spend?" 71 percent of the boys and almost 60 percent of the girls responded: "I earn it." The girls ran errands or did housework and babysitting for their parents and neighbors, while the boys, in addition to working for their parents, ran errands for strangers ("going to the store for a lady" meant from 1 cent to a nickel profit), sold papers or ice, caddied, and bootblacked. The working-class child, concluded the investigator, "sees a very close relation between money and service, and makes the receipt of one dependent on the performance of the other." As one young boy explained, "We must work to earn money."[105]

If a working child earned money through labor, what was to be the source of income once children stopped working? As the American economy turned out thousands of new consumer items, many of them directed at a juvenile audience, children's money became increasingly problematic. Michael V. O'Shea, professor of education at the University of Wisconsin and an expert in child welfare, remarked in 1915 that "there has probably been no aspect of family life which has been the cause of greater strain and stress than the problem of the child and his money." Working-class parents were not only relinquishing the income of their children, but also assumed significant new expenses of clothing and school supplies. Indeed, a 1903 investigation found few social class differences in children's spending habits. All children spent their money in school shops, purchasing supplies, but they also spent money on candy, toys, ice cream, theater tickets, and often tobacco and gambling. Regardless of class, boys spent more than girls. Concerned with children's "fever for spending," surveys investigated the "financiering of the child who is not a regular wage-earner." Articles began appearing on "The Child's Idea of Money," "The Child and Money," or "How Children Spend their Money."[106]

To be sure, middle- and upper-class children were already veteran paupers. As the *Outlook* remarked in 1903: "Servants, bootblacks, and the poorest class are rich in comparison with many young people who are dependent for their pennies . . ." Children, observed the article, "are often at their wits' ends to know how to get a dollar together."[107] When children from affluent families were asked how they obtained spending money, most responded: "It's given me," but not without first having to tease and cajole their parents or else beg "sympathetic relatives or friends, expecting a donation."[108] "Tipping" other people's children seems to have caused some controversy in the early twentieth century. When *Home Progress* asked its readers "What should parents do when guests in the house offer the children small sums of money?" responses ranged from warm approval to harsh condemnation. "My children," wrote a mother from Calmet, Michigan, "always explain to people that they are not permitted to receive money from callers, visitors, or people they meet in the street."[109]

The proposed solution to the economic insolvency of young children was an allowance to be provided by parents on a regular weekly basis. As early as 1893, the allowance was endorsed as "the best method . . . for giving children an income."[110] By 1930, the White House Conference on Child Health and Protection found that the trend in urban homes was "away from doling out driblets of money as needed, toward a regular allowance."[111] While the concept of the allowance was a middle-class invention, it was advocated by childcare experts and others as a solution for all children, regardless of class. For instance, Justice Mayer of the New York City Court, assured that an allowance would even serve as a crime deterrent for lower-class children. Lack of access to legitimate spending money, argued the judge, often turned decent, studious youngsters into thieves: ". . . the difficulty is that these children have no money to spend so that their desire to have what other children have—candy, soda water, neckties, children's fobs—cannot be gratified." With a small allowance, the child "would be saved from his initial wrong." Ironically, while money given to children by their parents was upheld as "safe" money, money earned by children was stigmatized by reformers as "dangerous" money, allowing the child an anomalous economic independence from its parents. The White House Conference found a relationship between delinquency and the source of spending money; adolescent nondelinquent boys were more likely to receive an allowance, while predelinquent boys were more likely to earn their money.[112]

But how could poor parents afford this additional gift of money? Although the evidence is limited, it suggests that the allowance became an expectation and sometimes a reality even among working-class families. As children lost their economic value, the nineteenth-century economic contract between parents and children had to be revised. Thus, parents were not only expected to forgo their children's wages, but they were expected to subsidize children's expanding spending habits, "from carfare to a ball ground to the highly coveted coin for a nickel show." The 1914 report of the West Side of New York, for instance, noted that although "these families have no very large sums of money to give their children . . . the wisdom of allowing a boy some spending money is recognized. . . . Money is given to school boys in small quantities and for definite things. 'If he gets a quarter a week, he doesn't get it all at once.' " Even prospective foster parents (recruited largely from the working class) were expected to provide their charges with a regular weekly allowance.[113]

It was difficult, however, to develop proper guidelines for the allowance money of a nonworking child. If wages were contingent on work, what did an allowance depend on? Could money be divorced from labor, and should it? From the start, the allowance was justified as educational money: "Considered educationally, ability in childhood to spend, to save, or to give away wisely from an income insures a happy manhood or womanhood."[114] By 1930, *Parents Magazine* expressed even more explicitly the noneconomic functions of children's money: "A sense of values is what we wish to develop in our children by the use of money. The way any one spends his income indicates what he considers valuable."[115] In the new consumer society of the twentieth century, the old lessons of thrift and saving were no longer sufficient. By teaching how to spend wisely, the allowance would train children as efficient shoppers: "If parents would only spend as much thought on teaching a child to spend money sensibly as they do in teaching him to save, how little there would be for him to learn when the time comes that every day means an expenditure. . . ."[116] In 1931, a Children's Bureau publication on "The Child and His Money," strongly warned parents not to transform their children into "little misers." As the *New York Times* observed, "The little boy who puts all his pennies in his metal bank no longer is ranked

... as the shining financial example for childhood." The new American ideal was a child "who spends wisely, saves wisely and gives wisely."[117]

A regular allowance served more than the child's best interest. For parents, it was an expedient arrangement to regulate their children's stepped-up requests for money. Women's magazines explained to their readers: "It is not . . . a child's fault when he teases for things, for almost always the child who teases is the one who asks for money as he goes along, perhaps receiving it, perhaps being refused. . . ."[118] In order to be effective, the allowance had to be a fixed "unearned" salary. Parental regulation of the expensive, nonworking child was further assured by closely supervising children's use of money. As Angelo Patri, an expert in child development, advised parents: "It will not do to give children money and allow them to use it without the oversight of some older person."[119] *Crestwood Heights,* a study of suburban life in the late 1940s provides some insights into parental techniques for supervising children's money; "The child may be allowed to 'buy on approval', that is, he can 'shop for himself,' but purchases are then accepted or returned by the parent. . . . Supervision in spending the allowance may be exercised on the grounds that the parent is 'forming the child's taste' or 'teaching him the value of money' or material objects."[120]

Converting money into an educational and moral instrument, however, was not easily accomplished. In order to preserve the traditional association of money with labor, the allowance was sometimes justified as an earned wage. *Harper's Bazaar,* for instance, recommended that children be trained "in the way in which money should come to any one—as the reward of labor." It suggested paying children, "by the day or week for keeping their rooms or bureau drawers in order, for being punctual at their meals, for having clean hands . . . or

for performing small duties about the house. . . ."[121] But this
solution led to an untenable new prospect—the monetization
of the home. Child labor reformers had long decried the perni-
cious effect "on premature minds of working for payment," in
factories and stores.[122] Ironically, once children were removed
from the market, their home became a place of employment.
After all, if parents were one of the few remaining legitimate
employers, where else could the child earn money? Parents
were warned against the dangers of commercializing the home
and urged to distinguish between the "principles of the home
. . . and [those] of the shop."[123] In 1911, the Rev. Dr. Hugh
T. Kerr in his *Children's Story-Sermons,* told a story that illustrates the ideal altruistic norm for household exchanges:

One morning when Bradley came down to breakfast, he put on his
mother's plate a little piece of paper neatly folded. His mother
opened it. She could hardly believe it, but this is what Bradley had
written:

> Mother owes Bradley
> For running errands . . $.25
> For being good 10
> For taking music lessons .15
> Extras. 05
> Total . . . . $.55

When lunch time came [the mother] placed the bill on Bradley's
plate with fifty-five cents . . . [and with] another little bill, which read
like this:

> Bradley owes mother
> For being good . . . . $.00
> For nursing him through his long illness
>   with scarlet fever. 00
> For clothes, shoes, and playthings 00
> For all his meals and his beautiful room .00
> Total that Bradley owes his mother . . $.00

Tears came into Bradley's eyes, and he put his little hand with the fifty-five cents in [the mother's] and said, "Take all the money back mamma, and let me love you and do things for you."[124]

For those who insisted on "paying" their children's allowance, the advice was to complement it with an occasional gift of "unearned" money, preferably on the Fourth of July, when "it is a real hardship for a child to take a whole dollar . . . for fireworks."[125] Another common rule was paying children exclusively for work that otherwise a stranger would be hired to do.

The preferred solution, however, was to firmly establish the allowance as "free" educational money just as domestic chores were expected to remain "free" unpaid instructional child work: "We . . . expect children to wash dishes or dust the furniture because . . . sharing in the work and responsibilities of the home is a needful part of their experience in home-making, and there is no thought of bargaining here."[126] By the 1930s, the differentiation of allowance from wages was un-equivocally endorsed. While recognizing that "it is not easy for either parent or child to draw a clear, logical line between allowance and earnings," the *Journal of Home Economics* con-cluded that a child's allowance "is of the nature of a right rather than a wage. He has earned the privilege of recognized membership in the family and of this status an allowance is a symbol." Allowances and wages were consequently two distinct categories of money; the former was a "right . . . earned by personality," the other, "specified sums that [the child] earns by specific acts."[127] The allowance, affirmed Sidonie Gruen-berg, Director of the Child Study Association of America, "is as 'free' as food and clothing, for the child must spend before he can earn."[128]

But it was difficult to maintain intact this culturally invented boundary between wage and allowance. It was broken not only by those parents who paid their children for house chores but, increasingly, by using the allowance to regulate children's behavior. *Parents Magazine* repeatedly warned against misusing the allowance "as an instrument of 'discipline,' or as a means of purchasing the child's obedience, or affection, or 'goodness.'" Among the ten key rules for children's proper financial training suggested by the Children's Bureau was not to "tip the child . . . for being 'good' or polite." In such cases, the allowance again became a wage no longer contingent on work, but as a payment for bringing in a good report card, practicing music, or even eating vegetables, taking a nap, or taking cod-liver oil.[129]

In the first three decades of the twentieth century, children's money was thus invested with new educational, moral, and social functions. In addition, as all children became primarily consumers, some former economic distinctions between working-class and middle-class children were blurred. While the spending money of the useful child had been derived from his or her wages, the allowance for economically useless children, regardless of class, came primarily from their parents' pocketbook. Defined as "the child's own portion of the family income," children's money, even when earned, also became progressively differentiated from adult money. For instance, older children who remained in the labor market were increasingly less likely to hand over their entire paychecks to the family.[130] This process of differentiation, however, was a gradual one. For instance, a 1918 survey of 150,000 sixteen, seventeen, and eighteen-year-old employed boys in New York State found that in Greater New York, 77.4 percent of the boys contributed more than ten dollars weekly toward family support. Similarly, national studies of newsboys conducted in the 1920s show that one-third to three-fourths of the children still contributed part or all of their money to their families. When newsboys were allowed to keep part of their wages, it was often spent in "useful" purchases, such as clothing or other necessities. For instance, the thirteen-year-old son of an Italian streetcar motorman who earned three dollars a week selling and carrying papers, "gave his money to his mother for groceries, keeping twenty-five cents for spending money. He had also saved ten dollars with which he had bought a suit of clothes." Another ten-year-old earned two dollars and forty cents a week, "bought his clothes, put 10 cents in the school bank, spent 10 cents 'for a show,' and gave the rest to his family." Newspaper carriers, on the other hand, who were more likely to come from middle-class families, usually spent their earnings on themselves. A publisher's eleven-year-old son, for instance, earned two dollars and fifteen cents a week on his route, "out of which he paid $1 a week for violin lessons, paid his carfare to work, kept 10 cents a week for spending money, and in four years had saved $95."[131] In his study *Children of the Great Depression*, Glen H. Elder, Jr., found that the economic function of children's money became newly significant in the 1930s. Severely deprived households depended on a portion of their children's earnings for basic expenses.

Yet, despite some exceptions, the new rules were increasingly accepted; children were entitled to unearned spending money, and when they earned some pocket money, it was theirs to keep. "Earning money can scarcely injure the child," confirmed Robert S. Woodworth, a Columbia University psychologist, "if the money remains his own or is conscientiously devoted to his advantage."[132]

In this new cultural and economic context, parents of successful child actors, particularly during the mid-1920s and 1930s Hollywood child star craze, were caught in a curious predicament. Their children not only worked, but made fortunes, often claiming their parents as dependents for income tax purposes. For instance, Jackie Coogan, at age eight, commanded a million dollars plus a percentage of profits for a four-picture contract with Metro. Shirley Temple's mother was paid $500 a week for managing her daughter, while Mr. Temple received a 10 percent commission as Shirley's agent. In her autobiography, Baby Peggy, another child star from the 1920s, recalls reporters' intense curiosity as to "how many dollars we were putting into our parents' pockets."[133] Hollywood "mammas" received even harsher press treatment than their predecessors, stage mothers.

In 1938, Jackie Coogan, then twenty three years old, sued his mother and step-father to recover the four million dollars he had earned as a child actor. But the defendants contended that under common law, Coogan's earnings as a minor child were their legitimate property, not his. The widely publicized lawsuit resulted in the 1939 passage by the California legislature of a Child Actor's Bill, better known as the "Coogan Act." The bill established that half of a child's earnings had to be set aside for the child in a trust fund or another type of savings. The Coogan lawsuit thus successfully challenged the historical rule of law that the earnings of minor children belonged to their parents.[134] The verdict reaffirmed the new cultural and economic contract between parent and child.

Parents of other child stars felt compelled to publicly justify their children's income by demonstrating its legitimate uses. For example, the Temples were "proud of the way they have arranged Shirley's finances. Her father says they have really taken very little money from her income for expenses."[135] The public was reassured that Shirley's money was safely invested. But the ultimate confirmation of good parenting was that even Shirley Temple received an allowance of four dollars and twenty-five cents a week. She was not the only one. Jane Withers, among many others, received a five dollar weekly allowance, and also "makes her own bed, does housework, and even runs errands."[136] In 1937, Louis B. Mayer offered thirteen-year-old screen star Freddie Bartholomew a $98,000 a year contract. A clause provided for a one dollar weekly spending allowance for Freddy. A Los Angeles judge involved with the arrangements commented "That probably is the best contract of them all."[137] The real earnings of these often millionaire children were thus neutralized with a legitimate educational income. The allowance permitted the comfortable fiction that the "deviant" useful child was not so different from its useless unemployed counterpart.

The transformation of children's economic roles during the first half of the twentieth century illustrates the interaction between economic and noneconomic factors in advanced industrial societies. Children were removed from the market between 1870 and 1930 in large part because it had become more economical and efficient to educate them than to hire them. But cultural guidelines profoundly shaped and directed the process of social change by differentiating legitimate from illegitimate occupations for children and distinguishing licit from illicit forms of child money. As children became increasingly defined as exclusively emotional and moral assets, their economic roles were not eliminated but transformed; child labor was replaced by child work and child wages with a weekly allowance. A child's new job and income were validated more by educational than economic criteria.

CHAPTER 4

From a Proper Burial to a Proper Education: The Case of Children's Insurance

One gets a glimpse of the frightful depths to which human nature, perverted by avarice bred of ignorance and rasping poverty, can descend, in the mere suggestion of systematic insurance for profit of children's lives.

From *How the Other Half Lives*, Jacob Riis, 1890

Children insured are loved the most and taken best care of. I think it a mean, contemptible slander in saying that the poor . . . love their children less than the millionaires.

Rev. O. R. Miller, East Boston, 1895

THE sacralization of children in twentieth-century America introduced fundamental changes in existing standards concerning the value of child life. The next three chapters turn to the analysis of three major institutions which, at the turn of the century, became increasingly involved with the price and value of children: the life insurance industry, tort law, and social welfare organizations concerned with adoption and foster care. Each of them was profoundly revolutionized by the transformation in children's economic and sentimental value. Nineteenth-century instrumental criteria for insuring useful children, compensating parents for their accidental death, or placing them for adoption, became not only obsolete, but morally offensive. As a consequence, pricing the priceless twentieth-century child turned into an unusual accounting procedure, as children's sentimental contributions to family life increasingly became the sole determinant of their "surrender" value at death and their "exchange" value in adoption.

The business of insuring children was launched in the 1870s by the powerful industrial insurance companies. Their low-priced policies were designed to reach a new working-class clientele. For three cents a week, for instance, a one-year-old child could be insured for ten dollars; a ten-year-old for thirty-three dollars. Children's insurance was a huge marketing success, but, unexpectedly, it also became one of the industry's most controversial products. Turn-of-the-century child-savers vehemently and publicly battled insurers in the courts and in the press. To its many opponents, the commercial valuation of child life was an unacceptable profanation of its sacredness. By making a child's death profitable, insurers were not only endangering children's lives, but, even worse, defiling the cult of child mourning by turning it into a mercenary commerce. Insurance was, from a child-saver's perspective, a regrettable extension of child labor, guaranteeing children's economic value even after their death.

Although monetary compensation for the death of a child was initially justified by the pecuniary loss for the parents, the final success of the industry was based on more than economic rationality. Children's insurance made its appeal primarily as burial insurance for poor children. It offered working-class parents a more dignified alternative than the dreaded pauper burial. The industry, therefore, was accepted as a legitimate partner in the construction of a new world for children that transcended social class distinctions. This chapter looks at the controversy over children's insurance and its resolution as a measure of the changing relationship between the economic and sentimental value of children.

Marketing Children's Insurance: A Brief Background

Ordinary life insurance companies that had operated in the United States since the latter part of the eighteenth century had confined their business to husbands and fathers of middle-class families. In 1875, John F. Dryden of the Prudential Life Insurance Company began insuring the lives of children under ten. It was part of what was called "industrial insurance," a major marketing innovation aimed at the rapidly expanding working-class population. Besides accepting the insurance of children and women, industrial life policies were available in small units—the average face value of a policy was about $100. It was primarily burial insurance. Before the Prudential, urban working-class families joined fraternal societies and mutual aid groups. The unsound financial methods used by these associations, however, resulted in frequent failures and little assistance for bereaved families. In addition, any support was for adult burials; few arrangements existed for the death of poor children.

Beginning in 1875, insurance agents visited the homes of prospective buyers, usually insuring their lives without medical examination and collecting premiums weekly on a house-to-house basis. They were effective. In four months, one thousand lives had been insured in Newark, including 329 children under ten. After one year of operation, the Prudential received about $14,000 in premiums. In 1879, two more companies, Metropolitan Life and the John Hancock Company began selling industrial insurance. Perhaps because the premiums of 5 or 10 cents per week were affordable, the business grew beyond all expectations. By 1895, there were $268 million of insurance in force and the Prudential alone received over $33 million in premiums. The company then employed 10,000 agents.[1]

A crucial component of that prosperity, children's insurance became firmly established; one million and a half children were insured in 1896. In fact, juvenile insurance was considered by some insurance organizers as the clue to the success of industrial insurance. In England, where children's insurance existed since 1854, four million children were insured by 1896. As one historian explains, " . . . burial insurance for working-class children had become a norm."[2] The first English company, the Prudential, had initially rejected infantile risks. At the end of their first year, however, the company's most successful agent attributed his profits to the fact that he had started an independent society to insure children's lives. Company officials decided to take over his business.[3]

The greatest growth of industrial insurance in the United States took place between 1882 and 1902; at the end of that period over three million children were insured.[4] It was also during those years that the trouble started. Between 1889 and 1902, there were at least eighty legislative attempts across the country to prohibit or restrict the insurance of children's lives; such insurance was considered to be against public policy and the public interest. In 1884, as sales multiplied, the legislative battle began when Governor Benjamin Butler of Massachusetts included in his inaugural address the first official suggestion to prohibit the insurance of children. In 1889, Governor Beaver of Pennsylvania revived the attack in his annual message to the legislature and a bill was introduced to make the insurance of children unlawful in the state. Although the bill was defeated, the antagonism persisted and additional bills were presented—and rejected—in Pennsylvania in 1897, 1903, and 1907. This tireless attack on the industry that insured children was nationwide. Every few years, bills were introduced in New York, Ohio, Illinois, Massachusetts, Wisconsin, and thirteen other states. In Colorado the opposition was finally successful, for in 1893 the insuring of children was declared illegal.

Insuring children was expensive to the parents. Although premiums were low, so were benefits. The industry had to guard itself against the higher mortality of the working class and particularly that of children. Costs were also increased by the need to subsidize an army of industrial agents in their weekly door-to-door collections. Industrial policies had little or no surrender value to its owners, and the lapse rate was extremely high. The battle against children's insurance, however, had little to do with these economic issues. It was a moral crusade by child-savers on behalf of poor children. An examination of the arguments and rationales used by the equally relentless opposition and defense in their testimonies to state legislatures, in the press, and other publications, reveals a struggle over the changing value of the lower-class child.

The Opposition: Child Savers versus Child Insurers

In 1874, only one year before the child-insurance business started, upper- and middle-class groups organized the New York Society for the Prevention of Cruelty to Children, the first and one of the leading institutions of the national child-saving movement. The almost twin births were more than an unrelated coincidence. In different ways, both organizations became involved in the changing value of the lower-class child. The primary goal of child-savers, pursued through a wide variety of programs, was to enforce a new respect for the sanctity of poor children's lives and create for them a special nonproductive world. To many child-savers, child insurers were the enemy. The insurance of children stood as an offensive symbol of the prevalent materialistic orientation toward childhood that they opposed; it was a form of commercial exploitation even more sordid than most, since it speculated on a child's death. Insurance was a mercenary trivialization of the cult of child mourning.

To its detractors, "Child-Insurance Companies," as they referred to the industrial insurance business, had "child-blood" on their hands.[5] Newspapers across the nation carried sensational articles about the dangers of making a child's death profitable. On March 26, 1878, the Trenton *True American* suggested that children's insurance be declared invalid as a "dangerous incentive to murder . . . It is not only the inducement which inhuman parents . . . find in insurance on their children to ill treat them or put them out of the way, but it is the tendency to cause them to neglect their children in their sickness and . . . the demoralizing effect produced by parents speculating on the lives of their children." Even within the insurance community some leaders warned that one "should shrink with horror from the ungodly speculation."[6]

The genealogy of the business did little to dispel fears. Children's insurance began as outright bets among sixteenth-century European businessmen on the lives and births of boys and girls. The evidence suggests that in England the insurance of children by burial clubs, which started in the 1830s and 1840s, was sometimes a sordid affair. In *Past and Present,* Carlyle relates an 1840 case of a mother and father arraigned and found guilty of poisoning three of their children to collect insurance money from a burial society adding, "the official authorities . . . hint that perhaps the case is not solitary, that perhaps you had better not probe farther into that department of things." Social critics denounced insurance as a "bounty on neglectual infanticide."[7] Until the 1870s, government regulation in England was weak and seldom enforced. Baby farmers, for whom the death of one of their children was already a pecuniary gain, made it doubly profitable by insuring the children they "adopted," often in more than one company. A case of this "unspeakable trade partnership between the insurance touter and the ghoulish baby farmer" was presented before the Royal Commission on Insurance in 1875; a child had been insured for the benefit of his guardian in eight societies for a total of thirty pounds. During another investigation that same year, a Manchester lawyer testified that in the 1840s, "it was publicly said in the town that the children had been purposely killed [for insurance money]; it was a regular trade."[8]

Comparative data from France reveals similar accusations against child insurance for dangerously raising the price of children above their emotional value. Anecdotes circulated of mercenary "nourrices" and heartless parents grieving over the recovery of a sick child because it meant the loss of insurance benefits. Indeed, sales booklets popular in both France and Belgium enticed customers quite candidly with the potential profits to be gained from a dying child. One popular pamphlet, for example, included a conversation between two working-class fathers with one outdoing the other in marveling over how much money they had received from the insurance company after the death of one of their children.[9] The available evidence is not conclusive enough to prove beyond doubt that child insurance and child murder were related. In England, for instance, the frequent allegations of foul play were seldom backed by documented cases of parental neglect or murder for the sake of insurance money. However, taking into account the high rates of infanticide in England and in Europe in the eighteenth and early nineteenth centuries, the inference was not unwarranted. If the death of a child, particularly an unwanted child, was a lesser event, the possibility of making money out of it could well become a tempting incentive.[10]

Until the 1880s, the opposition to child insurance in the United States remained sporadic and unorganized. But in 1893, the national American Humane Society for the Prevention of Cruelty to Animals and Children passed a resolution that "the practice of insuring the lives of children under 10 years of age, under any pretext, is against public policy." Member organizations were urged to secure prohibitive legislation making it a criminal offense to insure "or in any way offer a reward upon the death of a child."[11] The legislative battle was on. The fiercest fight took place in 1895, when the Massachusetts Society for the Prevention of Cruelty to Children introduced a bill to the legislature to prohibit the insurance of children under ten. For weeks the opposition and the defense argued their cases, making sensational front-page news with their alarming statistics and emotional pleas. Clergymen, physicians, judges, and politicians took the stand to denounce the "diabolical" practice of insuring children. Concerned citizens urged legislators to stop "the traffic in the lives of children" and the "merciless temptation of making young death a profitable event."[12] Charity workers presented heartrending accounts of families in extreme poverty whose sick children, often dying of starvation, received no care but whose insurance premiums were paid regularly. Insurance companies were accused of joining with mercenary parents to "feather [their] own nest at the cost of blood and tears and deaths of human beings." Charles C. Read, a vociferous critic, instructed legislators: "I do not know whether you have seen the building of the Metropolitan Company in New York . . . Go up . . . to the directors' room where the floor is soft with velvet carpets and the room is finished in rich red mahogany . . . and there you will find these gentlemen who think what a beautiful thing this child insurance is . . ." From every block of marble of that magnificent place peered "the hungry eyes of some starving child."[13]

Agents were also attacked as an unscrupulous "band of sharpers"; "the more they hustle, the more they make."[14] In fact, although agents' compensation plans established certain penalties for lapsed policies, the emphasis was on generous commissions for larger sales, encouraging quantity over quality. English agents, often imported by American companies for their experienced background, were even suspected of "baby-baiting," paying parents for the death of an uninsured child to attract new customers. Benjamin Waugh, president of the English Society for the Prevention of Cruelty to Children, quoted alleged admissions of agents that "we bait our hook with a dead child" or "I am glad of a funeral, I look out for one . . . I get business by funerals."[15] On October 15, 1895, the *New York Times* joined the ranks of outspoken critics, its columns exposing the child insurance business as an unconscionable "temptation to inhuman crimes" and insurance agents as "pests of society."

The moral condemnation of children's insurance, however, went beyond the arguments of possible child neglect or murder. For many child-savers, it was not the danger of death but the profanation of the child's life that was at stake. To them, the insured child was but another version of the working child, one earning by its death what the other earned by its labor. And indeed, the legality of children's insurance depended upon child labor. Life insurance is only justified by the existence of an insurable interest, a reasonable expectation of gain or advantage in the continued life of another person, and no interest in his death. Against objections that insurance was an illegal wager, nineteenth-century American courts ruled that the right of parents to the services and earnings of minor children gave them an insurable interest in their lives. Judicial approval thus rested entirely in the pecuniary bond between parent and child. In *Mitchell v. Union Life* the judge declared: "A father, as such, has no insurable interest resulting merely from that relation in the life of a child . . . But the insurance in the present case was effected by a father upon the life of a minor son. . . . The father is entitled to the earnings of his minor child, and may maintain action for their recovery. . . . He has a pecuniary interest in the life of a minor child which the law will protect and enforce."[16]

In the late nineteenth century, the monetary value of even very young lower-class children, many of whom started working before they were ten, made their insurance legitimate. Walford's influential *Insurance Cyclopedia* explained: "Regarding the practice [of insuring children] it may find some defense in the manufacturing districts where every parent has an interest in the prospective earnings of his child."[17] Insurance companies reminded state legislatures:

The industrial classes have the moral and legal right to insure their children, for it is well known that these children contribute to the support of their families at very early ages. . . . There is a just and reasonable expectation of advantage or benefit from the continuance of their lives and it logically follows that a proper justification inheres in the parents to protect that benefit.[18]

The vice president of Prudential Insurance Company explained that for identical premiums, eight- or nine-year-olds received higher benefits than one- or two-year-old children partly because "at the older ages, to speak in a commercial and what may seem a heartless way, there gets to be more of a money value in the life of a child." The expectation of assistance in the parents' old age was another argument legitimating insurable interest in a child's life, but it carried less weight.[19]

For child-savers, this economic approach to child life was unacceptable. Child insurance no less than child labor polluted the sanctity of a child's life by monetary considerations. Critics asked: "Can any reflecting citizen . . . justify himself in assisting . . . the unnatural practice of child insurance? . . . It is certainly not too much to claim that there should be no bargaining or trafficking in our Commonwealth under our auspices, in infant life which has been held sacred."[20] "No manly man and no womanly woman," declared the *Boston Evening Transcript* in 1895, "should be ready to say that their infants have pecuniary value." Insurance agents were despised for making the death of a child a matter of economics, a routine business transaction by which, as the English put it, "you exchange the child for the pound."[21] Regardless of individual motivations, the necessarily commercial involvement of agents with the life and death of little children was defined as morally deviant. Significantly, even the *Insurance Monitor,* an established insurance journal, was uneasy about the new business of child insurance: "When a strong man in the full vigor of his manhood, purchases a policy for the protection of his helpless family, the world . . . applauds the act . . . [but] what shall be said when that same man contracts for a pecuniary benefit upon the possible death of his prattling baby?" The journal strongly warned against parents "ready to traffic with their offspring as if they were horses or goats."[22]

Despite its dramatic impact, the evidence against children's insurance was weak and unconvincing. In fact, the striking feature of the legislative hearings was not the cases of neglect but the intensity of the accusers' fears; their unquestioned certainty that lower-class parents could be so cheaply bribed into destroying their children. In their moral outrage, and following the often distorted perceptions of middle-class observers, child-savers assumed that the economic ties between working-class parent and child could easily become mercenary ones. If they were willing to profit from the labor of their children, parents would be equally willing to profit from their death. "Until fathers and mothers cease to be brutal and drunken," warned anxious critics, "it is not safe to put them in the way of such temptation as this child insurance." In England, Waugh claimed that at least a thousand children were murdered every year for insurance money. He insisted that benefits be paid directly and only to undertakers, to deter parents who otherwise chose a "little funeral" for the sake of the "big drink."[23]

In 1895, after six weeks of heated debate, the Massachusetts bill to prohibit the insurance of children was defeated 149 to 23. With the exception of Colorado, all other states similarly endorsed the business. In some ways, the outcome was not surprising. It is true that powerful economic interests were at stake; the death of children had become big business not only for the insurance companies but also for the funeral industry. In fact, there were many complaints that undertakers raised their prices for insured customers, adjusting bills to insurance benefits. In 1905, Haley Fiske, vice president of Metropolitan Life, instructed all superintendents, "to prevent extortion or unfairness practiced upon our policyholder," urging them "to refuse information to undertakers."[24] Industrial insurance also saved cities, churches, and taxpayers' money previously spent in subsidizing pauper burials. Bishop Grafton of Fond du Lac, Wisconsin, noted for instance, that children's insurance "has wrought of late years a large absence of those appeals for help that the city clergy know so well, for aid in children's burials." The number of pauper burials was cut in half between 1880 and 1895, and city officials estimated a yearly reduction of about 20,000 pauper burials. At an average cost of seven dollars per burial, this saved the cities approximately $140,000 annually.[25] Yet, the success of children's insurance cannot be reduced to the clever manipulations of capitalist entrepreneurs at the expense of poor people. The basis for its appeal among the working class is a clue to the changing value of their children.

The Defense: Child-Insurers as Child-Savers

While the law routinely recognized the monetary value of children as the basis for a parent's insurable interest, the insurance business rarely pressed the issue outside the courts. Instead, insurance leaders themselves adopted their opponents' child-saving rhetoric, stressing the priceless emotional value of children above their cash value. Children's insurance was sold as a symbolic concern for the dying child; it was never marketed as insurance for the working child. This industry approach split child-saving organizations. While some members

attacked insurance as a mercenary business, many others en-
thusiastically welcomed it as a new partner in the defense of
childhood. In Massachusetts, for instance, the main spokesman for the opposition was Charles C. Read, attorney of the
Massachusetts Society for the Prevention of Cruelty to Children, and yet John D. Long, vice-president of the same organization, represented insurers. Refuting accusations that "I am
opposing the cause of little children," Long insisted that in
pleading for their insurance he was pleading for their welfare.[26]
Charges of neglect for the sake of insurance money were found
to be unsubstantiated. Insurance commissioners from every
state attested to the fact that no specific cases of abuse, cruelty,
or murder of children for insurance money had ever been
reported. In an open letter to the *Philadelphia Evening Bulletin* on December 12, 1894, J. Lewis Crew, secretary of the
Philadelphia Society for the Prevention of Cruelty to Children,
confirmed the irreproachable record of the industry. In its
periodic investigations, the society had found no criminal uses
of insurance even by baby farmers. Children were insured as
"a token of love and affection" and not for profit. In hearings
across the nation, leaders of child welfare organizations, lawyers, politicians, policemen, and physicians testified in favor of
the industry, while many clergymen praised it as a "grand
blessing."[27]

Ultimately, the debate over child insurance was a debate on
the value of poor children, a public assessment of their emotional versus their economic worth. Working-class family ties
went on trial. To insurance critics, the sacredness of child life
was compromised by parents willing to accept not only their
children's wages but also profit from their death. Working-class
parents needed instruction in proper love and laws to protect
their children against improper parenting. From this perspective, the legal prohibition of insurance was an extension of

child labor legislation. Supporters of the industry, on the other hand, defended the authenticity of love among the working class. The director of the Philadelphia Organized Charities called it a "gross libel" to say that "parents in the laboring classes deliberately make away with their offspring for the sake of securing ... thirty or forty dollars," adding that "among the poorer classes, parents are very fond of their children."[28] Attacking bills against insurance as discriminatory class legislation, insurance supporters rejected the "repugnant idea ... that the poorer classes ... do not have that natural affection for their offspring," insisting at every opportunity that "the natural love of parent ... beats as strongly under the coarser vest as under the costliest."[29]

Some misgivings about working-class affections, however, were apparent even among the staunchest insurance advocates, for they supported strict legal restrictions to prevent speculation with a child's policy. Initially, no premiums higher than three cents a week were accepted and no benefits payable until a child had been insured for three months. Children under one were not insurable. Until 1896, the maximum amount payable for a child twelve years old or younger was sixty dollars; benefits were then doubled. Until the 1920s, no higher premium than ten cents was accepted. Average death benefits matched undertakers' bills. In 1895, for instance, the average paid on an infantile insurance policy was 28 dollars, while the average cost of a child's funeral was 25 dollars.[30]

Despite these precautions, sympathetic child-savers saw child insurance primarily as a symbolic recognition of the emerging sacred value of poor children's lives. It was not the hope of ready cash but the desire for a proper mourning ritual that prompted working-class parents to invest their meager funds in premiums. In his testimony to the Massachusetts legislature, John D. Long, vice-president of the Massachusetts

Society for the Prevention of Cruelty to Children, dramatically asserted, "You cannot stop them from paying tribute to their dead until you blot out of their hearts their love for their children." The insurance press agreed: "Thousands of children are assured . . . and this is regarded in the light of a burial fund, to secure for the child in case of its death a decent Christian burial."[31] Child-savers admitted that "for a parent to speculate a profit from the death of his offspring is repugnant to the natural feelings," yet "a provision by insurance for the cost of sacred decencies to the relics and memory of the dead [children] is worthy and legitimate." Defending the "sentiment of respect for the body of a child" as a Christian sentiment, supporters elevated insurance to an act of piety: "If death should come into the family they want the household to be protected from harsh and profane influence and they want . . . a decent burial."[32]

Unlike ordinary adult life insurance, which was rejected by customers in its early stages, children's insurance was opposed by some middle-class critics but not by actual or potential buyers. Policyholders testified in defense of the business and signed petitions demanding the right to insure their children. The Boston Typographical Union, for instance, sent a resolution to the 1895 Massachusetts hearings stating that "The passage of such a law . . . limiting the age of children [for insurance] would be a detriment to the interests of all working men and a reflection upon their intelligence." Defending children's insurance as a "grand institution for the poor," Jacob Huack, a Denver shoemaker, wrote Colorado legislators in 1893:

I lost a child which never was insured, and do you know where that poor thing is buried? Away out in the prairie in a place called Potter's Field and there, among unknown men and women, lies that child of mine. It makes my heart ache . . . I take it as a personal insult when I hear people say that the poor would kill their little ones for a few pieces of silver.[33]

Working-class families increasingly dreaded a pauper burial, for themselves or even for the youngest of their children; it compounded tragedy with degradation. In New York's Potter's Field, for instance: "In the common trench of the Poor Burying Ground [the dead] lie packed three stories deep, shoulder to shoulder, crowded in death as they were in life, to 'save space.' "[34] Infants were often buried in mass graves. Yet a proper funeral cost money. In "Death Comes to Cat Alley," one of his stories about tenement life in New York City, Jacob Riis told about the death of a baby on Mulberry Street, "An undertaker had promised to put [little John] in the grave in Calvary for twelve dollars and take two dollars a week until it was paid. But how can a man raise two dollars a week, with only one coming in in two weeks, and that gone to the doctor."[35] Instead, a wooden dead-wagon drove the little pine coffin to the Potter's Field. In 1908, when young Marion was killed by a trolley car in the streets of New York, her grandmother told a reporter: "Yes, I think I am cornered . . . I tried to get our undertaker in Brooklyn to bury [her] . . . He buried a child of mine years ago and I thought he would bury the little one on credit. But he wants $30 cash in advance. The last money we had was in Marion's hands when she was killed. She was going to the store to buy 5 cents worth of milk. . . ." As a result of the newspaper story, "which touched the heart of all classes," Susan Meade, the grandmother, received eighty-seven dollars in contributions, from individuals and organizations, and the child received a proper burial.[36] But the happy ending was atypical. In testimony presented in support of insurance, charity workers related cases of children lying unburied for many days because of unsuccessful efforts to raise money among neighbors.

To working-class families, children's insurance, was therefore, a welcome alternative to a pauper burial. A Sister Pamela from the Child's Hospital in Albany, New York, told about the relief of poor parents, "If a child so insured dies . . . as [they] realize that there is money to bury their dead decently without calling on the 'City' for help and also without . . . running into debt."[37] As a form of thrift and self-help, insurance was superior to charity and more effective than informal methods of raising burial money. After losing a nine-month-old baby whose life was not insured, an Italian mother decided to insure the rest of her children: "I had to pay $95 for the funeral; with the drinks it came to $115 . . . I thought it was bad enough to lose the child without having to do without insurance money."[38] A systematic analysis of the budgets of two hundred working-class families living in New York's Greenwich Village, conducted between 1903 and 1905, found that 87 percent carried some insurance: "It is an obligation which must be paid before any other. A family is frequently willing to be dispossessed or to go without food or clothing or fuel in order to keep up the insurance." The 1909 report on the Condition of Woman and Child Wage-Earners, also found that among a certain group of workers, insurance was "one of the first payments to be deducted from the family income." Similarly, a 1914 Russell Sage report noted that life insurance had become almost universal and a budgetary priority for working-class families: "After the rent, a mother's next care is the life insurance payments. . . . This is an expense that is kept up until resources are at their last gasp. One family lived for weeks on bread and tea, meeting the insurance dues every week."[39]

What explains the success of children's insurance? Was it

simply a clever marketing invention by the insurance industry; the result of persistent agents as well as undertakers, who "sold" parents on giving their children a proper burial? Critics interpreted the new concern with children's funerals as just one more example of "mistaken" parental love among the working class:

> How can the true mother, though poor . . . take any comfort in . . . more elaborate funeral surroundings . . . if the first thought that comes to her . . . is, "Oh, if I had only spent the money . . . all through my child's little life . . . perhaps it would not have been lying here now." It seems to me that the showy hearse and the white casket would increase the agony tenfold to any mother who has the true mother love in her heart . . . and are we not trying to implant the true and holy mother love in all classes. . . .[40]

But the purchase of a child's policy was based on more than clever solicitation or an insensitive consumerism. The surge of concern with the proper burial of poor children in the late nineteenth century, which became the main sales appeal of the insurance industry, suggests that working-class parents adopted the middle-class cult of child mourning. The sentimentalization of childhood cut across social class distinctions; the sacred child was mourned with new intensity even in the poorest homes. When possible, the anonymity of the Potter's Field was broken with occasional memorial stones for a child, bearing inscriptions similar to those in ordinary cemeteries, "My beloved son," or "Asleep in Jesus, blessed daughter."[41] The evidence also suggests that working-class parents seldom considered insurance as coverage for the lost labor of their children; nonworking children were insured as much as working children.

Insurance sold primarily as a modern mourning device; it

"bought" a dignified death for children. One mother, who insisted on paying for two carriages for the funeral of her son even though no one rode in the second one, explained to a researcher in the 1903–05 study of New York wage-earners' budgets, "Sure, it's all I can do for him."[42] An investigation of Italian families in New York in 1914, described the home of one woman who had lost five children, "Over the mantelpiece hung a large, shiny photograph of the last baby lying in its casket. The casket had been very expensive, but it had been a great comfort to the mother to put so much money into it."[43] It was a sacred expense. As late as 1928, experts in family budgeting had trouble understanding its importance: "We who have the chance to compare policies realize that the better way for the family to place insurance is upon the main earner of the family, usually the father. . . . In practice the first question in the mind of the mother of the family . . . is 'who will pay for the funeral if the baby dies?' "[44]

Insuring the Sacred Child: From a Decent Casket to an Endowment Fund

The struggle over children's insurance reflects the cultural redefinition of childhood that began in the latter part of the nineteenth century. The business was caught in the transition. To its opponents, children's insurance was an extension of the old utilitarian view of childhood. Yet, child-insurers had an economic interest, if not a moral one, in the goals of the national child-saving movement. The new respect for the sanctity of children's lives was good for business. Insurance companies became active partners in the effort to prolong young lives;

they distributed free booklets instructing parents on proper care of their young children and even sent visiting nurses to the sick or to assist new mothers. The agent doubled as social worker, bringing "to workingmen's families a knowledge of the laws and rules of sanitation and hygiene, of the up-bringing and rearing of children."[45] Far from endangering child life, insurance saved children. Insurance advocates suggested that insured children received quicker and better medical attention than the uninsured. In his testimony to the Massachusetts legislature in 1895, John D. Long speculated, "Is not the doctor called a little sooner, and is he not a little readier to come to the sick child when there is an [insurance] fund?"[46]

Insurance officials also pointed out that children's mortality rates began to decline precisely during the same period as the number of children insured increased greatly. By 1896, the mortality of lower-class children had improved to the extent that companies were willing to raise benefits without significantly increasing premiums. The industry was quick to congratulate itself for the demographic improvement, suggesting that perhaps their business lifted the poor, "upon a higher plane of life."[47] In fact, insured children had lower mortality rates than the uninsured at comparable age levels. For instance, between 1897 and 1901, the expected mortality for American children one to two years old was 46.6 per thousand, while for customers of Prudential the mortality for that age was only 31.6 per thousand. For ages five to nine, the expected mortality during those years was 5.2 per thousand, but 4.4 for Prudential customers. Insurance companies did not require any medical examination for children, so the preferred mortality was not the result of selected lives. Similarly, children insured by the English Prudential, had lower mortality rates than predicted by standard life tables.[48]

The union of child-savers and child-insurers was formalized in the Child Welfare Conference of 1909, at which the president of Metropolitan Life, a guest speaker, called it "one of the anomalies of both insurance history and of child welfare history, that . . . since the introduction of industrial insurance . . . well-meaning men and women have taken occasion to condemn the insurance of children."[49]

The business continued to expand, and by 1928, 37.4 percent of all policies issued by the three largest insurance companies were for children. Postwar sales increased beyond expectations; in 1945 $10 billion worth of life insurance was in force for children under fifteen. By 1950 the total was $17 billion. A major national survey sponsored by the American Council of Life Insurance in 1976 found that 57 percent of all American children under fifteen have some kind of life insurance coverage. Even toddlers are insured. In 1978, Kinder-Care Learning Centers Inc., the nation's largest chain of daycare schools, launched Kinder Life, a subsidiary selling children's insurance at the company's 725 centers. By 1982, about 43,000 parents had bought the $5,000 policy on their child's life.[50]

The changing value of children's lives, however, transformed the legal foundations of the insurance business after the 1920s. The strictly pecuniary standard of insurable interest became progressively inadequate to measure the worth of the economically worthless child. As early as the 1880s, courts began recognizing the validity of ties of love and affection as a measure of the child's value. In a landmark decision, the judge in *Warnock v. Davis* declared:

It is not necessary that the expectation of advantage or benefit should be always capable of pecuniary estimation; for a parent has an insurable interest in the life of his child . . . The natural affection in cases of this kind is considered as more powerful—as operating more effica-

ciously—to protect the life of the insured than any other consideration.[51]

It was recognized that only in exceptional cases, such as child
actors (Shirley Temple, for example, was insured for $600,000
at the age of nine; Lloyds issued a five-week policy to nine-year-
old Jackie Coogan for a trip) did parents lose money when they
lost a child. Indeed, sustaining the legal fiction of pecuniary
loss would lead to the awkward conclusion that the average
child had a negative worth and its death was a benefit for
parents.

Other reasons for insuring children also emerged. Rituals for
the dying child became less necessary as lower-class children
began living longer. Instead there were new pressures to subsidize the living unproductive child. The marketing approach of
insurance companies mirrored the new status of children as
expensive consumer items; policies were now sold as "nest
eggs" for children. Endowments that matured by the age of
sixteen or twenty-one, creating funds for an education or a
dowry, became the most popular policies. Insurance was even
upheld as a vital element in a child's financial education, incul-
cating, "concepts and habits of foresight, planning and
thrift."[52] As it moved from burial coverage to an educational
fund, children's insurance gradually became also a middle-class
investment. While nineteenth-century insured children came
from working-class families, today 74 percent of children in
households with incomes between $20,000 and $24,999 have
some form of life insurance, compared with only 37 percent in
households with incomes below $6,000.[53] As children's insur-
ance was adopted by middle-class customers, and as mortality
rates declined, legal restrictions against speculative uses of insurance were relaxed first in the 1930s, and finally eliminated
altogether in more jurisdictions in the 1940s and 1950s.

While available records do not suggest significant sex differences in the insurance of children by industrial companies in the early period, after the 1920s middle-class parents insured their sons much more often than their daughters. As late as 1976, one successful female insurance agent remarked, "Unliberated though it may appear . . . I believe in making a distinction between insurance for girls and insurance for boys." She recommends whole-life policies for boys, which they will take over after they become self-supporting. But for girls, she prefers a limited pay plan insurance, explaining, "I would rather not commit . . . future husbands for paying for their wives' insurance."[54]

The success of children's insurance cannot be understood simply in economic terms. As an insurance writer avows, the purpose of insurance on children has always been "somewhat dubious."[55] Experts agree that funds for a child's education can be more profitably accumulated through investments other than a life policy. Mehr, an insurance specialist, considers that arguments to sell life insurance for children are "more effective in making the sale than in solving the buyer's problems."[56] The 1974 *Consumers Union Report on Life Insurance* remarks that children's insurance is irrational in economic terms. (Although in upper-income levels, child insurance may serve to reduce income and estate taxes.) A more recent *Consumers Report* is no less emphatic, denouncing life insurance for children as a "waste of money: The death of a child is a personal tragedy, but it is not a financial one and does not need to be covered by an insurance policy."[57] From the start, customers have been drawn by the symbolic appeal of a policy, a token of respect for the dead child in the late nineteenth century and one of love for the living child in the twentieth century. Agents' manuals and insurance-selling booklets recognize the noneconomic appeal. One booklet admits: "There are few tangible advantages for you in buying life insurance on your son. . . . You would be buying life insurance to pay him back his love, his trust, his respect, his confidence, you would be paying back for all those wonderful unforgettable moments that only a boy can share with his father." A 1951 manual instructs agents that the market for children's insurance is "as wide and as deep as the love of parents and grandparents for their children and grandchildren." Insurance advertisements have gradually hushed all reference to dying children and infant burials. Reminding agents that most parents insure children "because they expect them to live," instruction booklets strongly discourage any mention of a child's death.[58]

Insuring children became big business at the turn of the century. But it was a unique commercial enterprise, profoundly shaped by the sentimental value of its young customers' lives. As children were excluded from the workplace, insurance benefits from the death of a child could hardly be justified in economic terms, that is, as a replacement of a child's lost wages. Insuring the sacred, economically "useless" child turned into a semi-ritualistic business. At the turn of the century, it provided funds for a child's proper burial; later on, it served as a symbolic expression of parental love and concern.

CHAPTER 5

From Wrongful Death to Wrongful Birth: The Changing Legal Evaluation of Children

> We are not going to consider the value of babies as alarm-clocks for arousing the male parents . . . nor as gainers of prizes at the country fairs. Nor are we going to quote their market values south of Mason and Dixon's line in the days before the war. . . . But we are about to refer to some of those cases where judges and juries have been called upon to estimate the sums that will compensate for injuries arising from the negligence of others to life and limb of infants. . . . From "The Value of Children,"
> *The Central Law Journal*, 1882

> He said, "There is no way of amortizing the life of a child, is there?" I said, "I don't understand, Harry." And he said, "You can't declare that he cost so much and then divide that amount by his legal existence or by his estimated useful life, and at the end say there he is, he's dead but accounted for, written off; you can't because you should figure on that ultimate loss, shouldn't you?"
> From *Fertig*, Sol Yurick

IN 1896, the parents of a two-year-old child sued the Southern Railroad Company of Georgia for the wrongful death of their son. Despite claims that the boy performed valuable services for his parents—$2 worth per month, "going upon errands to neighbors . . . watching and amusing . . . younger child,"—no recovery was allowed, except for minimum burial expenses.

The court concluded that the child was "of such tender years as to be unable to have any earning capacity, and hence the defendant could not be held liable in damages." In striking contrast, in January 1979, when three-year-old William Kennerly died from a lethal dose of fluoride at a city dental clinic, the New York State Supreme Court jury awarded $750,000 to the boy's parents.[1]

The monetary disparity between the nineteenth- and twentieth-century decisions reflects more than inflation. It is a measure of the changing definition of children's value as seen through the legal process. The drama of a child's accidental death, described in Chapter 1, was not only played out in the streets or the train tracks; it was also staged in the very different, stark setting of a courtroom. Seeking monetary redress, parents confronted the defendants—usually a representative of a railroad company in the nineteenth century and trolley companies or automobile owners in the twentieth century. The translation of tragedy into lawsuit and of parental sentiment into cash was often awkward. The father of a fourteen-year-old boy killed in 1888 claimed a $3,000 loss protesting, however, that he "would not have lost [his] son for ten thousand dollars." Perhaps sensing the inadequacy of money, a San Francisco electrician who ran down a four-year-old little girl with his car in 1922, offered compensation in kind—his own child, five-year-old Isabel.[2]

How did American courts price the life of children? This chapter examines the different criteria used by the legal system to determine proper compensation for the accidental killing of a child. Nineteenth-century decisions relied primarily on economic guidelines: estimating the cash equivalent of the lost labor and services of a young child. But as children became economically useless, the accepted formula broke down. Pricing the twentieth-century sacred child confused legal experts and the courts. After much uncertainty and public controversy, new sentimental criteria were gradually developed to determine the cash value of an economically useless child.

≈ wives ???

Compensating Death with Money: A Brief Overview

The purpose of a civil suit in wrongful death cases is to determine equitable financial restitution for bereaved relatives. Unlike criminal cases, issues of moral guilt and punishment are irrelevant. Nineteenth-century juries were cautioned against "the feeling that the defendant ought to pay high for the gloom that had been brought upon a household . . . these sad occurences are necessarily incidental to our mode of life. . . . Money cannot atone for them. The law . . . simply tries to measure the pecuniary loss sustained, and it does not justify a recovery beyond a fair compensation for the injury."[3] Juries had wide discretion in estimating the amount of damages. In contrast to insurance benefits, wrongful death decisions were not bound by any fixed or precise mathematical rules. Thus, the price of each life was literally bargained in court. State legislatures, however, imposed restrictive ceilings to avoid extravagant awards. In 1893, for instance, ceilings ranging from $5,000 to $20,000 existed in twenty-two states. Moreover, concerned with the unpredictable response of judges and juries, superior court litigants often settled out of court, for much lower sums than the initial claim.[4]

The legal pricing of lives was not an American invention. In fact, the erratic evolution of wrongful death legislation has endlessly puzzled researchers. Early Anglo-Saxon law permitted the atonement of murder with a payment of money or goods, such as cattle or corn. The amount of this punitive payment (called *wergild* or blood-money) was determined on the basis of social status, not individual worth. Yet English law reversed itself in the seventeenth century, declaring that "the death of a human being cannot be complained of as an injury."[5] Until 1846, only recovery for injury was allowed, but not death. In sharp contrast, American colonial courts routinely awarded monetary compensation to the bereaved family in criminal proceedings. By the eighteenth and early nineteenth centuries, separate civil actions for death were recognized in New York, Connecticut, and a federal court in Maine. But after 1848, many American courts accepted the English decision denying a cause of action for death: "To the cultivated and enlightened mind, looking at human life in the light of the Christian religion as sacred, the idea of compensating its loss in money is revolting. . . ."[6] This led to an awkward situation. If severely injured, a person was allowed to sue and collect damages. But if that person died, the family was allowed no compensation. Thus, ironically, it was cheaper to kill than to maim a victim. In a subsequent turnabout, recovery for wrongful death was reinstated in the late nineteenth century, but was strictly limited to compensation for pecuniary damages. No recovery was allowed for the loss of society or for moral pain and anguish.[7]

With the dramatic increase in railroad, electric streetcars, and also industrial accidents, lawsuits rapidly multiplied in the last decades of the nineteenth century. Litigation was expensive, but lawyers accepted cases on contingent fees—allowing the poor to sue large corporations. Pricing young lives, however, posed a special challenge. The often conflicting opinions and decisions of judges and juries in child death cases provide unique insights into the changing price and value of American children.[8]

The Price of a Nineteenth-Century Child

How did nineteenth-century courts price the life of a child? Instructions to the jury were clear: The proper measure of damages for the death of a minor child was "the probable value of services of the deceased from the time of his death to the time he would have attained his majority, less the expense of his maintenance during the same time."[9] In 1896, when the wrongful death case of seven-year-old Ettie Pressman came to court (see p. 46), her father declared that he required his small children to work in order to help provide for the support of his household: "Yes, what I earn and what the children earn used together we have enough. They earn three dollars a week each. . . ." The court awarded him $1,000 for the loss of his daughter's services and earnings. The fiscal bookkeeping was explicit and unapologetic. Again, the jury awarded $5,000 for a twelve-year-old who was "intelligent . . . [and] money-making. [His] father owned . . . an opera house, during opera season [the boy] looked after all business, attended to fires, sold tickets . . . his services were worth . . . $50 a month."[10] Setting a fair market price for each particular child often involved the testimony of employers regarding the average earning capacity of children. As shown by the following cross-examination, the verdict often depended on skillful bargaining:

Q. . . . I ask you now, what do you think [this child] is worth in money? . . . you have a step-son about twelve years old: what would you consider him worth—$10,000 from five to twenty-one?

A. Yes, I would; boys between twelve and sixteen and twenty are worth $75 or $80 a month.

Q. Is this not rather an unusual thing, and an extraordinary boy who will get it?

A. I suppose it is not ordinary.

Q. Taking $720 per annum as the best rates a boy can earn on an average for the last six years of his minority . . . it would amount to $4,370. Deduct six years' expenses at $360 per annum, making $2,160, and it leaves the net earnings $2,210 . . .

The jury awarded $2,265 for the death of the five-year-old. Plaintiff's counsel had requested $10,000.[11]

Nineteenth-century American law thus put extraordinary weight on the economic worth of children. Significantly, four out of five of the earliest and leading civil actions for death concerned minor boys. In Maine, as early as 1825 (when England still denied all grounds for recovery at death), Moses Plummer was allowed to sue the master and mates of the brig *Romulus,* for the death of his twelve-year-old son, an apprentice aboard the ship. In Georgia, death benefits between 1852 and 1882 were recoverable *only* for a child's death.[12] Fewer claims were made for daughters, a predictable pattern considering the lower incidence of accidents among girls. The amounts collected, however, show no great variation between sexes; for both boys and girls, most awards ranged from $2,000 to $5,000.[13] In the nineteenth century, household services performed by an obedient daughter—obedience being particularly valued in both boys and girls—were of significant pecuniary value. After a seven-year-old girl was killed in a railroad accident in Indiana, the jury was instructed to consider the monetary value of "all acts of kindness and attention . . . nursing of sick members of the family . . . attending to the other children . . . which are reasonably expected to be performed by a daughter . . . and they are of value to the father, for, if not performed by her, other help must . . . be provided to perform them."[14]

Even very young children became marketable at death. While English courts refused compensation for children seven or younger, in America prospective damages were sometimes recovered for the death of a child "of such tender years as to be incapable of earning wages." For example, in the leading case of *Ihl v. Forty-Second St. and G.S.F.R.R.*, the court refused to award only nominal damages for the death of a three-year-old; the verdict was $1,800. The money value in such cases was based on an estimate of the child's future work potential. In *Oldfield v. New York and H.R.R.*, Hetty Downie, six years old, was killed by the cars of the New York and Harlem River Company. The court awarded her mother $1,300 on the basis that "the damages are to be assessed by the jury with reference to the pecuniary injuries sustained. . . . This is not actual present loss which the death produces . . . but prospective losses also." There were exceptions. In *Lehman v. Brooklyn*, recovery for the wrongful death of a four-year-old was denied: "The life of this little boy, however priceless may have been its value in other aspects, had no pecuniary value." Infants and children under two remained largely invisible and economically worthless.[15]

The greater vulnerability of lower-class children to accidental death was reflected in the social class of nineteenth-century plaintiffs. They were usually poor parents, often widows in "destitute circumstances." The financial status of bereaved parents was singled out by civil courts as a key factor in determining child death awards. In a landmark decision, the judge noted: "The circumstances of the parent suing . . . often becomes necessary evidence . . . to illustrate the acts of a child as useful . . . In this case the parents kept a dairy; all the family worked. The child, by attending to some duties, relieved the mother, so that she could engage in other necessary labor."[16] During cross-examination, the father of a twelve-year-old killed by a streetcar in 1899 bluntly conveyed his economic plight:

Q. Now, I wish you would tell the jury what your circumstances are, your means of taking care of yourself, and whether you are worth anything in the way of money?

A. I ain't worth anything and I cannot work either. My children have supported me a great deal.[17]

Poor children were often killed while playing alone or in the care of an older sibling. In contrast to the indictment of lower-class parents by the press and by child welfare organizations, courts were reluctant to define lack of proper adult supervision as parental negligence. An early decision explained why:

A large majority of children living in cities depend upon the daily labor of both parents . . . and these parents are unable to employ nurses, who may keep a constant and vigilant eye . . . we cannot hold, as a matter of law, that every time a child . . . steps into the street unattended, the mother is guilty of . . . negligence . . . Such a rule would depopulate a city of all its laboring inhabitants.[18]

Siblings were considered acceptable caretakers; a ten-year-old sister, "is entirely capable of protecting from harm a child of three; and the motherly instincts of little girls ten years old, usually endow them with both the thoughtfulness and courage to look out for babies."[19]

Middle- and upper-class parents had greater difficulty in justifying wrongful death awards. After all, the educated child required much expense and provided minimal monetary benefit. As an 1867 Wisconsin case concluded, "The children of such parents receive far more pecuniary aid . . . from their parents, than their parents from them."[20]

Overall, the principles of legal valuation of children in nineteenth-century death actions were remarkably similar to those of adults. The measure of damages in the case of a husband-father was the lost value of his probable earnings; for a wife, the anticipated worth of her household services; for a child the probable value of his or her services during minority less the costs of support. In each case, moral and sentimental concerns were excluded by custom and statute.

A Turning-Point: The "One Cent" Child Death Cases

The need for more precise and uniform monetary estimates of human life became apparent as wrongful death claims multiplied at the turn of the century. Actuaries pleaded with courts to incorporate their computations as necessary evidence. Physicians developed a "physical economics," "a mathematical formula for the normal earning ability of the body by which . . . a person may be either rated, or his economic value ascertained." Their search for a "standard money value for each man and woman, boy and girl," was greeted with enthusiasm by the press.[21] Yet, at no point was the economic rod for measuring life contested. The $2,601 money value of a ten-year-old working-class boy, for instance, was based on an estimate of his probable wages. But this unchallenged adherence to the nineteenth-century pecuniary rule was slowly being undermined. Computing the value of a sacred child required a different mathematics—a new formula to determine the economic loss created by the death of an economically worthless child. The tension between established legal principles and the changing value of children resulted in a series of unexpected, dramatic, and controversial child death cases.

The scandal cases first broke out in the late 1890s. On April 10, 1896, Melville Graham, five years old, was killed by a trolley car while playing with his friends in downtown Jersey City. His father, Abraham Graham, sued the Traction Company. A verdict of $5,000 from the jury was set aside as "absurdly excessive." A second trial on this case in 1898 had identical results; a $5,000 verdict was turned down by the judge who harshly chastised the jury for their "ignorance, prejudice, passion, corruption." According to indignant press accounts, Justice Gunmere concluded that, following the established pecuniary measure of damages, the child's life was worth no more than one dollar. Graham insisted, and a third jury again awarded him $5,000 only to be turned down by the court. When a fourth trial took place in 1900, the jury allowed $2,000, but in what was later described as an "amazing fit of pique," the court threw out the case altogether, allowing no damages.[22]

By that time, the Graham case had become a cause célèbre, making front-page headlines in New Jersey papers and provoking angry public reaction. At first, legal observers were puzzled. Judge Gunmere was simply abiding by the established economic principle of damages. Letters to the editor of the *New Jersey Law Journal* praised Gunmere's "courage, ability and impartiality." Some suggested that the public may have been provoked by the judge's "blunt, merciless way of putting a proposition of law."[23]

But the issue was not simply a matter of insensitive wording. After the second Graham trial in 1898, a scathing editorial in the *Jersey City Evening Journal*, significantly entitled "The Value of a Child's Life," explained why the public was outraged by Judge Gunmere's decision. Some people feared that if child life was so "cheap," there would be no protection against speeding trolleys and trains. Gunmere's assumption that children had lost all economic value was also dismissed as unjustified, "The couple who have ten sons are ten times as well off as the couple who are childless." But above all, the

Graham decisions were a profound moral offense: "Justice Gunmere ... has placed himself ... in a most unfortunate light before the people of this State. Admitted that children are an expense. ... Go further; admit that they are a burden and a drain, and a cause of worriment. ... Admit everything ... grant the logic of his statements ... and yet how can any man concur in such a view." The judge's decision was declared, "not only repugnant to human nature but ... as close to legal immorality as is any opinion that has been expressed ... from the State Bench."[24]

The same issue was being raised across the nation in a series of well-publicized child death cases. The controversy hinged over the shocking low awards for young children; six cents for a New York boy, ten dollars for a three-year-old in Nebraska, one cent for a twelve-year-old in Missouri. In 1895, an angry New York judge set aside a verdict of fifty dollars for the death of an eight-year-old. Ordering a new trial, Judge Pryor expressed his distress that a bright, healthy boy could be assigned the "price of a poodle dog."[25] A few years later, in "An Estimate of a Child's Value," a *New York Times* front-page story reported with astonishment another case, this time from Indiana. The jury had spent a record-breaking fifty-three hours to calculate the value of an eight-year-old boy: "The jury figured that from 8 to 10 years old the child would be able to make 45 cents a week ... [and] cost 84 cents ... From 10 to 12 it would make 75 cents and [cost] $1.25." The computation ended at age twenty-one. The tally was $599.95, far less than the $5,000 originally claimed by the father.[26]

Two leading New York cases attracted special public attention. In *Morris v. Metropolitan,* six cents was awarded for the wrongful killing of a boy by a streetcar. After a much noted appeal, Charles Morris, the father, obtained $7,500 in damages. The press welcomed the generous verdict as reassuring proof that a child's life was "worth over 6 cents." The Arnold case was less successful. At the 1911 New York State Fair, a racing car accidentally plunged into a crowd of spectators, killing four adults and nine-year-old Arthur Arnold. While the survivors of the deceased men collected between $5,000 and $10,000 each, an appellate court affirmed as "just and proper" a $500 award to Arthur's parents.[27]

Observers were jolted by the unprecedented verdicts. In reversing the Morris six-cent award, the judge noted how, "In almost uniform course, the award of damages for negligently causing the death of an infant has been of a substantial sum . . . we look in vain to find any logical relation between the verdicts which have been rendered in this class of actions . . . and this verdict . . . which offends the moral sense."[28] Yet the logic of the turning-point cases was impeccable. The sudden cheapness of the awards was partly the result of a new class of plaintiffs. The poor, sickly, or widowed parent demanding cash compensation for the lost earnings of a minor child was being joined by a host of middle-class parents. Why should they receive money for the death of an economically unproductive child? Charles Morris himself frankly declared in court that his son Leslie, ". . . never earned a dollar in his lifetime; I had never derived a pecuniary benefit to the value of one dollar from his services. . . . All the time, up to the date of his death, he had been a source of expense to me. I had him to support, board and clothe."[29]

The jury foreman candidly confirmed that the six-cent verdict had been reached because Morris was a wealthy man. If the measure of damages was "a business and commercial question only," nominal awards were justified. The courts were simply doing their job. Indeed, Tiffany's 1913 edition of *Death by Wrongful Act* (the single text on the subject), praised the "more logical view" of Graham-style decisions.[30]

But public outrage with these turn-of-the-century decisions had little to do with matters of legal proof or logic. It reflected the dilemmas created by the transformation in the economic and sentimental value of children. As with children's insurance, the legal pricing of a sacred child was to some extent a sacrilege. After all, if parents were expected to forego any immediate material gain from their children's labor, how could a windfall profit at the child's death be justified? "The Price of a Child," an editorial comment by the widely read *Current Literature*, suggested that "the highest instinct may . . . assert that the . . . bereaved parents should scorn recompense for an irreparable loss." Again echoing the concerns of child-insurance opponents, some lawmakers rejected substantial awards in child death cases, "because . . . that would put a premium on the death of the child and jeopardize its life in very many cases. . . ."[31]

At the core of the controversy, however, was not the possible greediness of parents but the more profound dilemma of determining the worth of children who no longer worked; that is, assessing value when price was absent. The *Current Literature* editorial speculated, "How much is the life of a child worth? At what price may a girl or boy be killed? Has a youthful life an actual value capable of being assessed in dollars and cents?" By denying compensation, or awarding nominal damages, the controversial wrongful death decisions challenged the value of the new sacred child. In 1899, a Kentucky decision significantly reduced the size of a child death award; the dissenting judge accused the majority of unethical materialism: "If a man like Gould, Vanderbilt, Rockefeller . . . had been killed, instead of the child Stock, the judgment must [*sic*] have been for millions of dollars. . . ."[32]

Indeed, the press celebrated those judges who recognized

that unlike the nineteenth century when price determined value, value would determine the price of a sacred child. A Justice O'Gorman was warmly praised for setting aside a nominal verdict in the death of a five-year-old child, as "so grossly inadequate and perverse as to shock the moral sense." The *Boston Morning Journal* noted, "There are considerations other than pecuniary, and parents and others who understand the value of a child life in the home will approve the ruling of Justice O'Gorman rather than that of Justice Gunmere."[33] As a Professor Rauschenbusch remarked some years later: "Is the baby worth a dollar? . . . For any eye that is not blind with coarse mammonism and unable to see value in anything that does not immediately earn net cash the baby is one of the most valuable and productive assets of the family . . . as a joy giver [the baby] is an incomparable success. . . ."[34] The monetization of a child's sentimental value had begun.

The New Ledger: Pricing the "Worthless" Child

By the 1920s and 1930s, the dilemma of compensating parents for the death of a child became magnified. As child labor legislation and compulsory education removed most children from the labor force, the sacralization of childhood increasingly cut across class lines. A 1916 Pennsylvania decision recognized the need for new standards when the life lost "may have . . . spent itself along the lines of those social, domestic or moral human relations that exhibit no commercial side."[35] Yet, the law stubbornly held on to principles grossly inadequate to evaluate the "useless' child. Public alarm and grief over the large numbers of children killed accidentally was muted by the routine economic ledger of most wrongful death decisions. The clash between legal dogma and social reality intensified as car accident cases (of children and adults) flooded the courts in the late 1920s. As one commentator observed:

Hardy indeed [is] the practitioner who would proceed to trial knowing that he would have to prove the deceased infant was a financial asset. . . . Is it just to allow a jury to speculate upon such a doubtful question in . . . a trial . . . which arouses such strong sympathies as one involving the death of a young child . . . with the proceedings punctuated by the lamentations of the mother?[36]

Law review articles repeatedly singled child death cases as unusually delicate and unsettling. Incipient legal criticism of the nineteenth-century measure of damages was partly based on the practical limitations of the pecuniary rule. Yet, a moral issue was also raised. The presiding judge in *Schendel v. Bradford* protested against "this cold-blooded calculating measure of human life. . . . Awarding pecuniary damages to the next of kin of a child six years of age is merely making a business commodity out of the child, and subjecting the loss of that child's life to the dollars and cents argument."[37]

Paradoxically, objections to the economic evaluation of adult human life had been largely overcome. New sophisticated measures were being developed to estimate the financial worth of the male wage earner and the substitute value of the housewife-mother. But when it came to child life, even statisticians were at a loss. Dublin and Lotka, who compiled the first estimate of capital value of males as a function of their age, acknowledged the difficulty: "The bringing up of children is not altogether a voluntary enterprise, entered upon [by] casting a balance sheet of the profit and loss to be expected. . . . We are brought face to face with a situation which cannot be completely discussed solely on the basis of present worth of net future earnings, but into which questions of sentiment inevitably enter. . . ." Another economic analyst similarly concluded that "sentiment alone can measure the value of the life of an infant." Yet, while defining the precise value of child life perplexed investigators, there was no doubt about the rapid and alarming increase in the cost of raising children. By 1930, it was estimated that a typical family with an income of approximately $2,500 per year would spend an average of $7,425 to raise a child to age eighteen.[38]

How did courts evaluate the "sacred" expensive twentieth-century child? After all, defendants could now easily demonstrate that the deceased child was a financial liability. Awards for minors engaged in a gainful occupation were contested as illegal violations of child labor legislation. Yet, all evidence points to an *increase* in awards for children after the 1920s. Even workmen's compensation for illegally employed minors was significantly expanded during this period. While some states refused all awards to young workers, Indiana, New York, and New Jersey offered double, and Wisconsin triple compensation for minors injured while illegally employed. To be sure, the legislative intent was to deter child labor by making children's injuries expensive. Yet, cheap awards were also condemned as a degrading monetary symbol of disrespect for children's lives.[39]

An analysis of legal articles, court cases, and statutes between 1920 and 1960 show that sentimental considerations entered wrongful death lawsuits in two ways—one explicit, the other implicit. A 1912 Florida statute recognized the uniqueness of child death cases by allowing an unprecedented and exclusive right of action to bereaved parents for the mental pain and suffering caused by the death of a minor child. In *Kelley v. Ohio R.R.*, judicial construction of a West Virginia statute allowing "fair and just" damages, similarly acknowledged parental anguish and distress; "[the defendant's] money it to pay for [plaintiffs] consolation . . . Why shall he not so when he has brought . . . a father and mother in sorrow o the grave? He has caused the grievous loss from which heart and soul suffers more than from pecuniary loss."[40]

In a few other states, by express statutory provision or by judicial construction, the term "pecuniary loss" was stretched to include compensation for the loss of society or companionship of a child. California pioneered the consideration of such nonpecuniary concerns as early as 1890. In *Munro v. Dredging*, consideration of a mother's sorrow was rejected by the court, yet the jury was instructed to determine the pecuniary value of the "loss of comfort, society and protection," caused by a son's death.[41] Significantly, the long-standing policy against compensating for noneconomic losses—balancing a "weight of gold with a weight of sorrow," was in many instances first breached by a child's wrongful death. To be sure, payments for moral damages were not restricted to children. But they became particularly necessary in child death cases where it was impossible to prove any pecuniary injury. As a result, verdicts increased. A Florida decision to award plaintiffs $12,500 explained the new rationale: "Those who have not brought a child into the world and loved it and planned for it, and then have it snatched away from them and killed can hardly have an adequate idea of the mental pain and anguish that one undergoes from such a tragedy. No other affliction so tortures and wears down the physical and nervous system."[42]

Most statutes and courts, however, still followed the pecuniary measure of damages based exclusively on loss of money and support. Yet, their rational bookkeeping was also upset by the invisible weight of noneconomic considerations. The best evidence for the implicit recognition of children's sentimental value is the substantial awards for a child's death even in those states that denied recovery for sentimental loss. Awards for adults also increased, but the relative increment was greater in child death cases, especially considering that verdicts for children often climbed from a zero base or meager nominal sums.[43] The courts favored larger awards by systematically disregarding testimony on the costs of raising a child. For instance, in an early Washington case concerning the death of a two-year-old girl whom the parents could afford and intended to educate, the defendant's efforts to introduce testimony on probable costs were deflected. The court upheld a substantial verdict despite reasonable evidence that parental expenses would exceed any prospective earnings by the girl. Similarly, in the death of a thirteen-year-old boy, evidence on the costs of "board, clothing, or personal expenses" was dismissed as "not material in cases like the one before us. Very few families keep a record of what it costs to raise children." A contested award was upheld. By 1943, it became evident that "the defendant's right to show expected costs in excess of expected benefits had been rendered completely ineffective."[44] Thus, whether by explicit or implicit recognition of the sentimental value of a child, the evidence shows that the "surrender" value of children at death increased even as their productive value in life declined.

In 1904, a controversial New Jersey decision made national headlines. The case involved the deaths of a sixteen-year-old boy and a nineteen-year-old girl both killed in a collision between a trolley car and a train. Initial verdicts of $6,000 and $5,000 respectively, were contested as excessive by the North Jersey Street Railway Company. In a new decision, Judge Adams upheld the boy's $6,000 award but reduced the girl's to $3,000, declaring:

A woman may become a bread-winner; a man must be one. If she devoted herself to the career of teacher as she . . . probably would if she had not married, she could after a few years have earned, if very successful, at most about $110 a month . . . taking the most optimistic view of Miss Werpupp's financial future, I think that Mr. Eastwood's expectations were at least twice as valuable.

One decade later, a New Jersey jury angered prominent women suffrage leaders with a similar discriminatory decision. In a legal suit against a manufacturer of condensed milk, a father was awarded $2,000 for the death of his three-month-old son, but only $1,000 for the boy's twin sister.[45]

Sex discrimination in child death cases, however, was not common. In a commentary on the New Jersey twins decision, one legal journal, for instance, found it "rather startling [that] such a difference [is] made in the value of the lives of children so young." Although statisticians calculated that a boy's prospective economic value was indeed double than a girl's at similar ages, jury decisions were not bound by empirical assessments.[46] Noting this sexual equality at death, a 1935 New York Law Revision Commission suggested that the clandestine inclusion of sentimental value tipped the balance for girls: "If pecuniary loss were the sole basis of the computation of damages, it would seem that the damages recovered for the wrongful death of a boy would be greater than those for the death of a girl."[47] Thus, the lack of differentiation between young girls and boys may be further evidence of the unique noneconomic valuation of child life.

The unresolved legal tension between the price and value of children exploded once again in the 1950s. In 1953, three-year-old John Martin Courtney was struck by an automobile driven by Edgar W. Apple on a public highway in St. Clair County, Michigan. In a decision reminiscent of the controversial turn-of-the-century cases, the court awarded $700 to the boy's parents, to cover funeral expenses. On appeal, the verdict was upheld as the just and logical outcome of deducting the cost of upkeep from the child's probable contributions. But this time a large segment of the legal profession protested against the "lamentable and ignoble" decision. One critic condemned the unseemly inference that "the casket had value but the dead boy buried in it was deemed worthless." Speakers at a 1957 conference on Wrongful Death and Survivorship (sponsored by the National Association of Claimants' Compensation Attorneys) urged the adoption of noneconomic criteria to determine a child's legal price, "Do we, as parents, bring forth children simply as little wage-earners? It must be conceded by the courts that normal parents . . . accept eagerly . . . the dollar cost of [their child] . . . not as a legal duty but as a joyful privilege. The money cost is more than repaid in the delight of having the child . . . in the pleasure of his society."[48]

Talbot Smith, the dissenting judge in the controversial 1956 case, emerged as a moral champion. In 1960, Smith revolutionized child death decisions in the landmark Michigan case of *Wycko v. Gnodtke,* concerning the accidental death of a fourteen-year-old boy. His decision to uphold a contested verdict of some $15,000 to the boy's parents served as a forum to indict the "child-labor" formula, as Smith dubbed the traditional measure of damages. If the modern child is a "blessed expense," how could courts insist on their "bloodless bookkeeping"? Smith introduced a new alternative; the worth of a child should be determined by past parental investment in his or her upbringing: "Just as with respect to a manufacturing plant, or industrial machine, value involves the costs of acquisition . . . maintenance, service . . . and renovation, we must consider the expenses of birth, of food, of clothing, of medicines, of instruction, of nurture and shelter." This "lost investment"

theory conveniently endowed the "useless" child with a contemporary form of economic value, yet it still avoided the direct pricing of sentimental worth. The *NACCA Law Journal* noted that Smith's "morally superior theory," reflected the position of most American courts, which "have balked at reading small children out of the death act by cruel adherence to the joyless theory that a child has no pecuniary value save as a wage-earner."[49]

Within the past twenty years, the trend has been toward a more explicit moral bookkeeping. Courts are involved in determining the pecuniary value of matters such as the joy of raising a child or even of a little daughter's goodnight kiss. In a 1961 landmark decision by the United States Court of Appeals, the traditional economic ledger was further undermined by the court's outspoken refusal to deduct the projected costs of raising the deceased seven-year-old boy to majority: "Such cold-blooded deduction . . . would treat an incalculable loss as a 'pecuniary gain.' What makes life worth living more than the privilege of raising a son? . . . Is it not still the law in that most sacred of relationships that it is more blessed to give than to receive?"[50] Indeed, insistence to comply with orthodox pecuniary statutes often results in a pathetic parody, as the plaintiff's lawyer earnestly projects the money value of a child's paper route or lemonade stand.

The wrongful death trial of an economically "useless" child evolves into an odd scenario, an unusual exercise in sentimentalized economics. While, in adult claims, expert witnesses can testify somewhat objectively on the replacement value of a housewife or a breadwinner, few equivalent specific functions exist for the contemporary child. Therefore, the child death trial hinges on determining the subjective emotional value of a *particular* child. As expressed in *Pagitt v. Keokuk,* "It depends on all the circumstances important in the lives of a particular parent and a particular child . . . the ability of the child to offer companionship and society and the ability of the parent to enjoy it."[51] Lawyers are urged to bring the child "back to life," dramatizing their brief with home movies and photographs showing the deceased child, "playing baseball, riding a merry-go-round, building sand castles at the beach, or seated on the floor in front of the Christmas tree rapidly solving a child's puzzle." To convey the uniqueness of the life lost, lawyers are also advised to visit the child's home "take some time to see the room where the child slept and carefully catalog every detail . . . from stuffed animals . . . to articles hidden under the bed."[52] The irony, of course, is that the irreplaceability of the child's personal qualities must be established with the purpose of converting them into their cash equivalent.

The quality and authenticity of parental grief also enters the jurors' ledger. The mother is the preferred lead-off witness in child death cases, followed by the father and any siblings. A suggested standard closing argument for the plaintiff's lawyer shows how such testimony is used: "You have seen and heard from the child's mother. You know about the deep concern she felt for this boy. . . . It is obvious to anyone who has seen these parents and heard them testify that they lived their lives for their children."[53] Where recovery for moral pain is allowed, psychiatrists usually testify on parents' mental distress. In *Seaboard v. Gay*, for instance, an eminent psychiatrist testified in the death of a twelve-year-old girl, the youngest of five children explaining: "A mother really invests a lot of herself into her children and especially into the baby of the family . . . it is like investing in Blue Chip Stocks . . . This is what a mother is going to give to society . . . if anything happens to that child . . . you lost your investment. That is why [mothers] have this prolonged neurotic reaction and long grief . . . after such a loss. . . ."[54] While the economically useful child was legally "owned" by the father, the "priceless" child is considered the mother's sentimental asset.

Child Death Awards: The Special Money

Despite increased recognition that sentimental loss has an economic equivalent, the legal fiction of pecuniary damages has not been altogether abandoned. Why does the law retain, even in name only, the nineteenth-century model of a useful child to value the twentieth-century useless child? Disparaged as "intellectual dishonesty" and a "miscarriage of justice," by most legal scholars, the "pocketbook" computation of child death losses still appears in a majority of wrongful death statutes. In some cases, the fiction of pecuniary loss is stretched in new directions. For instance, in the 1980 case of *Green v. Bittner*, the New Jersey Supreme Court ruled that a child's companionship in the parents' old age has economic value, "its value must be confined to what the marketplace would pay a stranger . . . for performing such services. . . . It is not the loss simply of the exchange of views . . . when child and parent are together; it is certainly not the loss of the pleasure which accompanies such an exchange. Rather it is the loss of that kind of guidance, advice and counsel which all of us need . . . the kind of advice . . . that could be purchased from a business adviser, a therapist, or a trained counselor." According to some observers, the possibility of uncontrolled and unreasonably high awards for emotional pain may have deterred statutory changes. They point nervously to the leading 1971 Florida decision, *Compania Dominicana de Aviación v. Knapp*, where the parents of a boy killed in an accident received 1.8 million dollars. The entire amount was allegedly based on the mental pain and anguish of the bereaved parents, who waived any claim in damages for loss of services.[55] However, a 1974 study testing the impact of different wrongful death statutes concluded that statutory differences were not an important determinant of variation in size of award, "the pecuniary loss doctrine has been softened to allow substantial recoveries, while in the all-inclusive loss states, restraint . . . has been exercised in assessing amounts for anguish."[56]

If pragmatic concerns are unwarranted, the persistence of pecuniary-loss statutes may be an indicator of underlying value and cultural concerns. In *The Philosophy of Money*, German sociologist Georg Simmel suggested that the traditional restriction of damages to pecuniary loss was paradigmatic of the function of money in the modern world. Money's vital importance was recognized by making only pecuniary loss compensable. But, on the other hand, this restriction limited the impact of money by recognizing it as an unfit equivalent for nonquantifiable human values. This apparent irreconcilability of money and personal values is breached when courts routinely quantify and monetize the emotional worth of human life. For many, this is a revolting development; "Such payments contribute to the corruption, degradation, and eventual permanent loss of all those non-material values which we claim to be precious."[57]

From this perspective, pricing a "sacred" child represents the ultimate boundary. In fact, many common law jurisdictions award no damages for the death of a young child, beyond funeral expenses. In Russia, no death actions exist for unproductive minors. Both the Soviet Union and the People's Republic of China denounce compensation for nonpecuniary loss as the ultimate capitalist exploitation; "Only the bourgeoisie thinks that mental suffering can be cured by money, and like commodities, can be exchanged by currency."[58] In the United

States, pecuniary loss restrictions preserve an illusory boundary between money and life values. But in reality, the sentimental pricing of children occurs, regardless of statutory limits.

The apparent triumph of the cash nexus in American child death actions, however, is deceptive. There is little understanding of the persistent involvement of noneconomic considerations. Lawyers, for instance, still consider the death of a minor child as the "toughest of all death cases."[59] An instruction manual warns of unusual complications in jury selection: "It will be difficult for jurors to comprehend the necessary correlation that money damages have to the life of a child." For many, the lawsuit is a desecration; the damages are "bloodstained."[60] A series of typical questions asked of prospective jurors further suggests the involvement of sentimental and moral issues in child death cases:

1. As I have told you, this is a case where the parents are bringing an action to recover damages for the death of their child. Is there anyone among you who feels that this is not a nice thing to do? That this would be in some way improper?
2. Is there anyone . . . who feels, that because money is such a common thing, that even though the law says that this is the only recompense parents may receive for their lost child, they should not ask for it?
3. Are you willing to accept the awesome responsibility of deciding for these parents, once and for all, what was the value of their little boy's life?[61]

Parents are also ambivalent. In an early 1909 case, a Mrs. Lauterbach refused to file a suit for damages in the death of her son because the idea that "a pecuniary benefit might result from such action was abhorrent." She finally relented, but with the proviso that any money would be donated to charity as a memorial to her son. Many parents are still reluctant to sue and middle-class plaintiffs tend to ritualize the monetary award by often donating it to charity, safety organizations, or scholarships for poor children. On the other hand, for a defendant, money can be a "final payment," symbolizing absolution. In 1911, a New York clergyman who ran over a little girl with his automobile sold all his belongings, turning the money over to the girl's parents. The court had found the pastor blameless and no damages were legally required.[62]

"Death money" is thus different than ordinary cash. Apparently, even the *wergild* had occasional symbolic overtones. According to Simmel, among some Malayan peoples, the word "blood-money" means, to get up or to stand up, suggesting that through a payment, the dead person will be resurrected to his people. French scholars, unlike their Communist counterparts, recognize the symbolism of money and contend that denying compensation for moral loss is a "philistine" decision. For them, monetary compensation asserts the existence of moral value. French scholars also refer to the uses of child death awards as a legitimating factor. "It is therefore not shocking to allow a father or a mother bereft of their child, to find some relief from their sorrow in the comfort they bring to [other] unhappy children."[63]

Child death money is also sacralized by the size of the award. Cheap verdicts are not only an inequitable compensation but "an insult to bereaving survivors."[64] Indeed, Simmel suggests that money in "extraordinarily great quantities," may attain a special distinctive quality; it is "imbued with that 'superadditum,' with fantastic possibilities that transcend the definiteness of numbers." Yet, notions of what constitutes a redeeming quantity are not universal but culturally defined. In civil law countries, which expressly allow compensation for the grief of losing a child, legal scholars advocate the "franc symbolique." A token sum of money is perceived as the only dignified equivalent for such purely emotional loss. Compensation for children in France rarely exceeds $3,000.[65]

The American child death trial is an unusual and uneasy mixture of secular funeral and lawsuit. A standard closing argument suggested for plaintiffs reminds the jury that parents are not simply seeking monetary redress but intend to "vindicate the memory" of their child, "It is your duty to close the book of the life of . . . [name of child]. He died a violent death, and you must ask yourselves whether he has rested quietly in these last years while this case has been in the courts . . . you know that if you do what is right . . . this boy will rest in peace."[66] Expected rules of behavior and "feeling rules" for parents further downplay the troublesome commercialization of grief. Emotional outbursts appropriate at the graveside become suspect in the courtroom; are parents trying to use their pain to raise the award? Lawyers are advised to prevent any "cheapening display of emotion" from their clients, and avoid "a spectacle featuring sackcloth and ashes, garment rending, and the whole panoply of grief embarrassingly displayed."[67] The concern to avoid an emotional scene is not just a matter of courtroom etiquette. It serves to prevent an overly direct and therefore mercenary correlation between grief and profit.

Shifts in the legal evaluation of children thus serve as a measure of the changing relationship between the price and value of children. The price of a nineteenth-century child determined its value; however, gradually sentimental value became the determinant of economic price. Paradoxically, as children's work time declined, their economic worth at death increased. It is not just a matter of inflationary trends. In fact, strict application of wrongful death statutes would, in most cases, lead to zero awards in child death cases. But new conceptions of childhood reshaped the ledger of twentieth-century American courts. Determining the cash value of a priceless child has become an unusual bookkeeping procedure—balancing a combination of "inestimable grief . . . and negative pecuniary loss."[68]

The priceless child is assigned dollar values at death for noneconomic contributions. Parents (whether directly or through legal subterfuge) are compensated for their sentimental loss. This extension of the cash nexus, however, does not represent the definitive test of money's "autocratic rule."[69] Sentimental factors intervene in the pricing process and shape the meaning and style of the child death trial, even the amount and uses of the benefits.

Child Life as a Debit: An Epilogue

In 1967, a California Court of Appeals made a novel and controversial entry in the legal valuation of children. Following a sterilization, Mrs. Custodio became pregnant with her tenth child. She and her husband sued the responsible surgeons on a number of grounds, and sought recovery for medical expenses, the wife's pain and suffering, plus an additional $50,000 for "costs and expenses to properly care and raise the said child to maturity." No damages were awarded because the suit was filed prematurely, before the birth. Yet, the court's opinion clearly endorsed the legitimacy of the parents' claim to "replenish the family exchequer so that the new arrival will not deprive the other members of the family of what was planned as their just share of the family income."[70] Before Custodio, no court had allowed recovery for the birth of an unplanned child. In the 1934 leading case of *Christensen v. Thornby,* where the husband underwent an unsuccessful vasectomy to protect his wife from a hazardous third pregnancy, the court denied recovery: "Instead of losing his wife, the plaintiff has been blessed with the fatherhood of another child." Similarly, in *Ball v. Mudge,* the costs of an unexpected birth were found to be "far outweighed by the blessing of a cherished child, albeit an unwanted child at the time of conception and birth." And in *Terrell v. Garcia,* the court concluded that: "The satisfaction, joy and companionship which normal parents have in rearing a child make such economic loss worthwhile. . . . Who can place a price tag on a child's smile?"[71]

Criticized by worried physicians, emotionally condemned by right-to-life organizations, wrongful birth seems to be gaining increasing legal approval.[72] As recovery is allowed in a small but growing number of cases, the price and value of child life is being dramatically reassessed. Unlike wrongful death decisions, where the emotional value of a child is considered greater than its price, in wrongful birth, price is superior to value. Indeed, the proper rule for damages has been the focus of much legal controversy. Relying on an "overriding theory of benefits," earlier cases invariably dismissed pecuniary costs. But with Custodio, and especially after the landmark case of *Troppi v. Scarf* (where a pharmacist negligently filled a birth control prescription with tranquilizers), the "blessing" ledger was replaced by an unsentimental cost-benefit rule. The jury is instructed to offset any emotional, physical, and financial expenses of the unplanned child with the value of all benefits derived from parenthood. Troppi concluded that, "The services and companionship of an unwanted child do not always have a dollar value equivalent or greater than the economic costs of the child's support, and the restrictions and pain and suffering caused by pregnancy and the obligation to rear a child."[73] Thus, paradoxically, while wrongful death decisions tend to disregard the costs of raising a child, these expenses re-enter the legal ledger in wrongful birth suits.

This economic realism, however, does not apply to all children. While the wanted child is indeed "priceless," the unwanted child is merely expensive. Thus, wrongful birth claims suggest that the sacralization of children is not an absolute process. As they become exclusively sentimental assets, children's value is increasingly dependent on parental attitude. Indeed, the decline in children's objective contributions corresponded to this increase in parental rather than societal determinants of value. The sacredness of the unwanted child is withdrawn when parents legally and publicly protest its birth, declaring it a civil wrong. It is perhaps no coincidence that the economic approach to child life was pioneered by Michigan, the same state that initiated the "lost-investment" formula in child death cases. Under certain circumstances, the child may be an unwanted, or even a bad investment.

This utilitarian downgrading of an unwanted child, however, remains a culturally deviant pattern. Even supporters of abortion hesitate before branding the already born child as an "emotional bastard." Few wrongful birth cases are brought to trial. Recovery for those that reach the court is often denied or limited by the judge or jury. Predictably, most plaintiffs settle out of court. The parents in *Troppi v. Scarf,* for instance, accepted $12,000, considerably less than their original request for $250,000. According to one legal commentator, "the emotional susceptibility" of juries to the joys of parenthood remains a serious obstacle for wrongful birth plaintiffs.[74] Dissatisfied with the cost-benefit ledger, some experts suggest that "child life" awards should depend on parents' physical, social, or economic circumstances. Thus, a "young married couple with a large bank account and a steady income, who desired sterilization because raising children would interfere with their Caribbean cruises," would not recover the full cost of raising the child. Already most successful plaintiffs are the parents of numerous children.[75]

The legal differentiation between the value of the wanted child versus the price of the unwanted child is primarily concerned with the rights of parents. Occasional expressions of concern with the potentially harmful emotional consequences for the child are confidently dismissed, ". . . it could be said that a child who was the subject of a wrongful conception recovery would have the satisfaction of knowing he was paying his own way."[76]

(handwritten marginalia: "(!)" and "but what if lose case...?")

CHAPTER 6

From Baby Farms to Black-Market Babies: The Changing Market for Children

Glorious and wonderful as babies may be . . . it is fortunate they are not in the market. If they were, how varied quotations would be, or rather how impossible it would be to establish any quotations at all! [yet] Who can tell what advantages might arise from treating infants as a commodity? If they were sold in the open market, would they not be better taken care of . . . better reared, better educated? . . . It is strange that the commercial consideration does not strike the nineteenth century.

"Babies Commercially," *New York Times*, August 12, 1877

Did you know that in this land of the free . . . there is a great baby market? And the securities which change hands . . . are not mere engraved slips of paper . . . but live, kicking, flesh-and-blood babies; babies for adoption. . . .

"The Baby Market," *Saturday Evening Post*, February 1, 1930

IN THE 1870s, there was no market for babies. The only profitable undertaking was the "business of getting rid of other people's [unwelcome] babies."[1] For about ten dollars, baby farmers took in these generally illegitimate children. Yet some fifty years later, adoptive parents were eagerly paying $1,000 or more to purchase an infant. As an article in *Collier's* put it: "It's the 1939 bonanza . . . there's gold in selling babies."[2] By the 1950s, a white, healthy infant sold for as much as $10,000. The creation of a market for babies was not the result of clever promotion and only partly a consequence of the increasing scarcity of children. This startling appreciation in babies' monetary worth was intimately tied to the profound cultural transformation in children's economic and sentimental value in the twentieth century.

Nineteenth-century foster families took in useful children expecting them to help out with farm chores and household tasks. In this context, babies were "unmarketable," and hard to place except in foundling asylums or commercial baby farms. But the redefinition of children's value at the turn of the century challenged the established instrumental assumptions. If child labor was no longer legitimate, a working home was an anachronism. And if children were priceless, it was obnoxious to profit by their misfortune. Thus, baby farming was singled out as a uniquely mercenary "traffic in children."

The breakdown of nineteenth-century arrangements was a difficult process sponsored by child welfare workers but resisted by adoptive parents. Yet gradually, adoption practices were revolutionized into a search for child love and not child labor. In a 1930 issue of the *Saturday Evening Post,* one observer marveled at the new altruism of adoptive parents: "What do they get out of this bondage? Worry, sickness, a procession of measles, mumps . . . chicken pox . . . scooters and muddy galoshes cluttering the hall . . . financial pressure to give these little strangers the best education in the land. Who would shoulder such burdens voluntarily? . . ." A parent's response: ". . . what we have done for that child is not a drop in the bucket compared to what it has done for us—the experiences, joys, emotions . . . it has put into our lives. . . ."[3]

Ironically, as children's labor value disappeared, their new emotional worth became increasingly monetized and commercialized. Sentimental adoption boosted babies' charms, and parents were willing to disburse large sums of money to obtain a baby of their own. The new market for children was shaped by children's noneconomic appeal. While in the nineteenth century a child's capacity for labor had determined its exchange value, the market price of a twentieth-century baby was set by smiles, dimples, and curls.

Working Homes and Baby Farms: The Nineteenth-Century Approach to Substitute Parenting

The legitimacy of child labor was essential to early nineteenth-century substitute care arrangements. In exchange for board, clothing, and some education, children were expected to assist the foster household in a variety of tasks. It was considered a fair bargain. After all, if children worked for their own parents, why not work for surrogate caretakers? The tradition had been established in colonial times with the widespread system of apprenticeship. Seventeenth-century parents placed their children with neighbors, relatives, and sometimes even strangers to learn a skilled trade. While for some, it was an instructional and elective indenture, for poor and dependent children it was the only way to secure a home. Authorities routinely bound out young orphaned or destitute children during their minority to households in the community where, under formal contract, a child earned its keep with productive labor. When the contractual agreement expired at age eighteen or sometimes twenty-one, the child left with some money, cattle, clothes, and a new Bible.[4]

Although abandoned by well-off families, indenture was still the preferred solution for the care of dependent children in the first three decades of the nineteenth century. Even when they were institutionalized in almshouses and, after the 1830s, shifted into orphanages, children's value as laborers determined the nature of their placement. After they reached the age of twelve or fourteen, most institutions placed children out as workers in foster families. During their institutional life, children also labored hard, sometimes even subsidizing their own stay by contributing with their work to the support of an asylum.[5]

The most renowned nineteenth-century program of placing children in family homes was directly contingent on children's economic usefulness. In 1854, the New York Children's Aid Society, organized by Charles Loring Brace, began sending needy city children to rural homes out in the Midwest and upstate New York. The plan met with extraordinary success as farmers promptly responded to the society's appeal for homes. Similar organizations were formed in cities all over the nation.[6]

Brace distinguished his plan of free family homes from the traditional indenture arrangement by the absence of a written contract and the retention of legal guardianship by the society or the natural parents. But free family homes meant only freedom from contract, not from work. By minimizing formal ties, Brace expected that families would more readily welcome children as working family members rather than as cheap laborers. Children's work contribution, however, was not in dispute. The Society's circulars were forthright, promising that, "These boys are, many of them, handy and active, and would learn soon any common trade or labor. They could be employed on farms, in trades, in manufacturing. . . . The girls could be used for the common kinds of housework."[7] The useful child was generally older than ten, and a boy: More than three times as many boys as girls were placed. The sex ratio was regulated not only by the demand for boys, but also by the supply of girls. One study of dependent children in New York City suggests that urban families were particularly reluctant to dispense with the domestic labor of their daughters.[8]

Recent evidence suggests that poor urban families used the Children's Aid Society as a quasi-employment agency for their children. Bellingham's analysis, for instance, shows that the most common single motive for surrendering custody of children to the organization was the children's need for a job: "Some wanted farm service positions . . . while others were trying to get training for a trade. Some wanted factory or domestic service jobs and a good number just wanted positions right in the city."[9] Thus, the instrumental aspects of nineteenth-century foster care served not only the interests of employers, but those of at least a segment of the children placed. The useful child found a legitimate place in the foster household economy no less than in his own working-class family.

The plight of nineteenth-century babies was the flip side of children's usefulness. If a working child was an asset, an infant was a liability. Unwanted babies, or those whose parents could not afford to keep them, were more likely to die than be adopted. Faced with almost insurmountable social and economic pressures, single, widowed, or deserted mothers had few available options. Abortion was not only expensive, but required connections, especially after the 1860s when it became an increasingly illegitimate and illegal practice. The few jobs available to women with children did not pay a living wage. Unprotected by insurance, and without the support of adequate public relief or private programs, many lower-class women abandoned their babies soon after birth in public places or in a foundling asylum where infant mortality sometimes reached between 85 and 90 percent.[10]

Baby farmers offered an alternative to those who could afford their fee. These usually middle-aged women built a profitable enterprise by boarding mostly illegitimate babies. With high rates of mortality, the turnover was quick, and business brisk. Mothers were relieved of their responsibility and assured of confidentiality. One baby farmer outlined her terms for a prospective customer: "I take Infants from Berth [sic] up and keep them in my own home until I place them in a good home and my terms is fifty Dollars and If you can't pay the fifty cash you can Pay thirty-five Dollars and the Balance weekly . . . you will never be troubled with the child after I take full charge of It until I have it adopted into a good home. . . ."[11] In an account of baby farming practices, the *New York Times* explained, "The mother is pleased with the prospect of ridding herself of a great incumbrance, and at the same time securing . . . a bright future for the child and eagerly agrees to the terms, even if exorbitant."[12]

The prospect of adoption for the infant, however, was seldom fulfilled. As a 1910 investigation discovered, the baby farm, "swarms with children whose numbers are added to weekly. Always they come and come, and rarely . . . are they carried away."[13] A baby had limited sales value; sometimes it took no more than 25 cents to obtain one. Thus, the baby farmer made her profits by charging mothers a "surrender fee," and only rarely by placing children. Unquestionably, it was a buyer's market. In an 1890 case, an agent of the New York Society for the Prevention of Cruelty to Children pretended interest in adopting a two-week-old baby. The baby farmer demanded two dollars but quickly settled for half. "She . . . urged him to take the infant at once and at his own price, for she could not attend to it."[14]

Even agents of reputable child-placing agencies were sometimes unwilling to forgo the profits involved in disposing of other people's unwanted children. During an 1897 interrogation by the New York State Board of Charities, the witness, Rev. W. Jarvis Maybee of the Children's Home Society, a national organization that placed children in free foster homes, admitted charging parents fifty dollars for taking their child. For illegitimate babies, the fee was doubled. As Jarvis explained, "We charge more for little babies because it is harder to get homes for them while they are young; we have to keep them."[15]

A Proper Home for the Sacred Child: Revising the Adoption Contract

Once the useful child was defined as a social problem, traditional solutions for the care of dependent children became untenable. Seeking a destitute child for its labor, or taking in a homeless baby for the sake of a cash bonus, equally transgressed the new sentimental value of children. If any child at all qualified as a "priceless jewel," the baby farm business could no longer be allowed to transform babies into "valueless chattels."[16] And how could families continue to employ a foster child when working-class parents were being forced to forgo the labor of their own children? Whether by indenture or in free foster homes, declared Homer Folks, a leading social worker, "Any plan which compels or allows these children to work when the others are at play or in school . . . is a disgrace to the people of any state."[17]

By the 1870s, child welfare workers had begun their campaign against the established instrumental approach to childcare and in support of "genuine homes . . . where a child would be received . . . from the real love of it. . . . "[18] Consequently, routine applications for a working child became suspect—the unseemly product of lower-class parents' misguided selfish motives. As William Pryor Letchworth, a member of the New York State Board of Charities, noted in his influential report on pauper and destitute children in 1874, "It is important that the person taking the child should feel an interest in it beyond a purely selfish one. . . . If this interest is not felt, the child has not found a home in the true sense of the word." Admitting that "it may seem difficult to secure this result under ordinary circumstances," Letchworth was confident that in a community "fully awakened," the change would come about.[19]

Baby farms were singled out as particularly offensive and deadly institutions. "It is time," urged a *New York Times* editorial in September of 1873, "that some active means were taken to put a stop to the practice of baby farming which in the vast majority of instances, is only another term for baby-killing."[20] Unnatural parents were accused of sending children out to "nurse," with the understanding that "they are to be 'put out of the way' by means that shall elude the law."[21] Since a rapid turnover of infants meant the arrival of new clients, and an additional payment, baby farmers were allegedly anxious "to get rid of the little milk imbibers as quickly as possible."[22]

But the threat posed by this "hiring out of babies," was only partly a matter of safety. Surely, in the nineteenth century, infant mortality was not much lower in officially approved almshouses and foundling asylums than in unlicensed baby farms. And, while mothers may indeed have been eager to "get rid of children that become incumbrances," it was not necessarily with the intent of infanticide. As even the alarmist editorials of the *New York Times* acknowledged, children were often put out to board permanently or only temporarily by "poor widows who desire to go out . . . to do . . . housework, where they find it very inconvenient to be incumbered by very young children."[23]

Baby farming was therefore denounced largely as a symbol of an antiquated and mercenary approach to adoption. Much as children's life insurance, the system visibly challenged the new sacred value of children by routinely pricing their lives. The parallels between both forms of "baby traffic" did not escape the New York Society for the Prevention of Cruelty to Children; "One way of getting rid of the infant was to insure it, neglect it, and so kill it off. Now it is . . . more profitable to buy and sell, and the system has become a kind of baby slave trade."

In the 1870s, the New York Society for the Prevention of Cruelty to Children was also heavily involved in a struggle against the "padrone" system, a particularly mercenary type of indenture. For a small sum of money, padrones "bought" young Italian children from their parents and brought them to the United States. It was a profitable investment; the children worked in the street, as beggars or musicians, handing padrones all their earnings. By the 1880s, the NYSPCC, with the cooperation of the Italian government, succeeded in stopping the padrones' business.[24]

Child welfare workers sought to replace mercenary foster parenting of any kind with a new approach to adoption more suitable for the economically "useless," sacred child. Institutional care for dependent children had gained great popularity in the nineteenth century. Even after the 1870s, when children were removed by law from almshouses, they were transferred to orphanages and other institutions. But by the 1890s, reformers began a forceful campaign in support of foster home care. In 1909, the White House Conference on Children officially declared foster homes the "best substitute for the natural home." As the concept of home care gained increasing recognition, it became imperative to rethink carefully children's proper place in the foster home. As Hastings Hart, another prominent social worker, explained, "We have a constant missionary work to do, to lead people to realize that they are not to take children for their own selfish gratification."[25] The *Children's Home Finder*, a publication of the Children's Home Society, appealed to its readers not to take a boy "for what you can get out of him, but, rather, for what you can put into him. . . ."[26] Prospective adopters were duly warned that raising a useless child was an expensive commitment: "It costs us comparatively nothing to secure a servant—the payment of a little coin, a paltry pittance. But to secure . . . a child . . . what anxious hours and days and months and years! . . . Think of the *time* bestowed . . . and the *money* spent."[27] Yet, new intangible benefits would make it all worthwhile:

Families . . . in need of a servant . . . have gone to . . . some "orphanage," . . . and asked for a boy or girl old enough to serve them. And what have they secured? Just what they asked for: a servant. . . . But their soul has not been enriched. . . . We . . . urge that such families make a great mistake in asking for a servant. We come to say that there is a *jewel* in that abandoned child.[28]

"When you receive a baby to raise," promised the *Children's Home Finder*, "you add to your possessions heaven's sweetest benediction." Even clergymen used their pulpits to persuade parishioners that the new accounting assured a positive balance: "Does the child pay? Yes, surely he pays—a hundred, a thousand fold. A man's children are his treasure. . . . What amount of money would buy them from us? This is . . . almost equally true of those children that come into our homes by adoption."[29]

To be sure, child welfare workers did not invent the sentimental value of an adoptive child. In fact, a significant minority of children placed by the Children's Aid Society were taken just for the sake of companionship.[30] But in nineteenth-century foster homes, the sentimental value of a child did not preclude the possibility of profitably employing that same child. Such an acceptable combination of children's economic and sentimental value was declared an illegitimate contradiction by child welfare workers. For them, the instrumental value of a child negated its sacred value. An 1869 report by the Massachusetts State Board of Charities warned that if sometimes, "the child who was taken as a servant secures a place in the affections of the family taking him, and so the connection ceases to be a mercenary one,"[31] such cases were exceptional.

Challenging the established exchange of child labor for childcare was often a frustrating effort. Officials of child-placing organizations shared their discouragement at the persistent offers of "situations," rather than homes. As Edward T. Hall told the National Conference of Charities and Corrections in 1899, "The beautiful, lovable homes that we read about, where people live who are lying awake nights ready to take to their hearts the undesirable children of society for the dear children's sake, are few and far between." Most applicants were after the best worker, not the most endearing child: "In the spring a farmer's fancy . . . turns to thoughts of a good, strong boy . . . who is not afraid to work. . . . At all seasons of the year the demand is good for girls . . . to take care of the children and work around the house."[32] As placement officials soon discovered, an acute "servant problem" at the turn of the century significantly increased the labor appeal of a young girl. Foster parents were accused of using new sentimental jargon to camouflage the same old instrumental designs, ". . . young married people . . . come and want a strong healthy girl to adopt. They want to take that child into their own family and treat her as their own. That sounds on the surface very beautiful. What does it usually mean? . . . They want cheap labor."[33]

The commercial treatment of infants was equally intractable. A 1910 investigation of New Hampshire baby farms ascertained that the "infamous barter in babies," remained a lucrative business, ". . . tiny defenseless babies, sometimes still unborn, are openly advertised as if on sale. . . . In the column headed Miscellaneous, sometimes listed with the Live Stock or Wogglebugs. . . ." Responses to a decoy newspaper advertisement offering, "A Blue Eyed Baby, 2 weeks old, to be given for adoption . . . bonus of $50," confirmed that the adoption of babies was still a matter of profit, not love. "Whether the incentive is the bonus often offered; the larger possibility of child-insurance; or the less apparent worth-whileness of speculating in a child's life cannot be exactly determined." The report estimated that a "tradeswoman in tiny lives," could make as much as $10,000 a year.[34]

Traditional solutions to substitute parenting were not maintained, as child welfare workers supposed, simply by the individual selfishness of foster parents or even the material greediness of baby farmers. Instead, the shift from instrumental to sentimental adoption was obstructed by the continuing legitimacy of children's usefulness. For working-class families, taking in a child was justified only if he or she paid its way with some form of work. Economically "useless" babies, therefore, still needed a subsidy to find a home. Leaders of the child-placing movement were themselves often unwilling to entirely proscribe children's usefulness. A good home, declared the superintendent of a Children's Home in Ohio, was a training school where children "are taught to become . . . useful men and women."[35] When the New York State Charities Aid Association instructed foster parents to treat children as family members, they meant children to be properly clothed, sent to school, and to church, but also "taught to be useful and fitted for a life of self support." The determination to reject applicants seeking child laborers therefore, did not mean that children should never again labor: "It is expected that our children will be taught to be helpful, just as if they had been born in the family."[36]

The transformation in the economic role of a child was thus just as complex and ambivalent in foster families as in natural ones. Some officers of child-placing agencies were even convinced that the new sacred value of children could be perfectly combined with their traditional work role. Recognizing that people would continue asking for useful children, Rev. M. T. Lamb, State Superintendent of the New Jersey Children's Home Society, maintained that, ". . . it is not wrong to want a child to help to do [the work] . . . We are simply trying to lodge in these good people's heart . . . that there is a golden opportunity to 'kill two birds with one stone,' that while they are securing some needed assistance . . . they are at the same time . . . receiving [that child] as a sacred trust." Foster parents were enticed by the paradoxical yet convenient likelihood that respecting the sacredness of children might increase children's labor potential, "the more prominently this higher object is kept to the front in the . . . treatment of this child, the larger returns will be secured in the lower realm . . . the boy . . . will do the best work. . . ."[37]

Most child-placing agencies sought to discriminate between illegitimate child labor and "good" child work for foster children. For instance, John N. Foster, Superintendent of Michigan's State Public School, distinguished "kind-hearted, well-meaning people . . . desiring a child to help 'mind' the baby, run errands, prepare vegetables," from families who took a child, "simply with reference to its commercial value . . ."[38] The distinction between types of work was not easy to make.

As Hastings Hart admitted: "It is often difficult to determine whether too much is required of a child. . . . It is only right that a child should render such reasonable assistance as would be required . . . in its own home, but it is altogether wrong that the child should be over-taxed. . . ."[39] Above all, it was essential to determine at what point the foster child ceased being a family member to become the family's servant. When was a child simply assuming its share of the "family burdens," and when was he or she transformed into a drudge, "to save the expense of hiring servants."[40] Supervisors were instructed to provide detailed reports on the amount of work performed by foster children: "It is not enough to know that a boy of ten carries wood and water; one should know how much wood he carries and how big and heavy the buckets are and what distance he has to go with them. . . ."[41]

Working homes persisted into the 1920s, mostly in rural areas, but as deviant exceptions. Despite some attempts to modernize the indenture contract, the arrangement was condemned as an unseemly bargain, "by which the foster home takes the child because it needs household help or farm labor and not because it is seeking an opportunity to extend education and affection to an unfortunate child."[42] Free homes were disparaged as "the wolf of the old indenture philosophy of child labor in the sheepskin disguise of a so-called good or Christian family home." The twentieth-century useful child was no longer a legitimate contributor to the household economy but had become an embarrassing survival of antiquated and unacceptable norms. In his influential book, *The Dependent Child*, Henry W. Thurston succinctly stated the critical new principle in fostering, ". . . the only way to safeguard the individuality of the child is to recognize that an immature boy or girl is a money liability and not an immediate money asset."[43]

As in natural families, the relationship of foster children to work and money was transformed in the twentieth century. New educational guidelines replaced earlier economic criteria. Child work became acceptable only as part of an "educational program." Child money was a means to teach children how to save and how to spend. In 1896, Homer Folks, then secretary of the New York State Charities Aid Association, had recognized the advantages of home care over institutions for the training of future consumers: "The relation between labor and the power to purchase is sharp and clear, and the children are . . . participating in discussions as to whether the family can afford this or that. . . ."[44] In an institution, on the other hand, children had little opportunity to learn the value of money. By 1910, agents supervising foster homes were instructed to determine whether the child received spending money. Experts in child-placing concurred that an allowance was the best means to teach "habits of economy and budgeting": "How better can he learn than through the wise use of money that is his own and which must be accounted for systematically?"[45] An allowance, noted Sophie Van Senden Theis of the New York State Charities Aid Association, not only provided the child with useful experience, but gave him a "certain standing among other children."[46]

An investigation of ten child-placing agencies conducted by the U.S. Children's Bureau in the early 1920s found that half of the agencies had established a policy that children "should have a small but stated amount of spending money." In some cases, agencies provided foster parents with funds for children's allowances, but often parents received no reimbursement for this additional expense. Establishing rules for children's money in substitute homes raised similar problems to those in natural families. While some mothers "paid" their children for performing household duties, most experts discouraged parents from paying a child for "his share of the routine household chores such as would be performed as a matter of course by their own children."[47] The financial obligations of older foster children were particularly complex. At least until the 1920s, it was expected that after children left school, they were entitled to wages as compensation for any labor required by foster parents. Yet, as Theis and Goodrich noted, the payment of wages generated a great deal of friction with foster families who were unwilling to pay a child for work their own children did for free. Concerned with the possibility that foster children would be treated as ordinary laborers, some agencies recommended an allowance in addition to wages. This unearned income differentiated a foster child from a paid worker.[48]

The ambivalent economic status of older foster children was vividly brought out in a 1924 lawsuit. In *Miller v. Pelzer* the plaintiff, a twenty-five-year-old woman, accused her foster parents who had taken her in their home as an infant, of wrongfully concealing her true parentage, thereby exploiting her services gratis. She claimed $2,500 for her unpaid labor after majority. But the judge ruled against her. Reaffirming the new sentimental standards of adoption, he declared that the emotional benefits of family life outweighed her pecuniary loss, "the home—the family relation—is of such vast importance that its benefits cannot be estimated."[49]

Boarding Homes: A Controversial "Dowry" for Useless Children

In the late 1860s, the Massachusetts State Board of Charities pioneered the concept of paying foster parents for the care of a child. These subsidized boarding homes stood at the crossroads between instrumental and sentimental adoption. Initially, boarding homes complemented the customary exchange of child labor for child care by financing primarily those unable to fulfill the traditional contract, "small children, the sickly, the troublesome and the vicious [who] are not readily taken by families, and will not be until some inducement . . . is offered. . . ."[50] A cash payment provided the necessary incentive to care for an economically unprofitable child. As Homer Folks explained: "The great majority of children who are returned after being placed in homes are returned . . . because of their inability to render a certain amount of service which the foster parents rightfully expected. In most cases the boy was not a bad boy, but a bad bargain." Board money made the bargain acceptable.[51]

But boarding homes also played a key role in the break up of nineteenth-century fostering practices. Concern shifted from a particular child's inability to labor, to the illegitimacy of all child labor. Paid parenting, then, presented the perfect alternative to working homes for all young children. In particular, it became urgent to find adequate placement for children between the ages of seven and eleven who were awkwardly caught in the transition from instrumental to sentimental adoption—too young to be placed as workers, yet too old to be adopted as "pets and means of amusement."[52] Boarding homes offered this in-between age group a substitute for the traditional indenture or free working home, thereby assuring them a prolonged period of "uselessness"; "if boarded [they] can be kept in school . . . shielded from overwork . . . by those who sometimes seek cheap labor in the person of a boy and a girl nearing the legal working age."[53] With some luck, it was even possible that a proper "dowry" would provide children with a passport to sentimental adoption; "[they may] awaken a sentiment which frequently deepens into a strong affection; and the child remains . . . after the payment of board has ceased. . . ."[54]

Yet, for its critics, the monetization of childcare was a dangerous new variant of the instrumental approach to substitute parenting. Supporters of free homes considered it "unfortunate that the appeal must be made to the mercenary side of our nature to induce the family to take a child." The boarding family, warned M. T. Lamb, of the Children's Home Society, "takes the child without a Christian motive in the taking; takes it for the pay offered for its board."[55] For Charles L. Brace, paid fostering turned "an act, which is at once one of humanity and prudence, into one purely of business."[56] Without proper regulation, what would prevent families from becoming "small institutions, and children being taken for profit"?[57] As a precaution, some child welfare workers urged closer supervision of boarding homes than of working homes: "The sum, though small, is enough to tempt the cupidity of the unworthy. . . ."[58]

Supporters of boarding homes denied that monetization necessarily led to commercialization. The term boarding itself, noted C. H. Pemberton, of Pennsylvania's Children's Aid Society, was inadequate: "it leaves out the greater part of what we want to express,—the special care, the training . . . and suggests the only one feature of payment."[59] Others pointed out that the modest board payments barely reimbursed parents for the expenses of raising a child. A well-known child-placing manual explained: "The amount paid for board is usually less than the commercial value of the service, implying a larger or smaller amount of unrequited philanthropic care, which in many cases is cheerfully and generously rendered."[60] To ward off commercialization, agencies were urged to reject any home "that does not give the boarded child much more than is paid by the board money."[61]

The legitimacy of boarding home care rested on the intangible, noneconomic clauses of the contract. The arrangement could not be settled as an ordinary business deal. For, if paid parenting was to become a legitimate collaborator in the sentimental approach to adoption, it was essential that the emotional link between foster parent and child transcend their financial bond. Otherwise, the boarding mother was indistinguishable from the much maligned baby farmer. In fact, some observers found little difference between mercenary and paid mothering. Wet nurses employed by the foundling asylums were often accused of regarding their infant boarders simply as a source of income. "In computing their assets . . . they will say: 'And if I could get a foundling to help me pay the rent, I could see my way clear for the winter.'" If one of their boarders got sick, these mothers' lamentations were exclusively over "her lost two dollars a week."[62]

Defenders of boarding homes did not deny the economic value of these "pay babies" or of older boarders for the mostly lower class, often immigrant foster families. As Jacob Riis recognized, "The money thus earned pays the rent of hundreds of poor families. It is no trifle."[63] Among poor New York women, explained a Russell Sage report in 1914, "every asset must be converted into its cash value. Even the death of a new baby may be an economic resource for the mother. Her breast milk is worth ten to twelve dollars a month, if she brings home a nursling baby." These foster mothers, however, escaped the stigma of baby farmers. The report concluded that "the little boarder is tenderly cared for and the whole family soon forgets that he is a stranger. When the time comes for him to return to the hospital the money loss is the least part of the foster mother's grief."[64] This emotional tie between boarding mother and child "cleansed" board payments. "Renting" out a baby to these mothers, usually Italian, was often more of a ritual event than a business deal. The New York State Charities Aid Association described the "fiesta" feeling when nurses arrived to pick up a baby:

Decked out in all the gold of which she is the proud possessor. She wears her brightest skirt and her gayest kerchief. She often brings her husband, two or three children . . . and usually a neighbor to "assist" at the high function of taking a baby. . . . It is a happy moment when the procession starts triumphantly homeward, the baby wrapped up in true bambino fashion, and the nurse radiant with happiness.[65]

A careful investigation of 122 infant boarding homes in 1907 confirmed the "kindly intelligence and very real affection displayed by these foster mothers." Yet, despite their overt praise, agencies viewed paid nurses with much condescension—fit for the temporary care of infants, but not for their adoption.[66]

Finding a proper home for the economically "useless" sacred child was a complex task. Once the instrumental link between foster parent and child was declared illegitimate, any form of profitable parenting became structurally deviant and therefore morally suspect. From that perspective, boarding homes were a reprehensible monetized version of working homes; the value of a child's services substituted by a cash payment from an agency. Despite every effort to depict boarding as a task of love and regardless of the individual motivations of foster parents, the contractual arrangement by which families received a fee for the care of a child, defined their task as partly commercial. Therefore, while boarding homes had an important part in the transition from instrumental to sentimental adoption, paid parenting remained an ambivalent occupation. A 1924 report on foster care, by the U.S. Children's Bureau, regretted the persistent popular notion that a paid foster mother "is either in dire need or so mercenary that she would starve the bodies of the little dependents." The widespread attitude that all boarding mothers "are commercial," noted the report, "makes it more difficult to attract the right sort of foster mother." Five years later, the bureau again found that despite the fact that "the contribution of foster parents . . . far outweighs any money compensation . . ." many communities still regarded foster parents "who accept pay for their services as grasping and actuated solely by money considerations."[67] Boarding homes were accepted slowly in the United States. The 1923 census showed that 64.2 percent of dependent and neglected children under care were still in asylums, 23.4 percent in free homes but only 10.2 percent in boarding homes.[68]

Blue-Eyed Babies and Golden-Haired Little Girls: The Sentimental Value of a Priceless Child

In 1921, the *New York Times* revealed "one of the most amazing stories of mother love." A Mrs. F. E. A. South of Atlanta confessed that the triplets, "supposedly 'born' to her on New Year's Eve, were not her own; that twin girls 'born' to her four years ago were not her own and that she had reared altogether eleven children whom even her husband believed that she bore, when in reality they were all adopted secretly. . . ." Love justified her deception, "I don't like movies, I don't like theatres . . . the greatest thing in my life are children . . . that is why I did it—because I love children. . . ."[69] In the 1920s and 1930s, sentimental adoption made sympathetic headlines as it rapidly displaced earlier instrumental fostering arrangements. A new consensus was reached. The only legitimate rewards of adoption were emotional, "an enlargement of happiness to be got in no other way."[70] As one grateful adoptive father told a reporter, "Talk about children owing their parents anything! We'll never be able to pay what we owe that baby."[71] Some well-publicized disputes over the custody of child movie stars in the 1930s became major scandals by visibly violating the new standards of sentimental adoption. These money-making children were sought for their riches, not their affection. For instance, the guardianship of English-born, thirteen-year-old Freddy Bartholomew, who earned $100,000 from his successful acting career in the United States, was bitterly fought in court between his aunt and his parents. Such cases were censured as callous attempts "by one party or the other to gain control of the child's earnings."[72] It was better for a child not to be adopted at all than to be taken for "sheerly mercenary reasons, for self-interest or greed."[73]

Legal adoption, rare in the nineteenth century, became increasingly popular in the twentieth century. A judge from the Boston Probate Court remarked in 1919, "the woods are full of people eager to adopt children—the number appearing to be in the increase."[74] By 1927, the New York Times reported that the new problem in adoption "has become one of finding enough children for childless homes rather than that of finding enough homes for homeless children." Despite greater regulation, and more thorough screening of adoptive parents, legal adoptions increased three-fold between 1934 and 1944, finally breaking a long-standing monopoly of institutional care for dependent children.[75]

The quest for a child to love turned into a glamorous and romanticized search as a number of well-known entertainment and political figures proudly and publicly joined the rank of adoptive parents. Minnie Maddern Fiske, a respected stage actress, told about her adoption of a thirteen-month-old baby, who made his stage debut in one of her tours. Al Jolson explained to the press his decision to adopt a child: "I think it is selfish to go through life without children." In the 1930s, Gracie Allen and George Burns, Mayor La Guardia, Babe Ruth, and Eddie Rickenbacker, among others, similarly announced their decision to adopt a child.[76]

The fairy-tale dimension of adoption was further magnified by many stories of poor waifs taken into the homes of generous, wealthy foster parents. A 1905 article in *Cosmopolitan* had already noted the fantastic prospect of transforming a little "plebeian" into a "lord"; "[the] little ones go from the . . . doorsteps and sewers, to comfort always, and sometimes to luxury."[77] In 1925, Edward W. Browning, a wealthy New York real estate operator, made front-page headlines when he advertised for a "pretty, refined girl" to adopt, thus opening up "the gates of fairyland for many a poor child." Browning allegedly received over 12,000 applications from all over the country. Each girl he interviewed was sent home in Browning's automobile, "with a chauffer in livery . . . and a footman to help them in and out of the coach, just like Cinderella."

The Browning case ended in a scandal after Mary Spas, the girl he adopted thinking she was sixteen years old, confessed to being twenty-one. Mary left Browning lured by an agent's offer to write her story for publication and the promise of a movie job. Browning, who claimed to have spent $20,000 for the adoption (including forty dresses for Mary), had the adoption nullified.[78] While the incident was exceptional, the social class of adoptive parents was indeed undergoing change. A comparison by the New York State Charities Aid Association of the occupations of 100 foster fathers between 1898 and 1900 with the same number of fathers in the period between 1920 and 1921, found that nearly three-quarters of foster fathers in the first period were in skilled, semi-skilled, or unskilled labor, or in farming, while in the latter period there was a predominance of men in business and office work. Sophie Van Senden Theis, author of the report, recalled how "Many of the plainest homes were used for the first children placed, for in those days the Agency had to take what it could get in the way of foster homes."

The shift in social class, detected by Theis, was tied to the sentimentalization of adoption. A study of adoptive parents in Minnesota during the period from 1918 to 1928 found that adoptive fathers surpassed the proportion of males in the general population in the higher occupational levels (professional, semi-professional, and managerial). But adoptive fathers of older, and therefore potentially useful, children were more likely to belong to a lower occupational category, in particular farming.[79]

Sentimental adoption created an unprecedented demand for children under three, especially for infants. In 1910, the press already discussed the new appeal of babies, warning, "there are not enough babies to go around."[80] The Home-Finding Committee of the Spence Nursery, an agency organized for the placement of infants, was surprised to discover that, "instead of our having to seek these homes, they have sought us, and so great is the demand for babies that we cannot begin to meet it." In 1914, Judd Mortimer Lewis, a Texas poet and humorist, achieved national notoriety by working as a one-man baby bureau, using his column in the Houston *Post* to find infants for "baby-hungry" parents. Babies, observed the *New York Tribune* in 1923, "are being taken into homes in numbers and for reasons that mark a new era in the huge task of caring for parentless children." By 1937, infant adoption was being touted as the latest American fad: "The baby market is booming. . . . The clamor is for babies, more babies. . . . We behold an amazing phenomenon: a country-wide scramble on the part of childless couples to adopt a child." Ironically, while the economically "useless" nineteenth-century baby had to be protected because it was unwanted, the priceless twentieth-century baby, "needs protection as never before . . . [because] too many hands are snatching it."[81]

The priceless child was judged by new criteria; its physical appeal and personality replaced earlier economic yardsticks. After talking to several directors of orphan asylums, the *New York Times* concluded that "every baby who expects to be adopted . . . ought to make it a point to be born with blue eyes. . . . The brown-eyed, black-eyed, or grey-eyed girl or boy may be just as pretty . . . but it is hard to make benevolent auxiliaries of the stork believe so."[82] But the greatest demand was for little girls. Soon after launching its popular Child-Rescue Campaign in 1907, promoting foster home care, the *Delineator* commented that requests for boys were half that for girls; "a two-year old, blue-eyed, golden haired little girl with curls, that is the order that everybody leaves. It cannot be filled fast enough."[83] Similarly, in its first thirty years of work, the New York State Charities Aid Association received 8,000 applications for girls, out of a total of 13,000. While working homes sought older girls for their domestic labor value, adoptive homes wanted little girls for their domestic sentimental value: "a doll on which they could tie pink sashes." In the 1920s, wealthy Americans even imported their "English-rose" golden-haired baby girls from London. Jews were apparently an exception. According to an interview with the assistant superintendent of the Hebrew Sheltering Guardian Asylum in 1910, three-year-old boys were in much greater demand among Jewish adoptive parents than little girls.[84]

Considering the widespread parental preference for a male first-born child, the popularity of adopted daughters was puzzling. As Hastings Hart observed in 1902, "When people pray for a child of their own, they are apt to pray for a boy; when they want it for adoption, they want a girl. It is an unexplainable fact that every one who is engaged in placing out children is familiar with."[85] Parents, suggested one adoption agency in 1916, "seem to feel that a girl is easier to understand and to rear, and they are afraid of a boy. . . ."[86] Twenty years later, the *Canadian Magazine* linked the persistent preference for girls to parents' fear of a lonely old age: "Girls do not break the home ties so early as boys and outside interests do not play so large a part in their lives." Why do "pretty little picture-book girls, go like hot cakes," speculated rhetorically a writer in the *Saturday Evening Post*, because they are "grand little self-advertisers and they know instinctively how to strut their stuff. . . . They stretch out their dimpled arms, gurgle some secret baby joke, smile a divine toothless smile . . . and women and strong men go mad, become besotted with adoration. . . ." Boys, on the other hand were promotional failures, "slower, more serious and aloof."[87]

The sex and age preferences of twentieth-century adoptive parents were clearly linked to the cultural revolution in fostering. While the earlier need for a useful child put a premium on strong, older children, preferably male, the later search for a priceless child led to babies and particularly, pretty little girls. It was not the innate smiling expertise of females, but established cultural assumptions of women's superior emotional talents which made girls so uniquely attractive for sentimental adoption. The new appeal of babies was further enhanced by the increasing acceptance, in the 1920s, of environmental theories of development. Couples considering adoption were now reassured that "heredity has little or nothing to do with our characters. It is the environment that counts. . . ."[88] Intelligence tests and improved methods of determining children's physical health, reduced the "old prejudice against thrusting one's hand in a grab-bag, eugenically speaking, and breeding by proxy."[89] Even the stigma of illegitimacy was turned into an asset by suggestions that "love babies" ·were particularly attractive and desirable.[90]

Ironically, as the priceless child displaced the useful child, the dangers of adoption shifted from economic to emotional hazards; the previously exploited little laborer risked becoming a "pretty toy." Prospective adopters were warned: "If you are planning to have a plaything to cuddle and pet and dress prettily, don't do it!"[91] Parents were also advised against seeking an emotionally or psychologically "useful" child. Experts now wrote about the dangers of "seeking compensation in children for frustrated affections," or unfulfilled ambitions.[92] If child placing agencies were less often confronted by requests for a sturdy working child, they now faced new expectations, as the couple who applied to the New York State Charities Association for a three-month-old baby, "who could eventually go to Princeton."[93]

Black-Market Babies: The Price of a Priceless Child

The sentimentalization of adoption had an unanticipated and paradoxical effect. By creating a demand for babies, it also stimulated a new kind of baby market. While nineteenth-century mothers had paid baby farmers to accept their unwanted baby, twentieth-century adoptive parents were willing to pay to obtain an infant. "Baby traffickers" thus found an additional line of business—making money not only from the surrender of babies, but doubling their profits by then selling them to their new customers.[94] As a result, the value of a priceless child became increasingly monetized and commercialized. Ironically, the new market price for babies was set exclusively by their noneconomic, sentimental appeal.

The traditional baby market continued into the second decade of the twentieth century. An influential investigation conducted by the Chairman of the Maryland State-Wide Vice Commission in 1914, reported that in many cases the adoption of children remained a "means of earning money; the child was entirely secondary and was taken simply for a price." Respondents to several decoy newspaper ads seeking a home for a one-week-old baby, requested sums ranging from $100 to $7,000 to take the child permanently. As one woman explained, "I love to care for a baby . . . but I would expect to be paid a fair price for my services." Two established maternity hospitals in Baltimore actively participated in this "commercialized traffic." Parents were asked to pay between $100 to $125 to be "relieved of all responsibility and relinquish all right and claim to the child." If a woman was too poor to pay with money, she paid with labor, working for one year as a maid in the hospital. The report uncovered the routine collaboration of physicians, nurses, midwives, and even clergymen who were willing, usually for a fee, to help a mother dispose of her infant.[95]

But by 1910, there had been signs that the structure of the baby market was changing and expanding. An article in *Cosmopolitan* referred to a "desultory and elusive traffic," with babies being sold for as much as one thousand dollars. A speaker at the 1913 National Conference of Charities and Correction remarked on the developing double baby market in California. Maternity homes and lying-in hospitals were finding that unwanted babies were a new source of revenue: "There are enough childless marriages to create a demand for promising babies, and therefore a market." The going price:

$200 per baby. In Chicago, the Juvenile Protective Association uncovered a "regular commercialized business" in 1917. As before, the unmarried mother "willing to pay any amount of money to dispose of her child," was charged from fifteen to sixty-five dollars by maternity hospitals or individuals to dispose of her baby. But the study also reported a different type of baby market. An "unusually attractive" infant sold for fifteen to one hundred dollars, paid in cash or installments. The new trade slogan of one baby seller was, "It's cheaper and easier to buy a baby for $100 than to have one of your own."[96]

In 1922, the dramatic findings of "A Baby a Day Given Away," a study conducted by the New York State Charities Aid Association, put commercialized adoption directly in the national public spotlight. The six months investigation of newspaper advertisements offering and requesting children for adoption, revealed an "indiscriminate exchange of children." An average of a baby a day was being disposed of in New York, "as casually as one would give away a kitten"; many sold at "bargain-counter" prices. It was not a peculiar New York arrangement.[97] In the classified advertisement column of almost any Boston newspaper, "together with items relating to automobiles, animals, amusements . . . may often be found the child offered for adoption."[98]

Three years later, the notorious prosecution of a New York baby farmer shocked the nation and further raised the visibility of commercial child placement. Helen Augusta Geisen-Volk was charged and indicted for child substitution and for starving infants to death. The young wife of a well-to-do manufacturer added fuel to the scandal by publicly confessing that unknown to her husband, Mrs. Geisen-Volk had sold her an infant for 75 dollars. None of the crimes committed by Geisen-Volk were new to the baby farming business; similar accusations were made as early as the 1870s. More unusual was the severity of the reaction and the degree of public interest in the case. Never before had a baby farming case, for instance, made several front-page headlines in the *New York Times*. [99]

Commercial child placement emerged as a significant social problem in the 1920s in large part because it violated new professional standards in adoption. Without proper supervision by a licensed child-placing agency, adoption could be dangerous both for children and their adoptive parents. The 1922 report by the New York State Charities Aid Association found many babies given away to "immoral and unfit homes . . . in some instances a baby was 'tried' in a new home every week for a period of six or seven weeks." Besides endangering children, such practices discredited "conscientious and intelligent home finding done by competent child-placing agencies."[100] But selling children undermined not only professional adoption; it also betrayed the new standards of sentimental adoption. It was a sacrilege to price a priceless child. Worse than a criminal, Mrs. Geisen-Volk was indicted by the judge as a "fiend incarnate." As a probation officer told reporters, ". . . the woman . . . has no maternal affections . . . [Babies] to her . . . are articles of merchandise to be bartered or exchanged. The defendant represents a revolting anomaly in humankind."[101]

Yet baby sales did not stop. Despite increased public regulation of childcare and the multiplication of adoption laws, including stricter licensing of boarding homes and new laws against adoption by advertisement, informal child placement persisted. A study of 810 children adopted in Massachusetts between 1922 and 1925 showed that two-thirds were adopted without assistance from social agencies. Similarly, of 1,051 adoptions in New Jersey during 1928, only 289 were sponsored by an agency.[102] Independent adoptions were often arranged by well-intentioned intermediaries, without involving profit. But in many cases, middlemen built a lucrative business by "bootlegging" babies.

Harshly denounced as an "iniquitous traffic in human life," and a "countrywide shame," the black market in babies flourished in the 1930s and 1940s.[103] As demand for adoptable children grew, the "booming" traffic in infants reached a new, third stage. It was now a seller's market. Therefore, the mother of an unwanted child no longer needed to pay to dispose of her baby. Instead, entrepreneurial brokers approached her, offering to pay medical and hospital expenses and often a bonus in exchange for her baby. Even in independent placements arranged without profit, it became common practice to pay the hospital and medical expenses of the natural mother.[104]

In 1955, a Congressional investigation conducted by Senator Estes Kefauver officially pronounced baby selling a national social problem. Its exact magnitude was unclear. While an estimated three out of every four adoptions were made independently of any agency, the percentage arranged for profit was unknown. Unquestionably, however, baby selling was no longer a small local business. In Memphis, a Mrs. Georgia Tann, executive of the Tennessee Children's Home Society, was found guilty of intrastate black marketing. Between 1930 and 1950 she placed over 1,000 children in some fifteen states, making more than a million dollars profit. In another case, Marcus Siegel, a Brooklyn attorney and baby broker, collected about $160,000 in only eighteen months of business. The price tag of a black market baby rose from an estimated $1,000 in the 1930s to $5,000 in the late 1940s. By 1951 some babies sold for as much as $10,000.[105]

The money value of infants was partly determined by a reduced supply. As the dramatic decline in the national birthrate, which began early in the nineteenth century, continued into the 1930s, fewer babies were available for adoption. Contemporary observers also suggested that the increased demand for babies was partly the result of higher rates of childlessness among American couples. In *The Conservation of the Family*, Paul Popenoe blamed higher infertility on a "meat diet, imperfect ventilation of houses, nervous strain of city life, spread of twin beds, [and] wearing of corsets."[106]

Growing concern with the preservation of the family unit further contributed to the baby shortage. After 1911, the mothers' pension movement allowed widows, and in some cases deserted wives or mothers whose husbands were physically or mentally handicapped, or in prison, to keep their children. Reformers also encouraged unmarried mothers to keep their babies. As a result, the supply of adoptable infants shrunk, and the waiting lists of adoption agencies grew longer. Unwilling to wait two or more years for a child, and impatient with the increasingly restrictive standards set by agencies, parents turned to the black market. As one 1951 exposé of baby selling noted, "Babies . . . are on the auction block because there are ten or more potential adopting couples in the country for every child available for adoption."[107]

But scarcity alone cannot determine value. A reduced supply raised the price of babies only because there was a growing number of enthusiastic buyers for white, healthy infants. The market exploited, but did not create the infatuation with priceless babies. In sharp contrast, older children found few customers. Deprived of their former labor value, they were excluded from the new emotional market. Therefore, while the agencies waiting lists for babies had the names of hundreds of impatient parents, it was virtually impossible to find homes for children older than six, who had become both economically and sentimentally "useless."[108]

Pricing the Priceless:
The Special Market for Children

The sentimentalization of adoption in the twentieth century, thus, led paradoxically to a greater commercialization and monetization of child life. As the market for child labor disappeared, a market price developed for children's new sentimental value. In 1975, a second Congressional hearing on black-market practices estimated that more than 5,000 babies were sold each year in the United States, some for as much as $25,000. Sellers retained bargaining leverage. As one black-market lawyer told a prospective customer, "Take it or leave it. I have five other couples."[109] The capitalization of children's value extended into legitimate child-placement. Reversing a long-standing policy by which "the question of a money transaction never comes up in negotiations for a child,"[110] many agencies in the 1940s introduced adoption fees.

An apparently profound contradiction was thereby created, between a cultural system that declared children priceless emotional assets, and a social arrangement that treated them as "cash commodities."[111] In the view of some economists, this persistent conflict between social values and structure should be resolved in favor of the market. Landes and Posner, for instance, advocate legalized baby-selling: "The baby shortage and black market are the result of legal restrictions that prevent the market from operating freely in the sale of babies as of other goods. This suggests as a possible reform simply eliminating these restrictions." An undiluted price system, they argue, would match adoptive parents with adoptable children more efficiently than agencies. In fact, studies comparing independent adoptions with agency placements find little, if any, differences in outcome. Landes and Posner dismiss "moral outrage" or "symbolic" objections against baby sales, as antiquated and impractical.[112]

Others strongly defend substitute parenting as a "gift" of love that should be regulated exclusively by altruism, not profit. As Senator Jennings Randolph told the Subcommittee on Child and Youth during the 1975 black-market hearings, "I cannot conceive of someone coldly and calculatingly selling another human being.... Many thousands of Americans want to provide parental love. It is certainly immoral ... for individuals to profit from that desire." In this ideological context, adoption fees are no more justified nor less venal than black-market purchases. For instance, in testimony presented to the Congressional Subcommittee, the director of an organization of adopted adults, rejected the claim that "monies collected by agencies are respectable while monies collected by independent agents are not:" "It . . . doesn't matter to the people involved . . . whether the fee was $5,000 or $25,000 and whether it was paid to an agency or to an independent agent. . . . No rationale of fees will relieve adoptive parents of the certain knowledge that they have bought a human being. . . ." From this perspective, the tension between values and structure can only be resolved by drastically eliminating every opportunity for a "system of merchandising adoptive babies."[113] In fact, some states have already banned all independent placements, even those not involving profit, in order to deter commercial baby markets.[114]

Ideological defense or rejection of the market equally ignores the interrelationship between market systems and values. Both positions presuppose, for better or for worse, the inevitable and unilateral power of the market. But a "free" independent market for babies is a theoretical illusion; cultural constraints cannot be simply dismissed as obsolete. On the other hand, denying the market any function at all ignores distinctions between types of markets. Not all markets are equal. As Bernard Barber notes, "As a result of . . . interdependencies with, or constraints from, both values and other institutional structures, economic exchange can be patterned in different ways."[115] From the start, the baby market was shaped by the cultural definition of children as priceless. It was not the contradiction, therefore, but the interaction between notions of children's pricelessness and pricing arrangements that resulted in the differentiation of legitimate and illegitimate baby markets.

The black market is unacceptable because it treats children in the same impersonal, economizing manner used for less sacred commercial products. For baby brokers, price and profit are dominant considerations: "If they were not selling babies, they would be selling whatever else was hot and produce [*sic*] a profit."[116] Black market practices are not only illegitimate but also illegal. In most states, it is a crime to accept payment for placing a child for adoption. Yet a different kind of market exists which is, in most cases, legal and compatible with sentimental adoption. In this "gray-market," placements are arranged "without profit by well meaning parents, friends, relatives, doctors and lawyers."[117] Within this context, professional fees for legal or medical services are acceptable. Justifying such payments during the 1975 Congressional hearings, the executive director of the Child Welfare League of America explained, "Money exchanges hands, but it is only to pay for actual costs. There is no thought of profit."[118] Not only do most adoption experts support the right to collect "reasonable fees for professional services," but certain statutes specifically allow legal fees and compensation for the mother's medical expenses. Thus, while the black market is defined as a degrading economic arrangement, a modified, legitimate market exists for the exchange of children. To be sure, the boundary between a legitimate market and a "dangerous" sale is not always easy to maintain. As a means of market control, parents in California are required to submit a detailed itemized account of their expenditures for a private adoption. Florida, on the other hand, limits lawyers' fees to $500.[119]

Adoption fees also constitute a separate market. From the start, agencies sought to define their work as consistent with sentimental adoption. Until the 1940s, only "gratitude donations" were accepted from adoptive parents. The Children's Home Society of Virginia, for instance, told parents, "that a gift from them in such an amount as they choose will be gratefully received, but that it must be made as a gift and not as payment for services."[120] The Society's directors refused to even discuss any definite sum with foster families. The boundary between adoption and purchase was preserved by defining the money as an elective gift and a symbol of gratitude, not a price. As Simmel points out in his discussion of marriage by purchase, "the gift contains something more personal—because of the indeterminateness of the gift's value and the individual freedom of choosing even if governed by conventions—than a definite sum of money with its uncompromising objectivity."[121]

The shift from donations to fees, was therefore, a sensitive matter. After all, as late as 1939, prospective adopters were warned, "Never pay anybody any money for a child—reliable agencies never ask fees."[122] Yet the system was accepted; the number of agencies charging a fee increased from 18 in 1949 to 105 in 1954. Despite opposition and predictions that fees would "degenerate into a price for placement,"[123] the adoption market retained its distinctive structure. Agencies did not turn into "efficient profit-maximizing firms," but still operate as nonprofit organizations. Their price is restricted to the costs of the services provided. Often, only a nominal fee is requested.

Some agencies employ a sliding scale, charging a token fee for lower-income families and a larger sum for those who can afford it.

In large measure, the differentiation between an adoption fee and a purchase price hinged on defining the payment as compensation for professional services. But a fee was also legitimized as a symbolic payment: a more efficient expression of gratitude than the traditional donations. "We believe that a financial payment is one of the ways that applicants to adopt children can fulfill their need to pay . . . many adoptive parents . . . fretted a good deal whether to give and how much . . . What we are now doing defines a tangible and specific requirement that is much fairer for applicants and for us."[124] Adoption fees were usually portrayed as a psychological crutch for parents, rather than a commercial device for agencies: "For any human being to be in the position of asking another . . . for a child . . . is to admit inadequacy. . . . Payment of the fee may ease some of the discomfort arising from this deeply humiliating experience."[125] Parents' voluntary contributions of additional monies to the agency, beyond the stipulated fee, further reinforced the boundary between the adoption market and other forms of economic exchange. Their elective gift of money served as a symbolic reminder that adopting a child is not an ordinary business deal.[126]

The uniqueness of a market involving children is also apparent in their "rental." Even after the 1930s, when boarding homes increasingly became the preferred method for temporary care of dependent children, the early dilemmas of paid parenting remained unsolved. Periodic efforts to raise board payments by defining the foster mother as an employee of the agency, met with resistance and ultimately failure. In the 1940s, for instance, a special committee from the Washington Council of Social Agencies, urged payment of a service fee to foster parents, "in return for the . . . contributions they make over and above the physical care and maintenance of the child." Such payments, explained the Director of a Children's Center in Connecticut, "would help identify the program as a service, rather than a charity."[127] But the service fee was opposed because it transformed mothering into a marketable job. Traditionally low board payments, besides being economical for the agency, certified the altruism of boarding mothers; "They are paid—but the amount they receive . . . does not in any way pay them for what they give to these homeless children. Motherly, loving care for a child cannot be bought . . . They deserve a specially high place in heaven, these boarding mothers."[128] Service fees reduced motherly altruism to an ordinary task. Kadushin explains the persistent resistance against defining foster parents as employees of the child welfare agency: "If the foster parent is an employee, then the child can view his stay in the foster home as a business transaction, [and] himself as a source of income."

A recent survey of the literature on foster parenting concludes that perceptions of the foster parent role remain "ambiguous and contradictory." The ambivalent role of foster parents has been traditionally aggravated by two contradictory expectations: foster parents were paid to provide a temporary, warm, familylike environment for children, yet excessive emotional involvement was discouraged and could legally terminate the arrangement. This, however, is changing with a more flexible and favorable attitude toward allowing foster parents to adopt the children in their care, if it is in the "best interests of the child."[129]

Adequate monetary incentive seems to have an effect on the number of foster homes available and even the success of fostering. Yet foster parents—most of whom are recruited from lower-middle class or working-class families—remain uneasy about asking for payment. Studies of their motivations remark that sometimes a parent "may state an entirely different reason than money as the primary one for wanting a foster child, stressing this to cover his subjective need for the money, which he is too ashamed to face."[130] Such discomfort is not a psychological symptom but comes from the awkwardness of selling what is defined as a personal, sacred task. Simmel explains how, "Personal performances demand something over and above their money equivalents . . . the acceptance of a money equivalent appears to disparage both the performance and the person."[131] Foster parents find ways to transcend the instrumental parenting contract. In many cases, for instance, parents use their own funds for a foster child's incidental expenses: extra clothing, transportation, allowance, toys, or parties.

The "gray-market," adoption fees, and board payments illustrate some of the cultural contours of the modern adoption market. Pricing the priceless child is a unique commercial venture; child 'rental' and child sales are profoundly constrained by twentieth-century conceptions of children. Ironically, even market ideologists and practicians ultimately justify baby selling by criteria other than profit. Payments are legitimized as symbolic expressions of sentimental concern. For Landes and Posner, for instance, "the willingness to pay money for a baby would seem on the whole a reassuring factor from the standpoint of child welfare."[132] Stanley Michelman, a noted baby broker, reportedly reassured his clients by pointing out the emotional payoffs of purchasing a child, "How would I feel if my father paid ten thousand dollars to adopt me? Boy, that guy really wanted me. . . . He paid that much for me, he really wanted me that much. . . . What could be a greater sense of self than that somebody sacrificed so much to have me? . . ."[133]

CHAPTER 7

From Useful to Useless and Back to Useful? Emerging Patterns in the Valuation of Children

Although one would not wish to return to an era of exploitative child labor . . . one still has the feeling that children in societies like ours are underemployed.

From "Children in Contemporary Society,"
Sarane S. Boocock, 1976

CHILD LABOR LAWS and compulsory education, announced E. S. Martin in a 1913 issue of *Harper's Monthly Magazine*, were quickly turning children into "the luxury of the poor and the indulgence of the better off."[1] But in the 1980s, the sacred, economically useless child may have become a luxury or an indulgence that the contemporary family no longer values, nor in fact, can afford. Ironically, some of the social solutions of the early twentieth century are now being redefined as new social problems. More specifically, writers and scholars from many disciplines are reappraising the useless child with concerned and often critical eyes.

To be sure, no one is advocating a return to nineteenth-century forms of child labor. But there is a growing interest in finding innovative ways to include children in the productive life of the community. There is also the issue of children's potential usefulness within the home. For example, should children participate more productively in the household division of labor? Is it reasonable or even feasible for a working mother to retain responsibility for the "real" jobs while children are carefully reserved educational chores (and fathers only slowly and reluctantly increase their share of domestic tasks)? And is it good for the child herself or himself to remain a privileged guest who is thanked and praised for "helping out," rather than a collaborator who at a certain age is expected to assume his or her fair share of household duties? Let us first briefly review the social construction of the sacred child in order to examine the possible future re-construction of childhood.

From Useful Worker to Sacred Child

Between the 1870s and the 1930s, the value of American children was transformed. The twentieth-century economically useless but emotionally priceless child displaced the nineteenth-century useful child. To be sure, the most dramatic changes took place among the working class; by the turn of the century middle-class children were already experienced "loafers." But the sentimentalization of childhood intensified regardless of social class. The new sacred child occupied a special and separate world, regulated by affection and education, not work or profit.

As previously discussed, the expulsion of working-class children from the market was a controversial process, vehemently supported by reformers but resisted with equal conviction by working-class and middle-class advocates of a productive childhood. It was partly a matter of conflicting economic interest but mostly an ideological dispute between two opposing views of childhood. The sacred child prevailed. Children were to be kept off the market, useless but loving, and off the streets, protected and supervised. The economic role of the child, however, did not disappear but was profoundly transformed, both in families or in adoptive homes. Child work and child money became defined primarily in educational not instrumental terms. A child was now entitled to an allowance; after all, how else could he or she learn to become a proper consumer? Children's token participation in household work was justified as moral training, seldom as a real labor contribution.

As the sentimental uniqueness of children was stressed, pragmatic pecuniary assessments of their value were considered not only impractical but morally offensive. Pricing the priceless child, therefore, became a complex task, creating confusion in legal thought and practice, controversy in the insurance business, and uncertainty in the "exchange" of adoptive children. New sentimental criteria were established to determine the monetary worth of child life. Courts began awarding damages for loss of a child's companionship; insurance was legally justified as coverage against the loss of affection; child sellers now sold a baby's cuteness and beauty. Ironically, both the "surrender" cash value of children at death and their "exchange" price increased even as children's economic value disappeared.

A profound paradox was created. The twentieth-century family was defined as a sentimental institution, "the antithesis of a market economy's concept of human relations," as Carl Degler aptly puts it.[2] Yet, even the family seemed to capitulate to the dominant cash nexus, as the value of its most precious member, the sacred child, was now routinely converted into its monetary equivalent. Had the child lost its economic value only to become another commercial commodity? My findings strongly suggest that the sentimental value of children served as a bulwark against the market. The historical development of the three institutions examined, shows that the insurance business, compensation for the wrongful death of children, and the sale of children were profoundly shaped by children's noneconomic value. Priceless values were being priced, but the pricing process itself was transformed by its association to value. In child death awards, insurance policies for children, and adoptive payments for a child, money is to a certain extent deprived of its economic worth. Instead, such monetary payments acquire powerful symbolic meanings. An insurance policy, for instance, never sold as a sensible investment but as a token of respect for the dying child in the nineteenth century, and later as a token of love for the living child. Damage cases for the economically useless child were surrounded by emotional ambiguities and settled in unusual ways. Similarly, payments for sacred adoptive children have seldom been conducted as ordinary business deals.

The Limits of the Market

The case of children is only one example of the complex interaction between the market and human values: On the one hand, there is a dramatic expansion of the cash nexus into previously unquantifiable aspects of social life, such as sentiments and emotions. But on the other, is the less well understood effect of noneconomic factors that constrain, limit, and shape money and the market. This book challenges established assumptions about the inevitable social effects of a money economy. The process of rationalization and commodification of the modern world has its limits, as money and the market are transformed by social, moral, and sacred values.

The pricing of the twentieth-century economically worthless child is thus a test case of the "sacralization effect" of values as a counterpart to the "commercialization effect" of money. It shows the reduction of the most precious and intangible values to their money equivalent, but it also demonstrates how economic rationality and the quantification process are themselves modified. Wrongful death awards, adoption, and insurance markets are shaped by cultural definitions of childhood. Thus, the sales value of an adoptive child or the economic value of the child at death are not determined only by ordinary utilitarian formulas, but depend on sentimental standards. In death and adoptive payments, money acquires different emotional and sacred meanings.

The economic world of the modern child further illustrates the importance of considering the symbolic functions of money as well as the noneconomic aspects of work roles. Children are unique economic actors. Their relationship to work and money is partly regulated by practical concerns; children are eager consumers determined to obtain a proper income either by negotiating an allowance or working for extra cash. But child work and child money are also shaped by noneconomic educational concerns. A job or an allowance are instructional devices that teach children the proper values and attitudes toward work and spending. The usefulness of children's chores is secondary; child work is supposed to train the child, not help the parent. The allowance does not depend on the efficiency or the quantity of child work but on a parent's beliefs of what is a proper amount.

As the French sociologist François Simiand recognized in a pioneering essay in 1934, money is a "réalité sociale." The symbolic functions of money have been recognized and analyzed by anthropologists but only with regard to primitive money in primitive societies. For example, in *The Phenomenon of Money*, Thomas Crump notes that money can equally represent the sacred or the profane; "since the conversion is purely symbolic, it lies within the power of any culture to effect it."[3] Yet, he restricts the sacralization of money to Eastern or primitive cultures. We know little about the symbolic and sociological dimensions of money in the modern Western world. How do cultural and social factors influence the uses and meaning of money? Child money is just one example; how does it differ from a housewife's "pin money" or a wage-earner's salary? What happens when child money is treated as a regular salary? For instance, the resistance to pay children for housework, as the reluctance to compensate housewives for their work, points to the use of money as a boundary. If domestic tasks are paid "real" money, then the family becomes another commercial setting.

The relationship between the market and noneconomic values is not static. In the nineteenth century, for instance, the economic value of children was legitimately combined with their sentimental worth, and the instrumental uses of child money were acceptable. The next section will discuss some possible future variations in the changing interaction between the price and value of children.

From the Sacred Child to Valuable "Housechild"?

The transition described in this book, from an economically useful to the economically useless child was not a precisely timed event, but a gradual and uneven process. As with all social change, the boundary between the two views of childhood was never clear-cut or absolute. Sentimentalized views coexisted with the instrumental valuation of children in the nineteenth century, while the economic value of children persisted long after it was declared illegal and morally offensive. To this day, the economic worth of a child is still a concern, particularly in rural areas and sometimes among the urban lower class. The National Child Labor Committee, for instance, estimates that at least 300,000 migrant children are at work in the United States. These children, as Robert Coles found out in his investigations, "take care of one another, pick crops fast, go fetch water and food at the age of two or three and know what size coins or how many dollar bills must be brought home."[4] Other children are currently being put to work by illegal prostitution rings, the highly lucrative child pornography industry, and by drug dealers who use young children as runners. At the opposite end of the occupational ladder, child actors and child models pursue profitable and often glamorous careers. The computer has recently introduced a new legitimate employment for skilled children, who can convert their expertise into a business. There have also been occasional social experiments to restore the useful child. For instance, a study of rural communes conducted by two sociologists in the early 1970s, describes the deliberate integration of children into the occupational and even social adult life of these hippie or posthippie settlements.[5]

But despite the occasional overlap of sentimental and economic views of childhood, the cultural legitimacy of the useful child was dominant in the nineteenth century while in the twentieth, the priceless child became the conventional norm. Economically useful children remain the exception. The labor market for most children, regardless of social class, is restricted to low-paying household chores, newspaper delivery, and occasional employment by neighbors to mow the lawn, shovel snow, or baby-sit. As a recent survey of 764 sixth-grade students in Oakland, California, points out, children's "principal source of income" is their parents. Indeed, if a child today earns "real" money, there are few rules for its proper management. One women's magazine warns parents of children employed in television commercials:

There is a moral dilemma for a parent about how much financial obligation commercial children have toward their families. One side of the argument says that what the child makes is the child's alone. Others argue that . . . the rest of the family has a legitimate claim to a share in the child's profits. Unfortunately, there are no set answers . . . your own conscience will help you decide.

When Brooke Shields was fifteen and earning some $10,000 a day for modeling, her mother solved the problem by putting the earnings in a trust, but not all of it. In the traditional manner of 1930s child stars, Brooke received a ten dollar weekly allowance.[6]

But are we today reaching a new historical stage in the relationship between the economic and sentimental value of children? Is the sacred, economically useless child outdated in the 1980s? There certainly seems to be a growing public uneasiness and puzzlement about the social situation of children in their families and in the larger society. This uneasiness and puzzlement is now being expressed in a variety of ways by several scholars and writers. Vance Packard, for instance, writes about "our endangered children," in an "anti-child culture;" Neil Postman mourns the "disappearance of childhood," while Marie Winn pities "children without childhood"; Letty Pogrebin asks "Do Americans Hate Children?," and Germaine Greer categorically asserts that modern society is "profoundly hostile to children."[7] The "child problem", however, is diagnosed in radically different ways by the observers of modern family life. Their proposed solutions, therefore, also differ, revealing diverse views of the price and value of children.

For some, the essential problem lies in the sharp contradiction in American society between the public and the private value of children. In *Broken Promises,* for example, W. Norton Grubb, an economist, and Marvin Lazerson, a historian, argue that the sentimentalization of childhood too often stops at the family's doorstep: "In contrast to the deep love we feel and express in private, we lack any sense of 'public love' for children." As a result, Americans "fail their children," by refusing to extend parental altruism to other people's children: "The saccharine myth of America as a child-centered society, whose children are its most precious natural resources, has in practice been falsified by our hostility to other people's children and our unwillingness to support them." While parents spend lavishly and "irrationally," on their own children, their altruism is paradoxically transformed into miserliness when it comes to public programs of child welfare. Irrationality is replaced by instrumental concerns. How much will public support cost? Will it pay off in the long run? The sacred child is thus a private luxury; children in need of public support are treated unsentimentally, assisted only if the investment is justified in economic terms.[8]

Letty C. Pogrebin, a founder of *Ms.* magazine, also denounces Americans' hypocritical approach to child life: "The society that kneels before the commercial altar of childhood in the adorable forms of Strawberry Shortcake, Peter Pan, . . . and Annie is the same society that murders its children, rapes them, starves them . . . poisons them, and hates them to death." Pogrebin diagnoses an epidemic of collective "pedophobia" in America today, "Though most of us make exceptions for our own offspring, we do not seem particularly warmhearted toward other people's children."[9] From this general perspective, the most urgent task is to replace collective indifference toward children by active public concern—new and better policies to improve child welfare. The sacralization of children should transcend the boundaries of the private family.

For other observers, however, the problem goes beyond public stinginess or collective insensitivity toward children. Without denying the need for more effective social policies, this second group of critics is also deeply concerned with the child's situation within the family. Here we find a sharp division between two opposite camps. On the one hand are those who fear that the sacred child is in danger of disappearing right from our own homes. Vance Packard, for instance, discerns a growing sentiment *against* children in the United States, expressed very concretely by those who refuse to have any children. Childlessness is emerging as an acceptable alternative to "child-creation." New instrumental considerations, claims Packard, may be depreciating the emotional benefits of the priceless child. Children are often feared as obstacles to "fulfillment," or a career, or as economic burdens, or even as impediments to marital happiness.[10]

As their emotional and practical costs increase, argue Marie Winn and Neil Postman, children are being rushed out too soon into adult-like behavior, clothing, language, entertainment, and even sexual activity and physical appearance. Indeed, Winn pronounces the "Age of Protection" dead, replaced by an "Age of Preparation": "Once parents struggled to preserve children's innocence . . . and to shelter children from life's vicissitudes. The new era operates on the belief that children must be exposed early to adult experience. . . ." Ideologists of the sacred child are convinced that the expulsion of children from a world "in which adults are adults taking care of children, while children are children, dependent upon and consequently unequal to adults," is a modern version of *Paradise Lost*, depriving children of safety and security.[11]

But while Winn and Postman nostalgically plead for the restoration of a "real" childlike childhood, another group of analysts is instead concerned by what they perceive as the unjustified and even dangerous survival, not the weakening of the Progressive ideal of a sacred, economically useless child. From this perspective, children's alleged integration into adult life occurs with illicit activities such as premature sexual involvement or drug use, or else is merely cosmetic; children may indeed wear the same brand-name jeans as their parents or watch the same television shows. But in any case, children's economic roles remain essentially unchanged. Spokesmen for this position strongly favor a profound re-evaluation of the useless child. While Progressive reformers insisted on the social and psychological hazards of a useful child, these contemporary revisionists point to the unanticipated social and psychic dangers of perpetuating children's uselessness.

For instance, in her controversial book, *Sex and Destiny*, Germaine Greer harshly denounces the lack of "interpenetration between the worlds of the child and the adult" as evidence of our profound antipathy to children: "At the heart of our insistence upon the child's parasitic role in the family lurks the conviction that children must be banished from adult society. Babies ought not to be born before they have rooms of their own." Greer contrasts her pessimistic view of Western childhood with a romanticized version of life in less developed countries: ". . . societies where adults and children laugh at the same jokes, . . . huge cities which are practically run by children, children who support their parents and their sibs by their skills and initiative, where children and adults inhabit the same cruel world and survive by clinging to each other." She compares the obnoxious "consumerism" of Western children with the saner familial context of child life in traditional societies: "The children may be grubby . . . but they have a clear sense of the group they belong to . . . They will not be found screaming for all the goods displayed in the supermarket. . . ."[12]

Since the 1960s, child liberation ideologists have also been outspoken critics of the economically useless child. For instance, in *Birthrights*, Richard Farson declared that the pursuit of children's rights includes "access to economic power . . . the right to work, to acquire and manage money, to receive equal pay for equal work . . . and to achieve financial independence." Children "cannot be denied the respect and dignity that can come from honest labor . . . cannot be excluded from the world of adults." While recognizing that economic discrimination against children is profoundly rooted in American culture, Farson insists that: "Just as the movement to abolish child labor was caused to some extent by a new way of thinking about children, so it is time to rethink what a child might be, might do."[13]

A much less ideological, yet equally fundamental rethinking and critique of the unproductive child is being conducted by sociologists, psychologists, and lawyers. One expert in the field of family studies observes, "Although nobody advocates . . . returning to the era of childhood exploitation, there is a growing recognition that the roles of self-denying adult and irresponsible child are frustrating for both parties."[14] Sarane S. Boocock, a sociologist, suggests we can no longer afford to treat the young as an "expensive consumer item," nor to keep children segregated from the productive life of the community. Children's rights, argues Boocock, have been overemphasized at the expense of children's obligations. The solution—". . . to develop innovative modes of . . . utilizing the full range of children's capacities."[15] Our underemployed children should be provided with a new set of jobs.

Psychologists support this view with evidence that economic dependency can be a psychological hazard to children. Jerome Kagan, for instance, argues that while the useful child could confirm his or her sense of value by making a material, visible contribution to the family's well-being, for the economically useless child, self-esteem depends primarily on psychological qualities; "he [can] not point to a plowed field or a full woodpile as a sign of his utility." As a result, such children may be unsure about their worth and overly dependent on expressions of parental love for self-validation. Indeed, in the 1960s, psychologist Mary Engel and her associates found that part-time jobs not only had no negative effects among boys between ten and fourteen years of age, but helped them in feelings of competence and personality development.[16]

Anthropologists contribute their own findings that support the value of real productivity for children in contrast to "token" chores. In *Children of Six Cultures*, Beatrice and John Whiting, found that child work in farming communities taught children responsibility and gave them "a sense of worth and involvement in the needs of others." But, note the authors, these children's jobs were not just make-work, but were directly related to the economy and welfare of the family. Similarly, in a unique study of the lives of children in Oakland, California during the Great Depression, sociologist Glen H. Elder, Jr., shows that the needs of economically deprived families created "urgent, realistic, and meaningful demands which were not in any sense contrived," for children's economic and labor contributions to the household. As a result, there was a "downward extension of adultlike experience" that increased children's independence, dependability, and maturity in money management. Elder concludes that, if the task is not excessive or exploitative, "Being needed gives rise to a sense of belonging and place, of being committed to something larger than the self."[17]

Some legal experts are even questioning the validity of child labor legislation. Until recently, these laws (both the Fair Labor Standards Act as well as the many state child labor laws) remained an unassailable "political sacred cow" seldom challenged and mostly unrevised. But now, Robert H. Mnookin, Professor of Law at the University of California at Berkeley, raises new questions, "Do these laws represent an undue restraint on the rights of young people? Why should children be treated differently from adults in the area of employment? Can we still justify the restrictions embodied in the child labor laws?" Indeed, futurologist Alvin Toffler predicts a possible campaign *for* child labor, when production returns to the home. In this "third wave" of our society, child labor laws may become an "anachronistic device," difficult to enforce in a domestic setting. The "electronic cottage," foresees Toffler, "opens an alternative way to bring youth back into socially and economically productive roles."[18]

Thus, the sacred child is in the spotlight, defended by some but newly challenged by others. Once again, as at the turn of the century, two views of childhood are being disputed, but this time, the reform group proposes to selectively increase children's useful adultlike participation in productive activities, while traditionalists cling to the Progressive ideal of a separate, domestic domain for children. It is no coincidence that this re-evaluation of a child's place is taking place just as the world of their mothers is being dramatically transformed. Almost 56 percent of married women with children under fourteen years of age are now employed. And the numbers keep growing. The sacred child is thus losing the undivided attention of its primary caretaker, and at increasingly younger ages. Between 1970 and 1980, for instance, the proportion of children under six years with working mothers increased to more than 40 percent. Indeed, married women with children under three are entering the labor market faster than any other group.[19]

Traditionalists, while professing support of women's rights, are uneasy about mothers relinquishing former responsibilities. As Marie Winn explains: "As women are no longer willing to sacrifice their own well-being and take an unfair share of the burdens of child care, too often no one at all steps in to take charge of the children." As both parents abandon the home for the workplace, contends Neil Postman, "children become something of a burden, and, increasingly, it is deemed best that their childhood end as early as possible." In *The Erosion of Childhood,* Valerie Polakow Suransky is even more emphatic, suggesting that women's liberation often results in the oppression and "commoditization" of children, "the expedient notion of the child as a commodity to be dispensed with and deposited in impersonal or inadequate childcare institutions."[20]

Are children in fact becoming emotionally dispensible in the 1980s, both economically and sentimentally useless to ambitious, or financially pressed, work-oriented couples? Families are clearly becoming smaller, and women are delaying child bearing, sometimes into their thirties. Yet few couples remain childless. One recent study of voluntary childlessness, for instance, shows that regardless of the costs of children, nonparenthood is *not* regarded as a privileged status. Voluntary childbearing is an indicator of children's persistent emotional value to parents. In an age of improved contraception, notes historian Carl Degler, "The present-day family's interest in children might well be considered to be higher than when the option of childlessness was much less practical."[21]

But if the emotional devaluation of children is doubtful, there may well be, however, a serious revaluation of their instrumental worth. That is, the potential usefulness of children is not just the bizarre discovery of a few unrealistic scholars. New family structures and an ideology of domestic democracy could indeed restore the useful child, at least within the household. According to experts, working mothers are not likely to return to full-time domestic employment. In addition, the rising divorce rate has led to a dramatic increase in the number of children living in single-parent families, usually with their mothers. By 1980, almost 18 percent of all children under eighteen were living only with the mother. Households can hardly remain static when their structure is being revolutionized. In the new family, there may be no place for a useless child.

A new egalitarian ideology of family life may further contribute to the transformation of children's value. In his history of women and the family in America, Carl Degler foresees a continuing tension between the family's interests and those of women. As he explains: "The central values of the modern family stand in opposition to [those] that underlie women's emancipation. Where the women's movement has stood for equality, the family historically has denied or repudiated equality . . . hierarchy has prevailed among father, mother, and children."[22] But values change, and the established hierarchy of family roles can break down with a new ideology of collaboration between husband, wife, and children. The demise of the full-time housewife may create a part-time "househusband" and "housechild."

Indeed, a manual has already appeared for parenting a useful "housechild." In a book significantly titled *The Cooperating*

Family, Eleanor Berman, mother of three, describes the reconstruction of her household after she divorced her husband. The "Berman experiment" began when Ms. Berman returned to work full-time and was unable to find adequate domestic help. Her three children took over the household responsibilities, including shopping, cleaning, and cooking. The "new system of cooperation" worked out: "I learned that my children were capable of far more responsibility than I had ever thought of giving to them. And rather than minding, they seemed to feel good about it." In this context, child work is still partly educational, "good" for the child, but also instrumental, useful to the mother and the family: "If we aren't afraid to let our children know . . . that we do need help, and that even as children they can be important in contributing to the well-being of people they care for, we may accomplish within our families a spirit of mutual concern. . . ."[23]

Despite Ms. Berman's enthusiasm, establishing new rules for child work, won't be a simple task. Most studies find, for instance, that despite the growing number of mothers in the labor force, and the increasing ideological approval of women's market work, the household division of labor remains largely unchanged—traditionally age and sex-typed. Children and their fathers may "help out," but for the most part, home duties remain a woman's job. Ironically, Ms. Berman suggests that this may be the "victim's" fault, the mother's "Queen Bee" syndrome, "allowing children to function at their full capacity within the home . . . diminishes the family's need for her, threatening her sense of worth. . . ."[24] But the evidence belies this explanation. It is husbands who are often reluctant and sometimes deeply resentful of increasing their household responsibilities. For instance, in a recent study of American couples, two sociologists discovered that "married men's aversion to housework is so intense it can sour their relationship.

The more housework they do . . . the more they fight about it."[25]

But what about children? The information is amazingly limited; we simply don't know much about what children do. Feminist research on the relationship between women's housework and market work deals primarily with gender inequality within the family and the lack of public childcare facilities. Children remain spectators of an adult struggle, seldom considered as possible contributors to a solution. While there has been much concern to liberate boys and girls from traditional sex stereotypes, age stereotypes have seldom been examined. The limited available evidence suggests, however, that children of working mothers follow their father's reluctant footsteps into productive domesticity, increasing only slightly or not at all their participation in household chores.[26]

Despite such predictable resistance, the useful child may make a comeback. While serious research largely ignores the issue, popular magazines are already discussing the renegotiation of established rules for child work. As *Working Mother* notes: "If a mother has always worked, it's one thing. It's another if she takes a job and suddenly dumps 'her work' on the family." A number of "harried working mothers" interviewed for the story complained that chores had become "the source of our major scenes." Parents and children are offered pointers on how to establish a new working relationship. In an article suggestively titled "Do Your Parents Ask Too Much of You?", *Seventeen* advises children of working mothers or divorced parents: "Try to look at things from your parents' point of view. If you don't do certain chores, who should do them? Do your parents, with all their responsibilities, really have time? . . . Examine the situation . . . to see what really is fair, and try to think of your family in terms of a unit with everyone having . . . something to contribute."[27]

New rules for child work will certainly involve a re-examination of the rules of child money. There is some indication that children themselves find a symbolic allowance simply too cheap for an inflationary economy. As one ten-year-girl of Wayland, Mass., commented in a survey conducted by *Money* magazine in 1981, "I don't think adults understand that sundaes cost $1.25, movies $1.50 and good records $5 to $6. A dollar used to be a big deal, but now—are you kidding?"[28] Yet, children have few options to increase their income. Considering the already high rates of teenage unemployment, an expansion of the labor market for children under fourteen is unlikely. Children's money will continue to come primarily from their parents' purses and occasionally from neighbors or family friends.

How will parents compensate children for their added household responsibilities? Will the allowance shift from a symbolic, educational payment for useless children into a straightforward salary for the useful "housechild"? The dilemmas of the early twentieth century still confuse parents in the 1980s. When it comes to paying their own children, even economists resort to noneconomic guidelines. One economist, for instance, awards his children raises, "as they show more responsibility and judgment. It has nothing to do with inflation." The study of sixth graders from Oakland, California discovered that parental practices regarding allowances revealed "little about the material resources of the family and much about basic child-rearing values." Poorer parents, for instance, were more likely to give children greater direct access to money than wealthier parents. Similarly, the 1981 *Money* magazine survey found that a nine-year-old girl from a welfare family in Orlando, Florida received one of the biggest allowances in her third-grade class.[29]

Many parents remain strongly opposed to treating children's

chores as a marketable commodity. As Ms. Berman puts it, "No child should expect monetary rewards for fulfilling his day-to-day obligations to his home and family." In many households, however, there is a differentiation between non-marketable household chores and jobs. As *Penny Power,* a consumer magazine for children explains, "work that you get paid for is something special. It's a job."[30] Thus, children perform two types of work, unpaid chores and compensated jobs. They receive two types of money, the allowance or occasional gifts of money as their share of the family income, and wages for special jobs.

The world of children is changing and their household responsibilities may be redefined by changing family structures and new egalitarian ideologies. The notion, inherited from the early part of this century, that there is a necessarily negative correlation between the emotional and utilitarian value of children is being revised. The sentimental value of children may now include a new appreciation of their instrumental worth. We need, however, much more research on the life of children. In 1980, for instance, more than eleven million children in the United States lived in poverty, often in female headed families. What does work and money mean for these children in contrast to children in affluent households, or in two-parent families? How do child work and child money vary by race or ethnic group, or by sex? At what age is a child ready to become a useful "housechild"? Is five too young, or twelve too old? How do children's contributions vary depending on their parents' occupation?

Useful children and the internal reorganization of the household are not the solution to the increased participation of mothers in the labor force. As almost every family expert points out, the United States urgently needs to support with adequate social policies the welfare of families with children, while the world of work must recognize and adjust to new family structures. But, perhaps, within the household, with proper guidance, new attitudes, and safeguards to prevent their exploitation, children may well become invaluable useful participants in a cooperative family unit.

NOTES

Introduction

1. Kathryn E. Walker and Margaret Woods, *Time Use: A Measure of Household Production of Family Goods and Services* (Washington, D.C.: Center for the Family of the American Home Economics Association, 1976), p. 38. On the costs of children, see Thomas J. Espenshade, "Raising a Child Can Now Cost $85,000," *Intercom* 8 (Sept. 1980): 1, 10–12.

2. Lynn K. White and David B. Brinkerhoff, "Children's Work in the Family: Its Significance and Meaning," *Journal of Marriage and the Family* 43 (November 1981): 793. See also Murray A. Straus, "Work Roles and Financial Responsibility in the Socialization of Farm, Fringe, and Town Boys," *Rural Sociology* 27 (Sept. 1962): 257–74.

3. Susan Muenchow, "Children and Money: Teaching Good Habits," *Parents* 58 (December 1983): 55.

4. Cited by Rose K. Goldsen, *The Show and Tell Machine* (New York: Dial Press, 1977), p. 194.

5. See Sheila B. Kamerman and Alfred J. Kahn, eds., *Family Policy* (New York: Columbia University Press, 1978).

6. Lawrence Olson, *Costs of Children* (Lexington, MA: Lexington Books, 1983), p. 58.

7. Lois W. Hoffman and Jean D. Manis, "The Value of Children in the United States: A New Approach to the Study of Fertility," *Journal of Marriage and the Family* 41 (Aug. 1979): 583–96. On the emotional value of children for working-class mothers, see Lee Rainwater, *And the Poor Get Children* (Chicago: Quadrangle Books, 1960).

8. William L. Parish and Martin K. Whyte, *Village and Family in Contemporary China* (Chicago: University of Chicago Press, 1978), p. 227. See also Beatrice B. Whiting and John W. M. Whiting, *Children of Six Cultures* (Cambridge, MA: Harvard University Press, 1977).

9. E. S. Martin, "Children as an Incentive," *Harper's Weekly* 48 (Dec. 10, 1904): 1889.

10. Felix Adler, "Child Labor in the United States," Annual Meeting of the National Child Labor Committee, 1905, cited by Robert H. Bremner, *Children and Youth in America* (Cambridge, MA: Harvard University Press, 1971) II, p. 653.

11. Joseph F. Kett, "Curing the Disease of Precocity," in *Turning Points*, edited by John Demos and Sarane Spence Boocock (Chicago: University of Chicago Press, 1978), p. S196.

12. Hoffman and Manis, "The Value of Children in the United States," p. 596.

See also Theodore W. Shultz, "The Value of Children: An Economic Perspective," *Journal of Political Economy* 81 (Mar.–Apr. 1973); S2–S13; Gary S. Becker, *A Treatise on the Family* (Cambridge, MA: Harvard University Press, 1981); Isabel Sawhill, "Economic Perspectives on the Family," *Daedalus* 106 (Spring 1977): 116–25; Fred Arnold et al., *The Value of Children* (Honolulu: East-West Population Institute, 1975).

13. For a critique of current theories of fertility, see Michael B. Katz and Mark J. Stern, "Fertility, Class, and Industrial Capitalism: Erie County, New York, 1855–1915," *American Quarterly* 33 (Spring 1981): 63–92; Boone A. Turchi, "Microeconomic Theories of Fertility: A Critique," *Social Forces* 54 (Sept. 1975): 107–25; and Judith Blake, "Are Babies Consumer Durables? A Critique of the Economic Theory of Reproductive Motivation," *Population Studies* 22 (March 1968): 5–25.

14. See, for instance, Joan Huber, "Toward a Sociotechnological Theory of the Women's Movement," *Social Problems* 23 (April 1976): 371–88; Wanda Minge-Kalman, "The Industrial Revolution and the European Family: The Institutionalization of 'Childhood' as a Market for Family Labor," *Comparative Studies in Society and History* 20 (Sept. 1978): 454–68. For a psychological approach to the history of childhood, see Lloyd deMause, "The Evolution of Childhood," in *The History of Childhood*, ed. by Lloyd deMause (New York: Harper & Row, 1975). On adolescence in a historical perspective, see Joseph F. Kett, *Rites of Passage* (New York: Basic Books, 1977); John R. Gillis, *Youth and History* (New York: Academic Press, 1981); Michael B. Katz and Ian E. Davey, "Youth and Industrialization in a Canadian City," in *Turning Points*, pp. S81–S119.

15. Philippe Ariès, *Centuries of Childhood* (New York: Vintage, 1962), p. 353.

16. See Barbara Laslett, "Family Membership, Past and Present," *Social Problems* 25 (June 1978): 476–90; Tamara Hareven, "Family Time and Historical Time," *Daedalus* 106 (Spring 1977): 57–70; Eli Zaretsky, *Capitalism, the Family, and Personal Life* (New York: Harper & Row, 1976).

17. Carl Degler, *At Odds: Women and the Family in America From the Revolution to the Present* (New York: Oxford University Press, 1980), pp. 73–74. On the domestication of women, see Barbara Welter, "The Cult of True Womanhood: 1820–1860," in *The American Family in Social-Historical Perspective*, ed. by Michael Gordon (New York: St. Martin's Press, 1983), pp. 372–92; Nancy F. Cott, *The Bonds of Womanhood: "Woman's Sphere" in New England, 1780–1835* (New Haven: Yale University Press, 1979).

18. Natalie J. Sokoloff, *Between Money and Love* (New York: Praeger, 1981), p. 214.

19. Winifred D. Wandersee, *Women's Work and Family Values, 1920–1940* (Cambridge, MA: Harvard University Press, 1981), p. 66.

20. Christopher Lasch, *Haven in a Heartless World* (New York: Basic Books, 1979), p. 13.

21. Lawrence Stone, *The Family, Sex and Marriage in England 1500–1800* (New York: Harper & Row, 1977), p. 105; Ariès, *Centuries of Childhood.*

22. Peter Uhlenberg, "Death and the Family," in Gordon, ed., *The American Family*, p. 170.

23. John Demos, "Infancy and Childhood in the Plymouth Colony," in Gordon, ed., *The American Family*, 1978 ed., pp. 157–65.

24. There are some significant exceptions. For some studies that explore the cultural dimension, see Neil J. Smelser and Sydney Halpern, "The Historical Triangulation of Family, Economy, and Education," in *Turning Points*, ed. by Demos and Boocock, pp. S288–S315; Robert Wells, "Family History and the Demographic Transition," in Gordon, ed., *The American Family*, 1978 ed., pp. 516–32; John Boli-Bennett and John

Meyer, "Ideology of Childhood and the State," *American Sociological Review* 43 (December 1978): 797–812; Philip Greven, *The Protestant Temperament* (New York: Signet, 1977). In his explanation of changing family types in England, Stone relies primarily on a cultural explanation, contending that the rise of "affective individualism" was the determining factor *(The Family, Sex and Marriage in England).*

25. On the other hand, I did not explore the controversy over abortion because this issue introduces a different, existential and philosophical, and also political dimension to the evaluation of child life.

26. Bernard Barber, "The Absolutization of the Market: Some Notes on How We Got From There to Here," in G. Dworkin, G. Bermant, and P. Brown, eds., *Markets and Morals* (Washington, D.C.: Hemisphere, 1977). See also Talcott Parsons and Neil J. Smelser, *Economy and Society* (New York: Free Press, 1956); Louis Dumont, *From Mandeville to Marx* (Chicago: University of Chicago Press, 1977).

27. Lester C. Thurow, *Dangerous Currents* (New York: Random House, 1983), pp. 216, 227; Kenneth E. Boulding, "Toward the Development of a Cultural Economics," in Louis Schneider and Charles M. Bonjean, eds., *The Idea of Culture in the Social Sciences* (New York: Cambridge University Press, 1973), p. 47.

28. See, for example, Gary S. Becker, *The Economic Approach to Human Behavior* (Chicago: University of Chicago Press, 1976); Jacob Mincer, *Schooling, Experience, and Earnings* (New York: Columbia University Press for the National Bureau of Economic Research, 1974); Louis Lévy-Garboua, ed., *Sociological Economics* (London: Sage, 1979).

29. Mark Granovetter, "Toward a Sociological Theory of Income Differences," in Ivar Berg, ed., *Sociological Perspectives on Labor Markets* (New York: Academic Press, 1981), p. 37. Economic sociology stagnates or develops only in "shreds and patches." Neil J. Smelser, *The Sociology of Economic Life* (Englewood Cliffs, NJ: Prentice-Hall, 1963), p. 2. This book provides a comprehensive historical overview and methodological synthesis of economic sociology. For an important but different approach, see Arthur L. Stinchcombe, *Economic Sociology* (New York: Academic Press, 1983).

30. Becker, *The Economic Approach,* p. 5. Becker explicitly disclaims any direct parallels between microeconomics and the Marxist structural economic approach, p. 9.

31. Georg Simmel, *The Philosophy of Money.* Trans. by Tom Bottomore and David Frisby (London: Routledge & Kegan Paul, 1978), pp. 365–66, 380, 390–91, 392, 407.

32. Karl Marx, *The Economic and Philosophic Manuscripts of 1844* (New York: International Publishers, 1964), p. 169.

33. Fred Hirsch, *Social Limits to Growth* (Cambridge, MA: Harvard University Press, 1978), p. 87; Peter M. Blau, *Exchange and Power in Social Life* (New York: Wiley, 1967), p. 63. See also Alfred Sauvy, *Coût et Valeur de la Vie Humaine* (Paris: Hermann, 1977).

34. Richard M. Titmuss, *The Gift Relationship* (New York: Vintage, 1971), p. 198.

35. In my earlier work, based on the development of life insurance, I stressed the effect of values on economic behavior. *Morals and Markets: The Development of Life Insurance in the United States* (New York: Columbia University Press, 1979) traced the impact of cultural factors, such as attitudes toward death, risk, and gambling on public acceptance of life insurance during the nineteenth century. My focus here is more directly on the interaction between economic and noneconomic factors. See also Charles H. Cooley, "The Sphere of Economic Valuation," *American Journal of Sociology* 19 (September 1913): 188–203.

Chapter 1

1. *New York Times,* July 23, 1903, p. 1; May 2, 1926, p. 17. The May Day event was sponsored by the American Child Health Association as part of a national program devoted to the life and health of children. See Phillip Van Ingen, *The Story of the ACHA* (New York: American Child Health Association, 1935).

2. George B. Mangold, *Problems of Child Welfare* (New York: Macmillan, 1924, first ed. 1914), p. 36.

3. Ibid., p. 123.

4. Lawrence Stone, *The Family, Sex and Marriage in England 1500–1800* (New York: Harper & Row, 1977), pp. 105–06.

5. Philippe Ariès, *Centuries of Childhood* (New York: Vintage, 1962), p. 39; Philippe Ariès, *The Hour of Our Death* (New York: Vintage, 1982), pp. 82, 90, 207.

6. Quoted by Mary Beth Norton, *Liberty's Daughters* (Boston: Little, Brown, 1980), p. 89. The age of the child influenced parental response. Norton notes that when older children died, parents lost their equanimity. [See also Peter Gregg Slater, *Children in the New England Mind* (Hamden, CT: Archon, 1977); Joseph E. Illick, "Child-Rearing in Seventeenth-Century England and America," in *The History of Childhood,* ed. Lloyd deMause (New York: Harper & Row, 1974), pp. 303–50; John F. Walzer, "A Period of Ambivalence: Eighteenth-Century American Childhood," in ibid., pp. 351–82.]

7. Ann Douglas, *The Feminization of American Culture* (New York: Avon Books, 1977), pp. 251, 243, 245–46; Ariès, *The Hour of Our Death,* p. 460. Among middle- and upper-class families, concern with child death seems to have intensified already by the late eighteenth century, Stone, *The Family, Sex and Marriage,* pp. 247–49; Ariès, *Centuries of Childhood,* p. 401.

8. Philippe Ariès, *Western Attitudes Toward Death* (Baltimore: Johns Hopkins University Press, 1974), p. 68; Ariès, *The Hour of Our Death*, p. 609.

9. Stone, *The Family, Sex and Marriage,* p. 249.

10. Ariès, *The Hour of Our Death,* pp. 90, 536.

11. Mangold, *Problems of Child Welfare,* p. 11. On the extension of middle-class responses to the lower classes in England and Europe, see Stone, *The Family, Sex and Marriage,* pp. 679–80; Ariès, *Centuries of Childhood,* p. 404; Edward Shorter, *The Making of the Modern Family,* (New York: Basic Books, 1975), pp. 195–96.

12. "Child Health," in Robert Bremner, ed., *Children and Youth in America* (Cambridge, MA: Harvard University Press, 1971) II, pp. 811–12; Kathleen W. Jones, "Sentiment and Science: The Late Nineteenth Century Pediatrician as Mother's Advisor," *Journal of Social History* 17 (Fall 1983):80–96.

13. Susan Tiffin, *In Whose Best Interest?* (Westport, CT: Greenwood Press, 1982), pp. 20–23; Sheila M. Rothman, *Woman's Proper Place* (New York: Basic Books, 1978), pp. 98–99.

14. Ibid., p. 104.

15. Bremner, *Children and Youth in America,* pp. 812–15; John Duffy, *A History of Public Health in New York City 1866–1966* (New York: Russell Sage Foundation, 1974), pp. 213–19; 466–67.

16. Ibid., p. 469; Bremner, *Children and Youth in America,* p. 1003; Tiffin, *In Whose Best Interest?* pp. 238–40; James Leiby, *A History of Social Welfare and Social Work in the United States* (New York: Columbia University Press, 1978), pp. 154–55. The Children's Bureau concentration on infant mortality was also safer politically; it was a far less controversial topic than child labor or delinquency. Mainly as a result

of intense opposition from the medical profession, the Sheppard-Towner Act was allowed to expire in 1929.

17. Mangold, *Problems of Child Welfare*, p. 61; Leiby, *A History of Social Welfare*, p. 154; Duffy, *A History of Public Health*, pp. 462, 471, 488.

18. David E. Stannard, *The Puritan Way of Death* (New York: Oxford University Press, 1977), pp. 55–56, 58.

19. Stone, *The Family, Sex and Marriage*, p. 420. Stone warns, however, against a "reductionist position that there is a simple and direct correlation between the level of mortality and the amount and degree of affect," and which ignores the intervening effects of cultural norms and societal expectations, p. 82.

20. Ariès, *Centuries of Childhood*, p. 40. He attributes the change to the cultural impact of Christianity and its discovery that the child's soul is immortal. See also Yasukichi Yasuba, *Birth Rates of the White Population in the United States, 1800–1860* (Baltimore: Johns Hopkins University Press, 1962). Maris Vinovskis suggests that death rates remained stable between 1800 and 1860, "Mortality Rates and Trends in Massachusetts before 1860," *Journal of Economic History* 32 (1972):184–213. Both agree, however, that mortality rates decreased significantly in the latter part of the nineteenth century.

21. Shorter, *The Making of the Modern Family*, pp. 203–4. For a similar hypothesis to explain improved child mortality among mid-eighteenth-century aristocratic English families, see Randolph Trumbach, *The Rise of the Egalitarian Family* (New York: Academic Press, 1978), p. 208.

22. Slater, *Children in the New England Mind*, pp. 19, 161; Stannard, *The Puritan Way of Death*, p. 51. There was one important difference between early Puritans and nineteenth-century parents' views concerning the spiritual worth of their children. Puritan beliefs in children's innately sinful nature and the prospect of infant damnation were replaced in the nineteenth century with a romantic concept of children as innocent beings needing protection instead of supervision and harsh control.

23. Significantly, a recent and important critique of both Stone's and Shorter's findings and arguments remains at the psychological, individual level, suggesting that "true" parental grief and love existed before the eighteenth century. See Linda Pollock, *Forgotten Children* (Cambridge: Cambridge University Press, 1983).

24. *New York Times*, Nov. 1, 1908, II, p.11.

25. See George Wolff, *Death From Accidents Among Children and Adolescents* (Washington, D.C.: U.S. Department of Labor, Children's Bureau, 1944); *The Mortality From External Causes 1911–1930* (New York: Metropolitan Life Insurance Company, 1935); "Childhood Mortality From Accidents," U.S. Children's Bureau Publication No. 311, 1949. For children under four, however, all five leading causes of death in 1910 were infectious diseases. By 1920, accidents ranked fourth among causes of death in this age group, climbing to second place in 1940.

26. Frederick R. Hutton, "The Dangers of Street Traffic and Danger Signals," *Scientific American* supplement 75 (Apr. 12, 1913):235.

27. Arthur Minturn Chase, "Children of the Street," *Outlook* 101 (July 27, 1912): 687; Allan Hoben, "The City Street," in *The Child in the City* (Chicago:Dept. of Social Investigation, Chicago School of Civics and Philanthropy, 1912), p. 458; Mary Mortimer Maxwell "An Englishwoman in New York Discovers the Great American Child," *New York Times*, Nov. 19, 1905, III, p. 6.

28. *Boyhood and Lawlessness* (New York: Survey Associates, 1914), pp. 10–11.

29. Ibid., pp. 11, 24–29, 35.

30. Christine Stansell, "Women, Children, and the Uses of the Streets: Class and

Gender Conflict in New York City, 1850–1860," *Feminist Studies* 8(Summer 1982): 309–35.

31. Cary Goodman, *Choosing Sides: Playground and Street Life on the Lower East Side* (New York: Schocken Books, 1979), p. 80.

32. Ibid. On the concern of Progressives with the Americanization of immigrant children, David J. Rothman, *Conscience and Convenience* (Boston: Little, Brown, 1980), pp. 206–07.

33. *Statistical Bulletin,* Metropolitan Life Insurance Co., (Feb. 1927), p. 1. See also "Children Killed in Street Accidents, New York City," *New York Times,* Feb. 2, 1913; Dec. 2, 1914, p. 5; and Frederick S. Crum, "Street Traffic Accidents," *Journal of the American Statistical Association* New Series No. 103 (Sept. 1913):473–528.

34. Fritz Blocki, "The Most Dangerous Job in the World," *Independent* 114 (May 30, 1925):605.

35. "Reduction in Child Deaths from Street Accidents in New York City," *The American City* 49 (Feb. 1934):17; *The Mortality From External Causes,* p. 53.

36. *Safety Education in Schools,* White House Conference on Child Health and Protection (New York: Century Co., 1932), pp. 8–9; *Pedestrian Traffic* (Washington, D.C.: American Automobile Association, 1939); *Statistical Bulletin,* Metropolitan Life Insurance Company (Aug. 1937), p. 1.

37. *New York Times,* June 7,1935, p. 20; *The Mortality From External Causes,* p. 57. Accidents remain the number one killer of children. After the 1930s, however, the accidental death rate of children under fourteen decreased in significance relative to other age groups, particularly those in the fifteen to twenty-four age range. *Accident Facts* (Chicago: National Safety Council, 1980); Albert P. Iskrant and Paul V. Joliet, *Accidents and Homicide* (Cambridge, MA: Harvard University Press, 1968), pp. 21–2.

38. "Trolley Accidents," *Outlook* 68 (May 25, 1901):202.

39. On the impact of differential visibility in the perception of social problems see Robert K. Merton, "The Sociology of Social Problems," in *Contemporary Social Problems* ed. by Robert K. Merton and Robert Nisbet (New York: Harcourt Brace Jovanovich, 1976), p. 16.

40. "Motormen and Street Boys," *New York Times,* July 15, 1904, p. 6.

41. *New York Times,* May 11, 1911, p. 1. While examples of mob reaction to a child death abound, I found few reports of similar response to adult death.

42. Blocki, "The Most Dangerous Job," p. 604. While homicide and suicide have been extensively studied, the sociology and history of accidents remain surprisingly unexplored. For some important exceptions see, Roger Lane, *Violent Death in the City* (Cambridge, MA: Harvard University Press, 1979); Lynda P. Malik, *Sociology of Accidents* (Villanova, PA.: Villanova University Press, 1970); Austin Porterfield, "Traffic Fatalities, Suicide, and Homicide," *American Sociological Review* 25(1960): 897–900; Barbara A. Hanawalt, "Childrearing Among the Lower Classes of Late Medieval England," *Journal of Interdisciplinary History* 8(Summer 1977):1–22.

43. "Motormen and Street Boys;" "Children in the Streets," *New York Times,* Dec. 9, 1904, p. 8.

44. Ibid.; *New York Times,* July 19, 1904, p. 6.

45. Ibid., Apr. 25, 1909, IV, p. 4.

46. Henry S. Curtis, *The Play Movement and Its Significance* (Washington, D.C.: McGrath, 1917), p. 314.

47. *Boyhood and Lawlessness,* p. 37; Chase, "Children of the Street," p. 689.

48. Ibid.; "Facilities For Children's Play in the District of Columbia," U.S. Children's Bureau Publication No. 22, 1917.

49. *New York Times,* Feb. 2, 1913.

50. *New York Times*, Oct. 13, 1913, p. 8.

51. Marcus Dow, "Accident Prevention as Relating to Child Welfare," Fourth International Congress on School Hygiene, IV (New York, 1914), p. 616; Frederick L. Hoffman, "Some Vital Statistics of Children of School Age," Ibid., p. 116.

52. See Lew R. Palmer, "History of the Safety Movement," in *Industrial Safety*, ed. by Richard H. Lansburgh, *Annals of the American Academy of Political and Social Science* CXXIII(January 1926):9–19.

53. "Children are the Chief Victims of Fatal Accidents," *Statistical Bulletin*, Metropolitan Life Insurance Co., (May 1925):3.

54. *Safety of Boston Elevated Railway Co.* Data Presented to the American Museum of Safety in Competition for the Anthony N. Brady Memorial Gold Medal. New York, 1925. On file at the New York Public Library; "Organizing Children for Safety," *Literary Digest* 48(Jan. 3, 1914):13–14; Jessica McCall, "The Safety Crusade in Brooklyn," *The American City* 12(Apr. 1915):305–08.

55. *Safety First for Children* (Safety First League, 1915). On file at the New York Public Library.

56. *Safety Education: A Plan Book for the Elementary School*, (Chicago, Board of Education, 1923) p. 10.

57. Dr. E. George Payne, *Plan of Safety Instruction in Public and Parochial Schools* (Chicago: National Safety Council, 1920), p. 3.

58. "Children's Day," *Safety* 9 (Oct.-Nov., 1922):218; "The Nation's Needless Martyrdom," *Literary Digest* 75 (Oct. 28, 1922):29.

59. "Children's Day," p. 218.

60. A. W. Whitney, "Introduction," in Payne, *Plan of Safety Instruction*, pp. 5–6. See *New York Times*, Mar. 24, 1926, p. 1; Mar. 29, 1926, p. 21; May 2, 1926, p. 17.

61. Ibid., Dec. 1, 1926, p. 29; Sept. 5, 1926, p. 12.

62. Ida H. Tarbell, "Who Is to Blame for Child Killing?" *Collier's* 70 (Oct. 7, 1922):12.

63. See *Safety Education in Schools*, White House Conference; Twenty-Fifth Yearbook of the National Society for the Study of Education; William G. Gann, "Role of the School in Traffic Safety," *AAAPSS* 328 (Nov. 1958):63–72; *New York Times*, Jan. 4, 1931, II, p. 1. Limited cross-cultural data suggests that the "child" problem was not exclusive to the United States. Indeed, Germany and England pioneered many school safety programs, Dennis O'Neill, "Traffic Accident Trends in Europe and the British Isles," *AAAPSS* 328 (Nov. 1958); "Road Safety for Children—And Others," *Justice of the Peace* 100 (May 2, 1936):291–92; Colin Ward, *The Child in the City* (London: The Architectural Press, 1978), pp. 116–125. On child accidents in Switzerland and Russia, see *New York Times*, Nov. 22, 1925, IX, p. 6; Apr. 22, 1935, p. 4.

64. Ibid., Mar. 24, 1926, p. 1.

65. Bernard Barber, "Place, Symbol, and Utilitarian Function in War Memorials," in *People and Buildings*, ed. by Robert Gutman (New York: Basic Books, 1972), p. 328.

66. Henry A. Boardmann, "God's Providence in Accidents: A Sermon," (Philadelphia, PA: Parry and McMillan, 1855). On file at Alexander Library, Rutgers University. *The Chapter of Accidents or Book of Caution to Children* (New York: M. Day, 1829), listed some common child accidents in the early nineteenth century: tumbling down the stairs, playing with knives, forks, scissors, candles, falling out of a window, kick of a horse, riding a wild horse, tossed by a mad bull, drowning, playing with firearms. See also Stone, *The Family, Sex and Marriage*, p. 210.

67. *New York Times*, Feb. 23, 1903, p. 3.

68. Tarbell, "Who is to Blame for Child Killing?" p. 12; Whitney, "Introduction," p. 6.

69. Dow, "Accident Prevention as Relating to Child Welfare,":614.

70. Hutton, "The Dangers of Street Traffic,":235.

71. *Statistical Bulletin*, Metropolitan Life Insurance Co. (Feb. 1927 and Feb. 1930); "Startling Death Rate in New York Streets," *New York Times*, Oct. 27, 1907, V, p. 1.

72. Louis I. Dublin, "Child Health Protection or Neglect: The Ultimate Cost to the Community," Transactions of the Fourth Annual Meeting of the American Child Health Association, Washington, D.C., 1927, pp. 201, 211.

73. See Dow, "Accident Prevention as Relating to Child Welfare," p. 612.

74. Marcus Dow, "A Nation's Neglect," *Outlook* 105 (Sept. 27, 1913):304; *New York Times*, Oct. 2, 1893, p. 4.

75. Pressman v. Mooney, 39 NYS 44(1896). Trial transcript, p. 49.

76. *Statistical Bulletin*, Metropolitan Life Insurance Co. (Apr. 1920, Feb. 1927, May 1925).

77. Tarbell, "Who is to Blame for Child Killing?" p. 12; *New York Times*, July 15, 1904, p. 6.

78. Ibid., Oct. 24, 1915, II, p. 16.

79. Ibid., March 30, 1909, p. 8; May 30, 1909, p. 6.

80. Ibid., June 25, 1928, p. 23. See *Safety Education in Schools*, White House Conference, p. 9, and Iskrant and Joliet, *Accidents and Homicide*, pp. 25, 40.

81. *New York Times*, Jan. 25, 1912, p. 10. See also Jan. 23, pp. 8, 20, 26.

82. Ernest Kahlar Alix, *Ransom Kidnapping in America* (Carbondale, ILL.: Southern Illinois University Press, 1978), pp. 39, 41, 174.

83. Cited in "Child Mortality from Automobile Accidents," *School and Society* 44(Oct. 24, 1936):547–48; "Herod and the Innocents," *Commonweal* 14(Aug. 19, 1931):375.

84. On the decline of child death rates, see *The Mortality From External Causes*, p. 57, and *Accident Facts*, 1930. See also Historical Statistics of the United States (Washington, D.C., 1975), p. 36.

85. *New York Times*, May 8, 1932, III, p. 7. For home accidents, see *Statistical Bulletin*, Metropolitan Life Insurance Co. (June 1933), p. 4; Iskrant and Joliet, *Accidents and Homicides*, p. 26.

86. Ruth Streitz, *Safety Education in the Elementary School* (New York: National Bureau of Casualty and Surety Underwriters, 1926), pp. 51–52; *Statistical Bulletin*, Metropolitan Life Insurance Co., (Sept. 1928) pp. 1–2; *New York Times*, Nov. 3, 1914, p. 9; Weaver Weddell Pangburn, "Playgrounds—A Factor in Street Safety," *AAAPSS* 133(Sept. 1925):178–85.

87. *Pedestrian Traffic*, pp. 69–70; Philip Davis, "Children and the Street," *Home Progress* 5(July 1916):514.

88. *Safety Education in Schools*, White House Conference, p. 24; Pangburn, "Playgrounds," p. 184; *Safety Education: A Plan Book for the Elementary School;* "The Nation's Needless Martyrdom."

89. *New York Times*, Dec. 19, 1926, p. 6; Roland B. Woodward, "Organizing Rochester's School Boys for Accident Prevention," *American City* 13(Sept. 1915): 208–9.

90. See *Statistical Bulletin*, Metropolitan Life Insurance Co. (Dec. 1922; Mar. 1933); *The Mortality From External Causes*, pp. 57, 60. Sex differences in accident rates persist. Iskrant and Joliet, *Accidents and Homicides*, p. 23. Racial differences in children's accidental death rate were low, except among infants under one year of age. Black children had a somewhat higher death rate than white children in all age-sex groups. More noticeable racial differences existed in death rates from all causes; rates

for nonwhite children being sometimes three times as high as those for white children. With the control of infectious diseases, accidents gained in prominence among non-white children. See Wolff, *Deaths from Accidents Among Children and Adolescents.*

91. Mark Baldassare, "Residential Density, Household Crowding, and Social Networks," in *Networks and Places,* by C. S. Fischer et al. (New York: Free Press, 1977), p. 112.

92. Cited in *Six Safety Lessons* (Washington, D.C.: Highway Education Board, 1921), p. 48.

93. Sarane Spence Boocock, "The Life Space of Children," in *Building for Women,* ed. by Suzanne Keller (Lexington, MA: Lexington Books, 1981), pp. 98–99; Elliot A. Medrich, Judith Roizen, Victor Rubin, and Stuart Buckley, *The Serious Business of Growing Up* (Berkeley, CA: University of California Press, 1982), p. 77.

94. *The Home and the Child,* 1931 White House Conference on Child Health and Protection (New York: Arno Press and The *New York Times,* 1972), pp. 10, 13, 23, 47–8, 52.

95. Boocock, "The Life Space of Children," pp. 105, 111. Data from the National Health Survey of children six to eleven years of age, conducted in 1963–1965, shows that less than 5 percent of children shared a bedroom or a bed with their parents and more than 40 percent shared a room with a sibling but slept in a separate bed. No class breakdowns were available. *Vital and Health Statistics* Series II, Number 108 (Washington, D.C.: U.S. Government Printing Office, November 1971), p. 3.

96. Jacques Donzelot, *The Policing of Families* (New York: Pantheon, 1979), p. 47.

97. Stephen S. Wise, "Justice to the Child," *AAAPSS* 35 (March 1910):1.

Chapter 2

1. For child labor statistics: See "Children in Gainful Occupations at the Fourteenth Census of the United States," (Washington: Government Printing Office, 1924); Grace Abbott, *The Child and The State* (Chicago: The University of Chicago Press, 1938) I: pp. 259–69; Raymond G. Fuller, "Child Labor," *International Encyclopedia of the Social Sciences* (1930): pp. 412–24.

2. A. J. McKelway, "The Awakening of the South Against Child Labor," *Proceedings of the Third Annual Conference on Child Labor* (New York: 1907), p. 17.

3. Josephine J. Eschenbrenner, "What Is a Child Worth?" National Child Labor Committee, No 236, p. 2.

4. Representative Sumners, cited in *The American Child* 6 (July, 1924):3.

5. Elizabeth Fraser, "Children and Work," *Saturday Evening Post* 197 (Apr. 4, 1925):145.

6. Michael R. Haines, "Poverty, Economic Stress, and the Family in a Late Nineteenth-Century American City: Whites in Philadelphia, 1880," in Theodore Hershberg, ed., *Philadelphia* (New York: Oxford University Press, 1981): p. 265; Claudia Goldin, "Family Strategies and the Family Economy in the Late Nineteenth Century: The Role of Secondary Workers," ibid, p. 284.

7. Editorial, *Journal of Home Economics* 7(Aug. 1915):371.

8. Daniel T. Rodgers, *The Work Ethic in Industrial America 1850–1920* (Chicago: The University of Chicago Press, 1978), p. 131.

9. John Demos, *A Little Commonwealth* (New York:Oxford University Press,

1972), pp. 140–1. See also Edmund S. Morgan, *The Puritan Family* (New York: Harper & Row, 1966), p. 66.

10. *Report on Condition of Woman and Child Wage-Earners in the United States,* VI (Washington, D.C., 1910), p. 48.

11. Niles' *Register,* Oct. 5, 1816, cited by Edith Abbott, "A Study of the Early History of Child Labor in America," *American Journal of Sociology* 14 (July 1908): 25. See also *Report on Woman and Child Wage-Earners,* pp. 49, 52; Stanley Lebergott, *Manpower in Economic Growth* (New York: McGraw Hill, 1964), pp. 48–51; Robert H. Bremner, ed., *Children and Youth in America* (Cambridge, MA: Harvard University Press, 1971) I: pp. 145–148. On child labor in nineteenth century England and France, see Louise A. Tilly and Joan W. Scott, *Women, Work, & Family* (New York: Holt, Rinehart and Winston, 1978). Employment in the early American mills apparently was not restricted to the children of the poor, but included the "children of farmers, mechanics, and manufacturers, in good pecuniary circumstances." Bagnall, *Samuel Slater and the Early Development of the Cotton Manufactures in the United States* (1890), cited by Forest Chester Ensign, *Compulsory School Attendance and Child Labor,* Ph.D. diss., Columbia University, 1921.

12. Fuller, "Child Labor," *IESS,* p. 419; Bremner, ed., *Children and Youth in America* II, p. 601.

13. John Modell, "Changing Risks, Changing Adaptations: American Families in the Nineteenth and Twentieth Centuries," Allan J. Lichtman and John R. Challinor, eds. *Kin and Communities* (Washington, D.C.: Smithsonian Institution Press, 1979), p.128. On the importance of the family as a work unit in the early stages of industrialization, see Neil J. Smelser, *Social Change and the Industrial Revolution* (Chicago: University of Chicago Press, 1959). Michael Anderson, *Family Structure in Nineteenth-Century Lancashire* (Cambridge: Cambridge University Press, 1971) and Tamara Hareven, *Family Time and Industrial Time* (Cambridge: Cambridge University Press, 1982) demonstrate the survival of the family as a work unit in the nineteenth and even twentieth centuries.

14. Ibid.

15. See "Child Labor and the Teachers," *New York Times,* July 8, 1905, p. 7, and Joseph M. Hawes, *Children in Urban Society* (New York: Oxford University Press, 1971).

16. Edwin Markham, "The Smoke of Sacrifice," *Cosmopolitan* 42 (Feb. 1907):397. See Philip S. Foner, *Women and the American Labor Movement* (New York: The Free Press, 1979), pp. 283–89. For a history of the National Child Labor Committee, see Walter I. Trattner, *Crusade for the Children* (Chicago: Quadrangle Books, 1970), and for an excellent account of child labor reform in New York State, Jeremy Felt, *Hostages of Fortune* (New York: Syracuse University Press, 1965).

17. On the effect of rising real income on the reduction of child labor, see Claudia Goldin, "Household and Market Production of Families in a Late Nineteenth Century American City," *Explorations in Economic History* 16 (1979):129. On the development of child labor and compulsory school legislation, see Ensign, *Compulsory School Attendance and Child Labor,* and Miriam E. Loughran, *The Historical Development of Child-Labor Legislation in the United States* (Washington, D.C.: Catholic University of America, 1921).

18. Paul Osterman, *Getting Started: The Youth Labor Market* (Cambridge, MA: The MIT Press, 1980), pp. 60–71. For additional economic explanations of the decline in child labor both in the United States and in nineteenth century England, see Allen R. Sanderson, "Child Labor Legislation and the Labor Force Participation of Children," *Journal of Economic History* 34(Mar.1974):298–99, and Clark Nardinelli,

"Child Labor and the Factory Acts," *Journal of Economic History* (Dec., 1980): 739–53.

19. *Niles' Register* (June 7, 1817):226; Joan Huber, "Toward a Sociotechnological Theory of the Women's Movement," *Social Problems* 23(Apr. 1976):371–88.

20. Osterman, *Getting Started*, pp.56–59; Selwyn K. Troen, "The Discovery of the Adolescent by American Educational Reformers, 1900–1920," in Lawrence Stone, ed., *Schooling and Society* (Baltimore: Johns Hopkins University Press, 1976), pp.239–51.

21. On early child labor legislation, see William F. Ogburn, *Progress and Uniformity in Child-Labor Legislation* Ph.D. diss. (New York: Columbia University, 1912); Loughran, *The Historical Development of Child Labor Legislation; Report On Condition of Woman and Child Wage-Earners in the United States* VI; Elizabeth H. Davidson, *Child Labor Legislation in the Southern Textile States* (Chapel Hill, NC: The University of North Carolina Press, 1939).

22. Elizabeth Sands Johnson, "Child Labor Legislation," in John R. Commons, ed., *History of Labor in The United States, 1896–1932* (New York: Macmillan, 1935), p. 446. For an excellent interpretation of the legislative aspects of the child labor controversy, see Stephen B. Wood, *Constitutional Politics in the Progressive Era* (Chicago: Chicago University Press, 1968) and Thomas George Karis, *Congressional Behavior at Constitutional Frontiers*, Ph.D. diss. (New York: Columbia University, 1951).

23. Davidson, *Child Labor Legislation*, p. 57.

24. The child labor amendment was also attacked as a Communist plot designed to nationalize American children. See Anne Kruesi Brown, "Opposition to the Child Labor Amendment Found in Trade Journals, Industrial Bulletins, And Other Publications for and By Business Men," M. A. diss. (Chicago, 1937); Katharine DuPre Lumpkin and Dorothy Wolff Douglass, *Child Workers in America* (New York: Robert McBride & Co., 1937), chapters 12, 13; "The Child Labor Amendment," *University of Texas Bulletin* No. 2529 (Aug. 1, 1925); Tom Ireland, *Child Labor* (New York: G. P. Putnam's Sons, 1937).

25. Reprinted in *Charities* 11(Aug. 8, 1903):130.

26. Fraser, "Children and Work," p. 146.

27. Iredell Meares, "Should the Nation Control Child Labor?" *Dearborn Independent*, Nov. 8, 1924. Reprinted in "The Child Labor Amendment," pp. 146,148.

28. Letter to the *New York Chamber of Commerce Bulletin* XVI, No.5 (Dec. 1924):50, cited in Brown, *Opposition to the Child Labor Amendment*, pp. 35–36.

29. Letter to the *Manufacturers Record*, LXXXVI, No.15(Oct. 9, 1924):91 cited in Brown *Opposition to the Child Labor Amendment*, p. 34.

30. Mrs. William Lowell Putnam, "Why the Amendment Is Dangerous," *The Woman Citizen* 9(Dec. 27, 1924):12; "The Twentieth Amendment," The Forum 73(Feb. 1925):281.

31. "What the Child Labor Amendment Means," in Abbott, *The Child and the State* I, p. 546; Lumpkin and Douglas, p. 219.

32. *Report on Condition of Woman and Child Wage-Earners* VII, p. 43; Mary Skinner, "Child Labor in New Jersey," U.S. Department of Labor, Children's Bureau Publication No.185 (Washington, D.C., 1928).

33. Tamara K. Hareven, "Family and Work Patterns of Immigrant Laborers in a Planned Industrial Town, 1900–1930," in Richard L. Ehrlich, ed., *Immigrants in Industrial America* (Charlottesville: University Press of Virginia, 1977), p. 63. On the relative importance of class versus ethnicity in determining the use of child labor, see John Modell, "Patterns of Consumption, Acculturation, and Family Income Strate-

gies in Late Nineteenth-Century America," in Tamara K. Hareven and Maris A. Vinovskis, *Family and Population in Nineteenth-Century America* (Princeton, NJ: Princeton University Press, 1978); Goldin, "Household and Market Production of Families"; and Miriam Cohen, "Changing Education Strategies Among Immigrant Generations: New York Italians in Comparative Perspective," *Journal of Social History* (Spring 1982):443–66. Until the 1920s, black children were less likely to be employed in the labor market than were immigrant children. See Elizabeth Pleck, "A Mother's Wages: Income Earning Among Married Italian and Black Women, 1896–1911," in Michael Gordon, ed., *The American Family in Social-Historical Perspective*, 2d ed. (New York: St. Martin's Press, 1978).

34. *Report On Condition of Woman and Child Wage-Earners* VII, p. 158; Goldin, "Household and Market Production," pp. 118–19.

35. Viola I. Paradise, "Child Labor and the Work of Mothers in Oyster and Shrimp Canning Communities on the Gulf Coast," U.S. Department of Labor, Children's Bureau Publication No.98 (Washington, D.C., 1922), pp. 11, 17.

36. "Industrial Homework of Children," U.S. Department of Labor, Children's Bureau Publication No.100 (Washington, D.C., 1924), p. 23.

37. "Child Labor, The Home and Liberty," *The New Republic* 41 (Dec. 3, 1924): 32.

38. *Report on Condition of Woman and Child Wage-Earners* I:p. 353.

39. Virginia Yans-McLaughlin, *Family and Community: Italian Immigrants in Buffalo, 1880–1930* (Ithaca, NY: Cornell University Press, 1971), p.193.

40. Sands Johnson, "Child Labor Legislation" p. 429; Felt, *Hostages of Fortune* pp. 22–23.

41. *New York Times*, Dec. 7, 1924, p. 19.

42. Cited in *The American Child* (Apr. 1925):6. Strong Catholic opposition to the Child Labor Amendment was also partly based on the perceived threat to parental authority. See Rev. Vincent A. McQuade, *The American Catholic Attitude on Child Labor Since 1891* (Washington, D.C.: Catholic University of America, 1938).

43. J. W. Crabtree, "Dr. Pritchett, Dr. Butler and Child Labor," *School and Society* (Nov. 8, 1924):585. Opponents of child labor invoked a variety of different arguments, from the physical and moral hazards of early employment to the economic inefficiency of employing young children. My discussion focuses on those arguments between the 1870s and 1930s, which centered on the changing definition of children's economic and sentimental value.

44. Quoted in *New York Times*, Feb. 2, 1925, p. 21.

45. Quoted in "The Nation and Child Labor," *New York Times*, Apr. 24, 1904, p. 6.

46. Felix Adler, "Child Labor in the United States and Its Great Attendant Evils," *Annals of the American Academy of Political and Social Science* XXV(May1905); Charles K. Gilbert, "The Church and Child Labor," in *The American Child* 9 (Aug. 1927):4.

47. A. J. McKelway, "The Evil of Child Labor" *Outlook* 85(Feb. 16, 1907):364.

48. Davidson, *Child Labor Legislation*, pp. 65–6; Elinor H. Stoy, "Child-Labor," *Arena* 36(Dec. 1906):586; "Education, Psychology, and Manufacturers," *The American Child* 8(Nov. 1926):2.

49. Quoted in *New York Times*, Feb. 2, 1925, p. 21.

50. "Potters' Clay," *The American Child* 8(Jan. 1926):3.

51. Marion Delcomyn, "Why Children Work," *Forum* 57(Mar. 1917):324–25.

52. Jacob Riis, "The Little Laborers of New York City," *Harper's New Monthly Magazine* XLVII(Aug. 1973):327.

53. Letter to the Editor, *New York Times*, Nov. 4, 1910, p. 8.

54. Alice L. Woodbridge, "Child Labor an Obstacle to Industrial Progress," *Arena* 10 (June 1894):158.

55. Editorial, *New York Times*, Dec. 17, 1902, p. 8.

56. Mrs. A. O. Granger, "The Work of the General Federation of Women's Clubs Against Child Labor," *Annals of the American Academy* 25(May 1905):104; A. J. McKelway, "The Leadership of the Child," ibid. 32(July 1908):21.

57. Quoted in Yans-McLaughlin, *Family and Community*, p. 190.

58. "The Cost of Child Labor," *National Child Labor Committee* 5(New York:1905):35.

59. Edward T. Devine, "The New View of the Child," *Annals of the American Academy* 32(July 1908):9. Reformers, however, recognized the need to subsidize nonworking children in families that could prove their financial need. In 1905, Child Labor Committees instituted a scholarship system in several cities to compensate needy families who kept a child in school, with a weekly payment equivalent to the child's foregone income. Apparently, most scholarships went to the children of widowed or deserted women.

Chapter 3

1. *Report on Condition of Woman and Child Wage-Earners in the United States* 7(Washington, D.C.,1910):15.

2. Raymond G. Fuller, "Child Labor Versus Children's Work," *The American Child* 3(Feb. 1922):281.

3. Theresa Wolfson, "Why, When, And How Children Leave School," *The American Child* 1(May 1919):61.

4. William Noyes, "Overwork, Idleness or Industrial Education," *Annals of the American Academy of Political and Social Sciences* 27(Mar. 1906):87. There was also a nostalgic recollection of apprenticeship as a lost form of "good" work.

5. Arthur D. Dean, "Child-Labor or Work for Children," *The Craftsman* 25(Mar. 1914):515.

6. Raymond G. Fuller, *Child Labor and the Constitution* (New York: Thomas Y. Crowell, 1923), p. 32.

7. Fuller, "Child Labor Versus Children's Work," p. 281.

8. Fuller, *Child Labor and the Constitution*, p. 28.

9. "Illiteracy Promoted by Perjury," National Child Labor Committee pamphlet No. 2(New York, 1905), p. 7.

10. See William F. Ogburn, "Progress and Uniformity in Child Labor Legislation," Ph.D. diss. New York: Columbia University Press, 1912, pp. 90, 103; "Child Labor," *White House Conference on Child Health and Protection* (New York: Century Co., 1932), pp. 27–30; Elizabeth Sands Johnson, "Child Labor Legislation," in John R. Commons, *History of Labor in the United States, 1896–1932* (New York: Macmillan, 1935), pp. 413, 428–30.

11. Edwin Markham, "The Smoke of Sacrifice," *Cosmopolitan* 42(Feb. 1907):393.

12. Thomas R. Dawley, *The Child That Toileth Not* (New York: Gracia Publishing Co., 1912), p. 140. Dawley's argument had some precedent. In 1909, Dr. Charles W. Stiles, an authority in hook-worm disease, announced that the health of children from poor farms significantly improved after working in cotton mills. See A. J. McKelway,

"The Mill or the Farm?," *Annals of the American Academy,* supplement (Mar. 1910):52–57.

13. Reprinted in Grace Abbott, *The Child and the State* (Chicago: University of Chicago Press, 1938), p.474.

14. Wiley H. Swift, "Is the Use of Children in Agriculture a Child Welfare Problem?" *Proceedings of The National Conference of Social Work,* 1924, p. 170.

15. "Child Labor," *White House Conference,* p. 213. Protected by their rural location, canners of fruits and vegetables sought and often won exemptions from industrial child labor laws.

16. "Child Labor in North Dakota," U.S. Children's Bureau Publication, No.129 (Washington, D.C., 1923):21–25,39.

17. Frances S. Bradley, M.D., and Margaretta A. Williamson, "Rural Children in Selected Counties of North Carolina," U.S. Children's Bureau Publication No.33 (Washington, D.C., 1918):85, 88, 99.

18. E. C. Lindeman, "Child Labor Amendment and the Farmers," reprinted in "The Child Labor Amendment," *University of Texas Bulletin* No. 2529(Aug. 1, 1925):87. For an overview of the studies of children employed in agriculture, see *White House Conference,* pp. 222–61.

19. Fred S. Hall, *Forty Years 1902–1942: The Work of the New York Child Labor Committee* (New York: The New York Child Labor Committee, 1942), p. 77.

20. Franklin N. Brewer, "Child Labor in the Department Store," *Annals of the American Academy* 20(1902):167–77.

21. Fuller, *Child Labor and the Constitution,* p. 76.

22. *White House Conference,* p. 147. On the regulation of street work, see ibid., pp. 164–68.

23. Edward N. Clopper, *Child Labor in City Streets,* (New York: Garrett Press, 1970, 1st ed. 1912), pp. 6–7.

24. Myron E. Adams, "Children in American Street Trades," *Annals of the American Academy* XXV(May1905):3.

25. *Survey* 30(June 14,1913):380.

26. Jacob A. Riis, *How the Other Half Lives* (New York: Dover Publications, 1971, 1st ed. 1890), p. 153.

27. Clopper, *Child Labor in City Streets,* p. 7. Besides newspaper selling, other common street occupations for children included peddling, bootblacking, messenger service, delivery service, running errands, and the tending of market stands.

28. Nettie P. McGill, "Child Workers on City Streets," U.S. Children's Bureau Publication, No.188(Washington, D.C., 1928):4.

29. Adams, "Children in American Street Trades," pp. 11,14.

30. Quoted in Clopper, *Child Labor in City Streets,* p. 15.

31. "Children in Gainful Occupations," Fourteenth Census (Washington, D.C.,1924):53.

32. McGill, "Child Workers in City Streets," pp. 6–7,36–7.

33. Charles W. Dabney, "Child Labor and the Public Schools," *Annals of the American Academy* 29 (Jan. 1907), p. 112. See *White House Conference,* pp. 128–9; "Children in Gainful Occupations," pp. 52, 59. Most street regulations also fixed a higher minimum age for girls than for boys. Domestic and personal service were other predominantly female occupations.

34. "Children in Gainful Occupations," p. 16.

35. Hall, *Forty Years,* p. 89. No precise figures of the number of child home workers exist.

36. "Industrial Home Work of Children," U.S. Dept. of Labor, Children's Bureau Publication No.100 (Washington, D.C., 1924):22.

37. Fuller, *Child Labor and the Constitution*, p. 87.

38. Noyes, "Overwork, Idleness or Industrial Education?"

39. Jessie P. Rich, "Ideal Child Labor in the Home," *Child Labor Bulletin* 3(May 1914):7.

40. George A. Hall, "Unrestricted Forms of Child Labor in New York State," *Proceedings* of the Twelfth New York State Conference of Charities and Correction, 1911, p. 104.

41. Rich, "Ideal Child Labor in the Home," p. 8.

42. Fuller, *Child Labor and the Constitution*, p. 28.

43. *Journal of Education* 78(Oct. 2, 1913):325.

44. 204 Mass. 18, 90 N.E. 394.

45. "Children on the Colorado Stage," *Survey* 27(Oct. 14, 1912):996. There is surprisingly little information on child acting. As the White House Conference on Child Health and Protection discovered in 1932: "There is no type of employment for children about which so little is known as about their employment in theatrical exhibitions and other public entertainments," p. 51.

46. "Children of the Stage," Editorial, *The Christian Advocate* 85 (Sept. 1, 1910), p. 1211.

47. Letter to the Editor, *New York Times*, Dec. 25, 1882, p. 2. See *Manual of the New York Society for the Prevention of Cruelty to Children* (New York: published by the Society, 1913), pp. 64–69.

48. "The Protection of Child Performers," *The Nation* 33(Dec. 29,1881):508.

49. "Children of the Stage," *New York Times* June 16, 1889, p. 16.

50. Arthur Hornblow, "The Children of the Stage," *Mumsey's Magazine* 12(Oct. 1894):33.

51. "Children of the Stage," Editorial *New York Times* Apr. 19, 1892, p. 4.

52. "Where Children Are Chosen for Positions on the Stage," *New York Times* Apr. 17, 1904, p. 22.

53. "Stage Children of America" (New York: Alliance for the Protection of Stage Children,1911), p. 1.

54. "Children Readmitted to Louisiana's Stage," *Survey* 28(Aug. 10, 1912):629.

55. *White House Conference*, p. 196; F. Zeta Youmans, *Stage Children and the Law* (Chicago: Juvenile Protective Association, 1923), p. 5. See also Benjamin B. Blydenburgh, "The Child and the Theatre," 18 *Case and Comment*(Mar. 1912):584–86. The confusion and conflict over the regulation of child acting was not uniquely American. For some comparative information, see George K. Behlmer, *Child Abuse and Moral Reform in England, 1870–1908* (Stanford, CA: Stanford University Press, 1982), p. 104, and "The Age of Admission of Children to Employment in Non-Industrial Occupations," *International Labour Conference* (Geneva: International Labour Office, 1931), pp. 19–28.

56. *New York Times*, Dec. 7, 1911, p. 12. No adequate sources exist on the exact number of children employed in theatrical productions. The 1920 census listing of 400 children between the ages of ten and fifteen under the category of "Actors and Showmen" is clearly an underestimate.

57. Hornblow, "The Children of the Stage," p. 33.

58. Elbridge T. Gerry, "Children of the Stage," *North American Review* 151(July 1890):18–19.

59. "Children on the Stage," *New York Times* Apr. 12, 1868, p. 11.

60. From a letter from Judge Brackett to Ligon Johnson, General Counsel of the

Theatrical Producing Managers, Apr. 11, 1910, on file at The Performing Arts Research Center. See Francis Wilson, "The Child on the Stage," *Collier's* 45 (May 21, 1910):19.

61. Everett W. Lord, "Child Labor on the Stage," *Survey* 24 (May 21, 1910):320. Although exceptionally successful child actors did receive large salaries, the rank-and-file were paid modest wages. See *White House Conference Report*, p. 193.

62. "Child Labor in Massachusetts," *Report of the Massachusetts State Child Labor Committee on the Legislative Campaign 1910*, p.10; Everett Lord, "Children of the Stage," National Child Labor Committee publication No. 137a, 1910.

63. Owen R. Lovejoy, "Employment of Children on the Stage," *Child Labor Bulletin* 1(Nov. 1912):78.

64. Henry Baird Favill, "Child Labor As Related To The Stage," National Child Labor Committee publication No.165, 1911, p. 15.

65. Wilson, "The Child on the Stage." Wilson (1854–1935), began his acting career at age seven. In 1913, he was named president of the newly formed Actor's Equity Association.

66. Gerry, "Children of the Stage," p. 17.

67. Letter to the Editor, *Survey* 24(June 18, 1910):496. While supporters of child acting opposed the prohibition of stage work, they recognized the need for proper regulation. See "Stage Children of America," p. 1.

68. Letter to the Editor, *New York Times*, June 26, 1910, p. 8.

69. "Children on the Stage," *New York Times* Apr. 12, 1868, p. 11.

70. "Lillian Russell's Juvenile Pets," *New York Herald* Jan. 10, 1892, p. 9.

71. Quoted in "Defending the Child Actors," *Literary Digest* 41(Nov. 12, 1910):861.

72. "Stage Children of America," pp. 7–8.

73. Quoted in *New York Times*, Dec. 7, 1911, p. 12. In 1914, the Professional Children's School opened in New York City, providing flexible schedules for child actors, which made it possible to formally combine stage work with an education.

74. Wilson, "The Child on the Stage."

75. "Children of the Stage," *Bellman* 10(Mar. 25, 1911):359.

76. Letter to Harry Powers, manager of the Power's theater of Chicago, on file at the Performing Arts Research Center.

77. Francis Wilson, letter to the editor, *Survey* 24 (June 18, 1910):498.

78. *New York Times* Apr. 12, 1868, p. 11. On female audiences, see Elsie Leslie, "Children on the Stage," *Cosmopolitan* 47(Sept. 1909):511; Margaret G. Mayorga, *A Short History of the American Drama* (Dodd, Mead, 1932), p. 265; Alexander Hume Ford, "Children of the Stage," (1903), on file at the Performing Art Research Center, p. 356.

79. "Stage Children of America," p. 16.

80. Mary E. Leonard, "Children On The Stage And Off," *New England Magazine* 42(June 1910):494.

81. Eleanor Robson, "Happy Experiences of the Child Who Acts, and His Beneficent Influence on Grown-Up Actors Upsets Old-Fashioned Theories," *New York Times* Dec. 15, 1907, VI, p. 1.

82. Ibid. There is little information on the gender of children on the stage. It appears that at the turn of the century young girls were more likely to appear on stage than boys, often taking male parts.

83. "The Show-Child: A Protest," *Longman's Magazine*. Reprinted in *Living Age* 208(Jan. 11,1896):113.

84. F. Zeta Youmans, "Childhood, Inc.," *Survey* 52(July 25, 1924):462.

85. See Jeremy Felt, "The Child Labor Provisions of the Fair Labor Standards Act," *Labor History* 11 (Fall 1970):467–81; "Second Thought On the Child Labor *Amendment,*" 9 *Massachusetts Law Quarterly* 15–21 (July 1924); "Comments," 7 *Fordham Law Review* 223–25 (May 1938); Anne Kruesi Brown, "Opposition to the Child Labor Amendment," Ph.D. diss., Chicago, 1937, pp. 46–49.

86. Rich, "Ideal Child Labor in the Home," p. 4. Interestingly, two of the legitimate occupations employed middle-class children. Newspaper carriers, for instance, were likely to come from more prosperous families than city newsboys. Nettie P. McGill, "Children in Street Work," U.S. Department of Labor, Children's Bureau, Publication No. 183 (Washington, D.C., 1928), p. 38. Although information on the social class of child actors is limited, it appears that particularly in the twentieth century, acting involved middle-class as well as lower-class children. See Ford, "Children of the Stage;" "What of the Stage Child?" (Minneapolis, MN: Women's Cooperative Alliance, 1929).

87. McGill, "Child Workers On City Streets," U.S. Department of Labor, Children's Bureau Publication No.188 (Washington, D.C., 1928), p. 37; "Your Boy's Christmas Money," *Ladies' Home Journal* 27(Nov. 1, 1910):1. The newspaper industry gladly encouraged the definition of newspaper work as education and not "real" labor.

88. John Mason, "The Education of the Stage Child," *New York Dramatic Mirror* (Mar. 8, 1911):5.

89. Lillian Davidson, "Idle Children," *Home Progress* 6(June 1917):474.

90. Helen C. Candee, "In the Beginning," *Outlook* 49(May 5, 1894):787.

91. Henriette E. Delamare, "Teaching Children to be Helpful at Home," *Home Progress* 3(Nov. 1913):115.

92. "The Home and the Child," *White House Conference on Child Health and Protection,* 1931 (New York: Arno Press & The *New York Times,* 1972), p. 90.

93. Amey E. Watson, "The Reorganization of Household Work," *Annals of the American Academy of Political and Social Science* 160(Mar. 1932):174.

94. Miriam Finn Scott, "The Perfect Child," *Ladies' Home Journal* 39(June 1922): 30.

95. Ethel Packard Cook, "All Hands Help," *Parents Magazine* 9(July 1934):19.

96. William F. Ogburn, "The Changing Family with Regard to the Child," *Annals of the American Academy* 151(Sept. 1930):23.

97. "The Adolescent in the Family," *White House Conference on Child Health and Protection,* 1934 (New York: Arno Press & The *New York Times,* 1972), p. 37.

98. Mary Beth Norton, *Liberty's Daughters* (Boston, MA: Little, Brown, 1980), pp. 23–24. See Thomas D. Elliot, "Money and the Child's Own Standards of Living," *Journal of Home Economics* 24 (Jan. 1932):4–5.

99. Edward T. Devine, "The New View of the Child," *Annals of the American Academy* 32 (July 1908):9. See Editorial, *Journal of Home Economics* 7 (Aug. 1915): 372. On the development of industrial education in the early decades of the twentieth century, see Marvin Lazerson and W. Norton Grubb, *American Education and Vocationalism* (New York: Teachers College Press, 1974).

100. Tamara K. Hareven, *Family Time and Industrial Time* (New York: Cambridge University Press, 1982), p. 189; Thomas Dublin, *Women at Work* (New York: Columbia University Press, 1979), pp. 174–5.

101. *Report on Condition of Woman and Child Wage-Earners in the United States* (Washington, D.C., 1910) 1:352–54; Ruth S. True, *The Neglected Girl* (New York: Survey Associates, 1914), p. 48; *Boyhood and Lawlessness* (New York: Survey Associates, 1914), pp. 68–69. See also Louise Bolard More, *Wage-Earners' Budgets* (New

York: Henry Holt and Company, 1907), p. 136. John Modell suggests that late nineteenth-century American-born working-class families may have treated children's wages differently from other sources of income, that is, "all dollars were not equal." Child income was not spent as freely as, for example, wages earned by the father. In Irish families, on the other hand, children's wages were more likely to remain undifferentiated from general family income, "Patterns of Consumption, Acculturation, and Family Income Strategies in Late Nineteenth-Century America," in *Family and Population in Nineteenth-Century America*, ed. by Tamara K. Hareven and Maris A. Vinovskis (Princeton, NJ: Princeton University Press, 1978), pp. 220–25.

102. *Report on Condition of Woman and Child Wage-Earners in the United States* 7(Washington, D.C., 1910):94–97. *Boyhood and Lawlessness*, p. 69; Katharine Anthony, *Mothers Who Must Earn* (New York: Survey Associates, 1914), p. 136.

103. See Hareven, *Family Time and Industrial Time*, p. 189; Louise C. Odencrantz, *Italian Women in Industry* (New York: Russell Sage, 1919), pp. 175–77; Leslie W. Tentler, *Wage-Earning Women* (New York: Oxford University Press, 1979), pp. 89–90; *Report on Condition* 7:95–96. In *Children of the Great Depression* (Chicago: University of Chicago Press, 1974), Glen H. Elder, Jr. found that girls were more likely than boys to be given money when needed rather than receiving a regular allowance, thus increasing their financial dependence on parents. (pp. 72–73).

104. *Boyhood and Lawlessness*, p. 69.

105. Gertrude E. Palmer, "Earnings, Spendings and Savings of School Children," *The Commons* 8(June 1903):3–6.

106. Ibid., pp. 1, 7–10; introduction to Edwin A. Kirkpatrick, *The Use of Money* (Indianapolis: Bobbs-Merrill, 1915), p. 1.

107. Helen B. Seymour, "Money Matters with Young People," *Outlook* 48 (Sept. 23, 1893):553.

108. Ibid., Palmer, "Earnings, Spendings and Savings," p. 3.

109. *Home Progress* 6(Nov. 1916):141.

110. Seymour, "Money Matters," p. 553.

111. "The Adolescent of the Family," p. 38.

112. See *New York Times*, Nov. 7, 1903, p. 2, and "The Adolescent in the Family," p. 229.

113. *Boyhood and Lawlessness*, p. 68. On foster children, see chapter 6, and for contemporary data on allowances and social class, see Conclusions.

114. Seymour, "Money Matters," p. 553.

115. Frances F. O'Donnell, "Every Child Needs an Allowance," *Parents Magazine* 5(Mar.1930):18.

116. Mercedes Lake, "Teach The Children Business Principles," *The Delineator* 89(July 1916). On consumerism and the family economy, see Robert S. Lynd, "Family Members as Consumers," *Annals of the American Academy* 160(Mar.1932):86–93.

117. *New York Times*, July 4, 1931, p. 11; "Have You a Little Miser in Your Home?," *The Literary Digest* 110(July 18, 1931):44.

118. Lake, "Teach the Children." In *Middletown* the Lynds note the economic friction generated by the issue of "spending money," between parents and their penniless yet spendthrift teenage children, (p. 141). Robert S. Lynd and Helen M. Lynd, *Middletown* (New York: Harcourt Brace Jovanovich, 1956).

119. Angelo Patri, "Your Child's Allowance," *The Delineator* 102(Jan.1923):3. A tightly supervised money education was also undertaken by schools after 1915. On

thrift education programs, see *Addresses and Proceedings of the National Education Association* 1920, pp. 117–133.

120. John R. Seeley, R. Alexander Sim, and Elizabeth W. Loosley, *Crestwood Heights* (New York: John Wiley & Sons, 1967, first ed. 1956), p. 188.

121. Benedict Burrell, "The Child and Money," *Harper's Bazaar* 33(Nov. 3, 1900): 1721.

122. Charlotte Perkins Gilman, "Child Labor in The Schools," *Independent* 64(May 21, 1908):1135.

123. Burrell, "The Child and Money," p. 1721.

124. Reprinted in Sidonie M. Gruenberg, "Learning the Use of Money," in *Guidance of Childhood and Youth*, ed. by Benjamin C. Gruenberg (New York: Macmillan, 1926), pp. 121–22.

125. Burrell, "The Child and Money," p. 1721.

126. "Teaching Children the Use of Money," *Parents Magazine* 6(Dec. 1931):48.

127. Elliot, "Money and the Child's Own Standards of Living," p. 4.

128. Sidonie M. Gruenberg, "The Dollar Sign in Family Life," *Parents Magazine* 9(Dec. 1934):85–86.

129. "Teaching Children The Use of Money," p. 47; "How Children Earn Money," *Journal of Home Economics* 26(Jan. 1934):289; "Have You a Little Miser in Your Home?."

130. Sidonie M. Gruenberg, quoted in *New York Times*, Feb. 10, 1932, p. 25. See also Tentler, *Wage-Earning Women* p. 92.

131. Nettie P. McGill, "Child Workers on City Streets," U.S. Children's Bureau Publication No. 188 (Washington, D.C., 1928), pp. 29–30, 39. See also Howard G. Burdge, *Our Boys*, Ph.D. diss., Columbia University, 1921, p. 215.

132. Dr. R. S. Woodworth, "From the Psychologist's Point of View," *The American Child* 8(Oct. 1926):4. This new approach to parent-child economic relationships also modified parents' expectations of support in their old age. As an article in the *American Home* put it: "Children should not be regarded as so many human annuities for which the care during their early years counts as payments of premium." Dorothy Blake, "My Children Owe Me Nothing," 14(Nov. 1935):491.

133. Diana Serra Cary, *Hollywood's Children* (Boston: Houghton Mifflin, 1979), p. 91. See also Norman J. Zierold, *The Child Stars* (New York: Coward-McCann, 1965) and "Child Movie Stars Make Millions—For Others!" *Chicago Sunday Tribune*, July 18, 1937.

134. Harry Hibschman, "The Jackie Coogan Case," 72 *United States Law Review* 214 (Apr. 1938). Coogan's victory was mostly symbolic; he was only awarded $126,000. For two earlier cases that also challenged the parental right to a working child's wages, see Rounds Brothers v. McDaniel 133 Ky. 669, 118 S.W. 956 (1909) and Jacobs v. Jacobs, 130 Iowa 10, 104 N.W. 489 (1906).

135. "Whose Is The Money A Child Film Star Earns?" *Sunday News*, Apr. 24, 1938, p. 55. On file at The Performing Arts Research Center. A study conducted by the National Child Labor Committee in 1941 discovered that the earnings of most child actors were used for their own expenses and training, in dancing, music, or dramatic lessons. Anne Hood Harren and Gertrude Folks Zimand, *Children in the Theater* (National Child Labor Committee, 1941), pp. 52–54.

136. "Guarding Their Pots of Money," *Silver Screen* (1938). On file at The Performing Arts Research Center. Jackie Coogan himself had received an allowance of six dollars and twenty-five cents a week.

137. *New York Times*, Oct. 24, 1937, IV, p. 2.

Chapter 4

1. John F. Dryden, "Industrial Insurance is Family Insurance, of Which Infantile Insurance is an Essential Part: Is it Against Public Policy?," Testimony presented before the Committee on Insurance of the Massachusetts Legislature, Mar. 1895; p. 22. On file at Metropolitan Life Insurance Co., New York; Solomon S. Huebner, *Life Insurance* (New York: Appleton, 1921), p. 276.

2. George K. Behlmer, *Child Abuse and Moral Reform in England, 1870–1908* (Stanford, CA: Stanford University Press, 1982), p. 131.

3. *History of the Prudential Company* (London: Holborn Bars, 1880), p. 12.

4. Frederick H. Hoffman, *Life Insurance for Children* (Newark, NJ: Prudential Press, 1903), p. 4.

5. Benjamin Waugh, "Child-Life Insurance," *Contemporary Review* 58(July 1890): 59.

6. Elizur Wright, *Politics and Mysteries of Life Insurance* (Boston: Lee & Shepard, 1873), p. 65.

7. Behlmer, *Child Abuse and Moral Reform*, p. 121; Thomas Carlyle, *Past and Present* (New York: Charles Scribner's, 1918), pp. 4–5; Johan Huizinga, *Homo Ludens* (New York: Harper & Row, 1970), p. 73; Florence Edler de Roover, "Early Examples of Marine Insurance," *Journal of Economic History* 5 (May 1945): 196. Two early ambitious attempts to insure children's lives failed in sixteenth- and seventeenth-century Europe. In 1565 Berthold Holtzschucher promoted compulsory insurance for all children. After the birth of their child, parents had to deposit a specific sum of money; at marriage, the child would collect three times the amount deposited. If the child died the deposit, with interest, was turned over to the authorities. With high infant mortality, the plan promised significant revenues for the community. Yet it failed, as did a similar scheme developed by George Obrechet in 1603; A. Fingland Jack, *An Introduction to the History of Life Insurance* (New York: E.P. Dutton, 1912), pp. 207–10.

8. Alexander Colin Campbell, *Insurance and Crime* (New York: G. P. Putnam's Sons, 1902), p. 283.

9. René Goupil, "De la Considération de la mort des personnes dans les actes juridiques," Ph.D. diss., Université de Caen, Faculté de Droit, 1905, p. 101; L. François, "L'Assurance populaire en particulier l'assurance des enfants," in *Reports, Memoirs and Proceedings of the Fifth International Congress of Actuaries*, ed. by Alfred Manes (Berlin: Mittler, 1906), p. 10; Albert Quiquet, "L'Assurance des enfants en France," in ibid., pp. 85–95. In Germany, Holland, Denmark, and Belgium opposition to children's insurance was milder and there were few legal restraints. Aage Hostrup, "Industrial and children's insurance in Denmark," ibid., pp. 17–20; I.M. Vas Dias, "L'Assurance populaire et l'assurance des enfants," ibid., pp. 115–29; Julius Wendt, "Die Kinderversicherung," Ibid., pp. 39–57.

10. Behlmer, *Child Abuse and Moral Reform*, p. 123. On infanticide, see Thomas McKeown, *The Modern Rise of Population* (New York: Academic Press, 1977); William L. Langer, "Checks on Population Growth: 1750–1850," *Scientific American* 226(1972):93–99.

11. Charles Coolidge Read, "The Insurance of Children," Testimony presented before the Committee on Insurance of the Massachusetts Legislature, Apr. 4, 1895, pp. 19–20. On file at Metropolitan Life Insurance Co., New York.

12. Alexander McKenzie, Letter from First Church in Cambridge to Metropolitan Life Insurance Co., Mar. 16, 1895. On file at Metropolitan Life Insurance

Co., New York; Marquis James, The *Metropolitan Life* (New York: Viking, 1947), p. 122.

13. Read, "The Insurance of Children," pp. 4, 51.

14. Read, "The Insurance of Children," p. 39. Haley Fiske, "The Insurance of Children," Testimony presented before the Committee on Insurance of the Massachusetts Legislature, Mar. 20–21, 1895, p. 4. On file at Metropolitan Life Insurance Co., New York.

15. Waugh, "Child-Life Insurance," p. 54.

16. 45 Maine 105 (1858). See also Loomis v. Eagle Life Co. 6 Gray 396 (1856). Although these landmark cases concerned minors over fourteen, they served as legal precedent for insuring younger children.

17. Cornelius Walford, *Insurance Cyclopedia* (London: Layton, 1871).

18. Statement by the representative of Prudential Life Insurance Company at the 1893 hearings before the Insurance Committee of the Colorado legislature. Frederick H. Hoffman, *History of the Prudential Life Insurance Company* (Newark, NJ: Prudential Press, 1900), pp. 198–99.

19. Dryden, "Industrial Insurance is Family Insurance," p. 16. See 15 Hun. 74 (1878).

20. Letter by Chas. F. Donnelly, printed in Read, "The Insurance of Children," p. 28.

21. Waugh, "Child-Life Insurance," p. 41.

22. *The Insurance Monitor* 29 (Feb. 1881):88.

23. Waugh, "Child-Life Insurance," p. 41; M. J. Savage, Testimony presented before the Committee on Insurance of the Massachusetts Legislature, Mar. 29, 1895, p. 28. On file at Metropolitan Life Insurance Co., New York.

24. Report on the Examination of the Metropolitan Life Insurance Company, State of New York, Insurance Department. (New York: J. B. Lyno Co., 1911), p. 33. See Quincy L. Dowd, *Funeral Management and Costs* (Chicago: University of Chicago Press, 1921).

25. Hoffman, *Life Insurance for Children;* Bishop Grafton, Letter to the Milwaukee Sentinel, Dec. 28, 1902. On file at Metropolitan Life Insurance Co., New York.

26. John D. Long, "The Insurance of Children," Testimony presented before the Committee on Insurance of the Massachusetts Legislature, April 4, 1895, p. 1. On file at The Metropolitan Life Insurance Co., New York.

27. Ibid., pp. 14, 35; Extracts from Official Reports of State Commissioners and Superintendents of Insurance between 1880–1901. Pamphlet on file at Metropolitan Life Insurance Co., New York.

28. "Child Insurance as Regarded by Anti-Cruelty and by Charity Societies," 1897. Pamphlet on file at Metropolitan Life Insurance Co., New York.

29. Report from the Insurance Commission of Wisconsin, June 1, 1904, in "Child Insurance in the Legislatures," 1909. Pamphlet on file at the Metropolitan Life Insurance Co., New York, p. 4; *Weekly Underwriter*, July 24, 1880.

30. Hoffman, *History of the Prudential Life Insurance Company*, pp. 108–9, 220, 225–28; Long, "The Insurance of Children," p.13.

31. Ibid., p. 11; *The Spectator*, Mar. 13, 1890.

32. Haley Fiske, "Industrial Insurance," *Charities Review* 8(Mar. 1898):37; Bulletin of the Bureau of Labor, 1906, pp. 613–14; Fiske, "The Insurance of Children," p. 24.

33. Cited in Hoffman, *History of the Prudential Life Insurance Company*, p. 279.

34. Jacob A. Riis, *How the Other Half Lives* (New York: Dover Publications, 1971, 1st ed. 1890), p. 136.

35. Jacob A. Riis, *Out of Mulberry Street* (New York: Century Co., 1898), pp. 205–9.

36. *New York Times*, Oct. 23, 1908, p. 6; Oct. 24, 1908, p. 8.

37. Letter reprinted in Fiske, "The Insurance of Children," pp. 8–9.

38. Louise C. Odencrantz, *Italian Women in Industry* (New York: Russell Sage Foundation, 1919), p. 201.

39. Katharine Anthony, *Mothers Who Must Earn* (New York: Russell Sage Foundation, 1914), pp. 138–39; *Report on Condition of Woman and Child Wage-Earners in the United States* 4(Washington, D.C., 1910):304; Louise Bolard More, *Wage-Earners' Budgets* (New York: Henry Holt and Co., 1907), pp. 42–3.

40. Read, "The Insurance of Children," p. 24.

41. Frederick L. Hoffman, "Pauper Burials and the Internment of the Dead in Large Cities," presented at the National Conference of Social Work, June 4, 1919, p. 48. On file at the New York Public Library.

42. More, *Wage-Earners' Budgets*, p. 145.

43. Ruth S. True, *The Neglected Girl* (New York: Russell Sage Foundation, 1914), p. 100.

44. Margaret J. Bacon, "Savings and Insurance and Their Relation to the Family Budget," Proceedings of the Twenty-Ninth New York State Conference on Social Work, Rochester, New York, 1928, p. 98.

45. Lee F. Frankel, "Industrial Insurance and its Relation to Child Welfare," Child Welfare Conference Proceedings, 1909, p. 9. On file at Metropolitan Life Insurance Co. Companies did not insure babies in their first year of life until the 1920s when infant mortality began to decrease significantly. Black children were not insured until 1881 and even then received lower benefits than white children. Racial discrimination was explained as a "commercial matter," namely, the higher mortality rate among blacks. Dryden, "Industrial Insurance is Family Insurance," p. 30.

46. Long, "The Insurance of Children," p. 10.

47. Dryden, "Industrial Insurance is Family Insurance," p. 6.

48. Hoffman, *"Life Insurance for Children,* p. 23; Dr. Hugh Jones, "The Perils and Protection of Infant Life," *Journal of the Royal Statistical Society* 57(1894):1–98; Behlmer, *Child Abuse and Moral Reform,* p. 133.

49. Frankel, "Industrial Insurance," p. 1.

50. See Walter E. Thornton, "Juvenile Insurance," in Abstract of the Proceedings of the Fiftieth Annual Meeting of the Association of Life Insurance Medical Directors of America, 26(1940):68; Dr. W. H. Scoins, "Juvenile Insurance," in Report of the Sixty-seventh Annual Meeting of the National Fraternal Congress of America (1953), p. 122; *Consumers Reports* 47(Jan. 1982):5.

51. Warnock v. Davis, 104 U.S. 775 (1882).

52. Thornton, "Juvenile Insurance," p. 33.

53. "Families and Their Life Insurance: A Study of 2,134 Massachusetts Families and Their Life Insurance Policies," Prepared for the Temporary National Economic Committee, 76th Cong., 3d sess. (Washington, D.C.: Government Printing Office, 1940), p. 61; David W. Gregg, *Life and Health Insurance Handbook* (Homewood, IL: Irwin, 1964), p. 105; *The 1949 Buyer* (Hartford, CT: Life Insurance Agency Management Association, 1950).

54. June M. Milan, "Juvenile Insurance—An Invaluable Tool to Open Bigger Sales," *Life Association News* 71 (June 1976):79.

55. Julius Vogel, "Juvenile Insurance," Proceedings of the Home Office Life Underwriters Association, 1969, p. 60.

56. Robert I. Mehr, *Life Insurance* (Dallas, TX Business Publications, 1977), p. 118.

57. *Consumers Union Report on Life Insurance* (New York: Bantam Books, 1974); *Consumers' Reports* 47(Jan. 1982):5.

58. *Young Lives and Life Insurance*, 1964; William L. Willard, *Juvenile Insurance Today* (Indianapolis, IN: Research & Review Service of America, 1979); *Give Your Son A Hand*, 1958 sales booklet on file at Metropolitan Life Insurance Co., New York; H. P. Gravengaard, *Juvenile Insurance* (Cincinnati, OH: Diamond Life Bulletins, 1951).

Chapter 5

1. *New York Times,* Jan. 20, 1979, II, p. 1; Southern Ry. v. Covenia, 100 Ga. 46, 29 S.E. 219 (1896).

2. Pennsylvania Coal Co. v. Nee, 9 Sadler 579, 13 A. 841 (1888). The San Francisco case was reported by the *New York Times* as an "offer sure to be scorned," Oct. 24, p. 16; Oct. 22, p. 14, 1922.

3. Louisville & Nash. R.R. v. Creighton, 106 Ky. 42, 50 S.W. 227 (1899). In addition to compensatory damages, some states allow punitive damages based on the degree of the wrongdoer's culpability. For a clear explanation of the differences between tort and crime see William L. Prosser, *Law of Torts*, 4th ed. (St. Paul, MN: West Publishing Co., 1971), pp. 7–9.

4. Robert A. Silverman, *Law and Urban Growth* (Princeton, NJ: Princeton University Press, 1981), pp. 114–15. The trend has been toward removing all restrictions or increasing maximum awards. By 1975, only Kansas and West Virginia retained statutory ceilings.

5. Baker v. Bolton, 1 Campb. 493, 170 Eng. Reprint 1033 (1808). On the *wergild*, see Georg Simmel, *The Philosophy of Money*, trans. Tom Bottomore and David Frisby (London: Routledge & Kegan Paul, 1978), pp. 355–59.

6. Hyatt v. Adams, 16 Mich. 180 (1867).

7. American death statutes were patterned after Lord Campbell's Act of 1846 that initiated the right of recovery for wrongful death in England. The Act was interpreted as restricting recovery to pecuniary losses. For critical analysis of the evolution of wrongful death legislation, see Malone, "The Genesis of Wrongful Death," 17 *Stanford Law Review* 1043 (1965); Smedley, "Wrongful Death—Bases of the Common Law Rules," 13 *Vanderbilt Law Review* 605 (1960); Hans A. Fischer, *Los Daños Civiles y su Reparación* (Madrid: Librería General de Victoriano Suarez, 1928), pp. 229–39.

8. On the rise of accident litigation at the turn of the past century, see Lawrence M. Friedman, *A History of American Law* (New York: Simon and Shuster, 1973), pp. 422–23 and, on industrial accidents, Carl Gersuny, *Work Hazards and Industrial Conflict* (Hanover, NH:University Press of New England, 1981). This chapter is based on an extensive qualitative analysis of a variety of nineteenth- and twentieth-century primary and secondary sources including court decisions, wrongful death statutes, law review articles, instruction manuals for lawyers, trial transcripts, and treatises on torts and family law. Francis B. Tiffany's two editions of *Death by Wrongful Act* (St. Paul, MN: West Publishing Co., 1893, 1913) provide useful data for the nineteenth and early twentieth century. Stuart M. Speiser's *Recovery for Wrongful Death* (New York: Lawyers Co-Operative Publishing Co., 1975) is a well-researched, indispensable source for contemporary materials. The selection of court cases was guided by the English

and American Annotated Cases and by the American Law Reports. Law review articles helped to determine landmark or controversial decisions for each historical period. Researchers interested in developing precise monetary estimates of human life have been discouraged by court decisions. Compensation formulas have been found inconsistent and lacking an "analytic thinking process." Richard Zeckhauser, "Procedures for Valuing Lives," *Public Policy* XXIII (Fall 1975), p. 450. Indeed, wrongful death damages are determined by a jury which is not bound to any fixed mathematical formula. No uniform death statute exists, adding interstate variation to court decisions. But if jury discretion prevents precise correlations between monetary values and life values, it offers an important source of sociological information. For instance, in determining child death awards, juries are guided by implicit and explicit social conceptions of children's sentimental and economic value. This chapter traces significant changes in such conceptions.

9. 12 American State Reports 371 (1889).

10. Gulf, C. & S.F. Ry. v. Brown, 33 Tex. Civ. App. 269, 76 S.W. 794. See also the early leading case of O'Mara v. Hudson River R.R., 38 N.Y. 445 (1868). Pressman v. Mooney, 5 A.D. 121, 39 N.Y.S. 44 (1896). Trial transcript, p. 22.

11. Little Rock & F.S. Ry. v. Barker, 33 Ark. 350 (1878).

12. Plummer v. Webb, 19 Fed.Cas. 894 (No. 11234); Shields v. Yonge, 15 Ga. 349 (1854). The two other child death cases were Ford v. Monroe 20 Wend. 210 (1838) and James v. Christy, 18 Mo. 162 (1853). In allowing recovery for a child the courts often used the analogy of a master's right of action for the wrongful death of a servant. The fifth early American decision concerned a husband's right to sue for the wrongful death of his wife, Cross v. Guthery 2 Root 90, 1 Am. Dec. 61 (1794).

13. See Tiffany, *Death by Wrongful Act*, pp. 196–207; 18 *English and American Annotated Cases* 1225–1231 (1911).

14. Louisville, N.A. & C. Ry. v. Rush, 127 Ind. 545, 26 N.E. 1010 (1891). Some early leading decisions concerned the death of young daughters. In Oldfield v. New York & H. R.R., 14 N.Y. 310 (1856), $1,300 was awarded to the parents of a six-year-old girl; in Houghkirk v. Delaware & Hudson Canal Co., 92 N.Y. 219 (1883), a market gardener and his wife received $5,000 for the loss of their six-year-old daughter.

15. Ihl v. Forty-Second St. and G. S. F. R.R., 47 N.Y. 317 (1872); Oldfield v. New York and H. R.R. Co., 14 N.Y. 310 (1856); Lehman v. Brooklyn, 29 Barb. 234 (1859); Tiffany, *Death by Wrongful Act*, p. 198. On the tendency of nineteenth-century American courts to allow recovery for young children, see "The Value of Children," and "The Pecuniary Value of Life and Limb," 1 *University Law Review* 55 (1893).

16. Brunswig v. White, 70 Tex. 504, 8 S.W. 85 (1888). The verdict was $7,500.

17. Cincinnati St. Ry. v. Altemeier, 60 Ohio St. 10, 53 N.E. 300 (1899).

18. Chicago v. Major, 18 Ill. 349 (1857). See also 160 Pa. 647 (1894). Courts, however, often denied the right of recovery to children injured while trespassing on a trolley or on other street-railway property by defining it as contributory negligence. Silverman, *Law and Urban Growth*, p. 104.

19. Chicago & N.W. Ry. v. Des Lauriers, 40 Ill. App. Ct. 654 (1890). A 1981 N.Y. State Court of Appeals decision offers a contemporary version of this legal endorsement of family baby-sitting. Denying a cause of action for negligent supervision between minor siblings, the court explained that entrusting a child with the well-being of a sibling "might be part of the training of a child in an effort to inculcate responsibility or affection.... These are some of the "stuff" that binds families together." Smith v. Sapienza, 52 N.Y.2d 82, 417 N.E.,2d 530, 436 N.Y.S. 2d 236 (1981).

20. Potter v. Chicago & N.W. Ry., 21 Wis. 377 (1867).

21. "What is the Value of a Human Life in Dollars?" *New York Times*, July 1, 1906, III, p. 6. See also Miles M. Dawson, "Valuation in Actions for Damages for Negligence, of Human Life, Destroyed or Impaired," *Proceedings of the Fourth International Congress of Actuaries* (New York: Actuarial Society of America, 1904), pp. 928–39, and Erastus E. Holt, "Physical Economics," *Journal of the American Medical Association* XLVII (July 21, 1906), pp. 194–203.

22. Graham v. Consolidated Traction Co., 62 N.J.L. 90: 40 A. 773 (1898), 64 N.J.L. 10 44 A. 964 (1899), 65 N.J.L. 539, 47 A. 453 (1900).

23. 21 *New Jersey Law Journal* 292, 349 (1898).

24. *Jersey City Evening Journal* July 21, 30, 1898, p. 4; Nov. 12, 1900, p. 1; *Jersey City News*, Nov. 14, 1899, p. 3; Nov. 14, 1900, pp. 2, 23; *New Jersey Law Journal* 354 (1900).

25. *New York Times*, Jan. 15, 1895, p. 14. See Lee v. Publishers George Knapp & Co., 137 Mo. 385, 38 S.W. 1107 (1897 one-cent verdict); Silberstein v. Wm. Wicke Co., 22 N.Y.S. 170 (1892, six-cent award); Sceba v. Manistee Ry., 189 Mich. 308, 155 N.W. 414 (1915, $71 award); Snyder v. Lake Shore & Mich. S. Ry., 131 Mich. 418, 91 N.W. 643 (1902, $250 award); and J.L. Bernstein, "Is It Cheaper to Kill?," 74 *New Jersey Law Journal* 113.

26. *New York Times* Jan. 23, 1899, p. 1.

27. Morris v. Metropolitan St. Ry., 51 A.D. 512, 64 N.Y.S. 878 (1900); *New York Times*, May 12, 1900, p. 16; July 11, 1901, p. 12, and Arnold v. State of New York, 163 App. Div. 253.

28. 64 N.Y.S. 880.

29. Morris v. Metropolitan, trial transcript, p. 20.

30. *New York Times*, May 12, 1900, p. 16; McGarr v. National & Providence Worsted Mills, 24 R.I. 447, 53 A. 320 (1902); Tiffany, *Death by Wrongful Act*, p. 358.

31. Sceba v. Manistee Ry., 189 Mich. 317, 155 N.W. 414 (1915); *Current Literature* 32(Jan. 1902):5.

32. Louisville & Nash. R.R. v. Creighton, 106 Ky. 53, 50 S.W. 227 (1899); *Current Literature* 32 (Jan. 1902):6.

33. "The Value of a Child," *Boston Morning Journal*, Nov. 20, 1901, p. 4.

34. Professor Walter Rauschenbusch, "Is the Baby Worth a Dollar?," *Ladies' Home Journal* 27(Oct. 1, 1910):19.

35. McCleary v. Pittsburgh Rys., 47 Pa. Super. 366 (1911) reversing judgment of $147 for the death of a six-year-old boy.

36. Aaron Stern, "Action for Wrongful Death in New York," 12 *New York University Law Quarterly Review* 390(1935). Proper compensation for automobile accidents became a serious problem for victims of all ages. See "Compensation for Automobile Accidents, A Symposium," 32 *Columbia Law Review* 785 (1932).

37. Schendel v. Bradford, 106 Ohio St. 387. 140 N.E.155 (1922). For responses to child death cases, see Stern, "Action for Wrongful Death in New York"; "Damages —Measure of Damages in Case of Death of Minor Child," 13 *Virginia Law Review* 392 (1926–27); "Comments—Actions for Wrongful Death in Pennsylvania," 2 *University of Pittsburgh Law Review* 167 (1936); "Death—Measure of Damages Under Wrongful Death Statutes—Elements of Compensation for the Death of a Minor Child," 16 *Minnesota Law Review* 409 (1932); Leo V. Killian, "Wrongful Death Actions in California—Some Needed Amendments," 25 *California Law Review* 170 (1936); "Damages: Recovery by a Parent for Wrongful Death of a Child," 25 *California Law Review* 103 (1936); New York Law Revision Commission, *Reports, Recommendations, and Studies* 215 (1935).

38. Louis I. Dublin and Alfred J. Lotka, *The Money Value of Man* (New York: Ronald Press, 1930), pp.48–49 and chapter 3; William F. Ogburn, "The Financial Cost of Rearing a Child: Standards of Child Welfare," U.S. Children's Bureau Publication No. 60, 1919; George M. Crogan, "Value of Human Life in Dollars can be Expressed," *New Jersey Law Journal* 1, 1936. On earlier objections to the monetary evaluation of life, see Viviana A. Zelizer, *Morals and Markets: The Development of Life Insurance in the United States* (New York: Columbia University Press, 1979).

39. See "Ten Stories for Legislators," *The American Child* 7(Mar. 1925):1, 6–7. On compensation for illegally employed minors, Ellen Nathalie Matthews, "The Illegally Employed Minor and the Workmen's Compensation Law," U.S. Children's Bureau Publication No. 214, 1932. Employers also supported fixed extra-compensation plans as potentially cheaper than a civil suit for damages.

40. 58 W.Va. 216 (1905), cited by Speiser, *Recovery for Wrongful Death*, p. 335. The case concerned an older son whose parents were financially independent. The Florida statute was upheld as constitutional in Davis v. Florida Power Co., 64 Fla. 246 (1912).

41. Munro v. Pacific Coast Dredging & Reclamation Co., 84 Calif. 515, 24 P. 303 (1890). See also Bond v. United Railroads, 159 Calif. 270 (1911) and "Wrongful Death Actions in California." The Wisconsin statute allowed a sum "not exceeding twenty-five hundred dollars for loss of society, and companionship." 14 ALR 2d 499–500.

42. Winner v. Sharp, 43 So. 2d 634 (1949). On the trend to award substantial damages for children in California and Florida, see 25 *California Law Review* 103 (1936) and Ed Reichelt, "Damages—Measure of Damages Recoverable by Parents for Wrongful Death of Infant," 2 *Baylor Law Review* 350. Reichelt notes that "parental losses for wrongful death of minor children . . . come within a distinct category and merit special attention as distinguished from other death claims." On the general recognition by tort law of emotional distress in the 1920s and 1930s, see G. Edward White, *Tort Law in America* (New York: Oxford University Press, 1980). There are two major types of nonpecuniary losses: loss of companionship and comfort, and mental anguish and grief of survivors.

43. On larger child death awards in pecuniary-loss states, see New York Law Revision Commission; Briscoe B. Clark, *Law of Damages* II (New York: E. Thompson Co., 1925); Dublin and Lotka, *The Money Value of a Man* (1946 ed.), p. 95; "Damages for the Wrongful Death of Children," 22 *University of Chicago Law Review* 538 (1955); 14 ALR 2d. 550 (1950); 22–3 *NACCA Law Journal* 123. As with all social or legal change, the trend toward more substantial verdicts was gradual; nominal sums were still awarded by some courts.

44. 22 *University of Chicago Law Review* 544. Pecuniary value was added to the "worthless" child by often including post-minority benefits in the assessment of damages. See Ginocchi v. Pittsburgh & L.E.R.Co. 283 Pa. 378, 129 A. 323 (1925); and Atkeson v. Jackson Estate, 72 Wash. 233 (1913).

45. 19 *Law Notes* 63 (1915); Werpupp v. N.J. St. Ry.; Eastwood v. same, Essex Circuit Court, May 13, 1904. See 27 *New Jersey Law Journal* 172 (1904); *New York Times*, May 14, 1904, p. 1.

46. See 19 *Law Notes* 63 and Louis I. Dublin, "Child Health Protection or Neglect: The Ultimate Cost to the Community," *Transactions of the Fourth Annual Meeting of the American Child Health Association* (Washington, D.C., 1927), p. 204.

47. New York Law Revision Commission, p. 61. Other studies confirm the absence of major differences by sex in child death awards; Michael O. Finkelstein, "Compensation for Wrongful Death," in *Quantitative Methods in Law* (New York: Free Press,

1978), p. 259 and Kathryn A. Belfance, "The Inadequacy of Pecuniary Loss as a Measure of Damages in Actions for the Wrongful Death of Children," 6 *Ohio Northern University Law Review:* 522. The 1904 New Jersey decision (but not the 1915) may be partly a result of the victims' age. Because they were teenagers, the judge based the assessment of damages on future earnings. Sex differences in the amount of *adult* compensation, particularly between male wage-earners and housewives, are very large. See "Legal Worth of a Woman, By Sections and Entire," 48 *Albany Law Journal* 455 (1893); Thomas F. Lambert, Jr. "How Much is a Good Wife Worth?" 41 *Boston University Law Review* (1961).

48. Craig Spangenberg, "Proof of Damages for Wrongful Death—The Worthless Child," *Wrongful Death and Survivorship,* Report of the NACCA Sixth Circuit Regional Meeting and Seminar (Cincinnati, 1957), pp. 65–66; Thomas F. Lambert, "History and Future," ibid., p. 22. The case was Courtney v. Apple, 345 Mich. 223, 76 N.W. 2d 80 (1956).

49. NACCA *Law Journal* 26–27, pp. 211–12. See Wycko v. Gnodtke, 361 Mich. 331, 105 N.W.2d 118 (1960).

50. Hoyt v. United States, 286 F.2d 356 (5th Cir., 1961). For states allowing recovery for moral pain or loss of companionship by statute or by judicial construction in 1971, see Speiser, *Recovery for Wrongful Death* I, pp. 308–37. The uniqueness of child death cases was further recognized by Washington's and Oklahoma's revised death statutes which include recovery for the destruction of the parent-child relationship. See Ellen M. Hamilton, "Wrongful Death of Children in Oklahoma: Statutory Expansion of Recoverable Damages," 11 *Tulsa Law Journal* 98 (1975). The trend in child injury cases is similar, Jean C. Love, "Tortious Interference with the Parent-Child Relationship: Loss of an Injured Person's Society and Companionship," 51 *Indiana Law Journal* 590 (1976).

51. Pagitt v. Keokuk, 206 N.W. 2d. 700(1973), cited by Speiser, *Recovery for Wrongful Death* 1, p. 515. Economists may project a child's future earnings and teachers can also testify on the child's academic "quality" as a measure of value.

52. 20 Am. Jur. Trial 697; Allan R. Earl, "The Wrongful Death of a Child," *Trial Diplomacy Journal* 4(Fall 1981):37. See also Leonard Decof, "Damages in Actions for Wrongful Death of Children," 47 *Notre Dame Lawyer* 197 (1971).

53. 20 Am. Jur. Trial 723.

54. Seabord Air Line R.R. v. Gay, 201 So. 2d. 241(1967). Earlier statutes often provided that a father "or in case of his death, or desertion of his family, or imprisonment," then the mother could recover damages. Current statutes include both parents as beneficiaries. Tiffany, *Death by Wrongful Act;* Speiser *Recovery for Wrongful Death,* II, pp. 146–47.

55. 251 So. 2d. 18 (1971); Speiser, *Recovery for Wrongful Death* I, p. 335, fn. 36. On Green v. Bittner, 85 N.J. 1, 424 A. 2d. 210, see 7 *Family Law Reporter* 1 (1981). See also Charles R. Johnson, "Wrongful Death and Intellectual Dishonesty," 16 *South Dakota Law Review* 37 (1971); Belfance, "The Inadequacy of Pecuniary Loss."

56. Finkelstein, "Compensation for Wrongful Death," p. 257.

57. Paul Brennan, "Monetary Compensations of Death," *Society* 17(Nov.–Dec. 1979), p. 62; Simmel, *Philosophy of Money.*

58. Institute of Civil Law, Central Political Juridical Cadre's School 339, cited by Harvey McGregor, "Personal Injury and Death," *International Encyclopedia of Comparative Law* XI, chapter 9, pp. 20, 103–4.

59. Warren C. Shrempp, "Death of a Child," Proceedings, Nebraska State Bar Association. Reprinted in 47 *Nebraska Law Review* 389(1968). On the controversial

aspects of jury verdicts in child death cases, see William J. Weinstein, "Jury Verdicts–Excessive or Inadequate," 39 *Michigan SBLJ* 15(1960).

60. Lambert, "Damages for Wrongful Death," p. 308; 20 Am.Jur.Trial, 681.

61. Ibid, p.682.

62. *New York Times,* May 29, 1911, p. 1; Nov. 17, 1909, p. 6.

63. Henri et León Mazeaud and André Tunc, *Traité Théorique et Pratique de la Responsabilité Civile Délictuelle et Contractuelle,* 5th ed. (Paris: Editions Montchrestien, 1957) pp. 390, 392 (personal translation). On moral damages see Robert H. Brebbia, *El Daño Moral* (Rosario, Argentina: Orbir, 1967); Stuart M. Speiser and Stuart S. Malawer, "An American Tragedy: Damages for Mental Anguish of Bereaved Relatives in Wrongful Death Actions," 51 *Tulane Law Review* 1 (1976). Simmel, *Philosophy of Money,* p. 357.

64. Stanley B. Kent, "Damages in Wrongful Death Actions," 17 *Clev-Mar. Law Review* 238. On the continuing trend toward larger verdicts in child death cases, see 30 *NACCA Law Journal* 195–98; 49 ALR 3d 935.

65. Fischer, *Los Daños Civiles,* p. 256; Mazéaud and Tunc, *Traité Théorique,* pp. 396–97; Max Le Roy, *Evaluation du Préjudice Corporel* (Paris: Librairies Techniques, 1966), pp. 105, fn.19; 112; McGregor, "Personal Injury and Death," pp. 20, 113–14. See also Simmel, *Philosophy of Money,* pp.273, 406.

66. Am.Jur.Trial 721, 726.

67. Decof, "Damages in Actions," p. 207; 20 Am.Jur.Trial 588. On the social regulation of emotions, see Arlie R. Hochschild, "Emotion Work, Feeling Rules, and Social Structure," *American Journal of Sociology* 85(Nov. 1979):551–75.

68. 22 *University of Chicago Law Review* 549. The wrongful death of retired elderly persons offers strong parallels with child death actions. With the aged, however, the court can rely on a record of past earnings, on Social Security benefits or private pension plans, as well as homemaking responsibilities. See 52 ALR 3d. 289; 81 ALR 2d. 949; 13 POF 2d. 197; Speiser, *Recovery for Wrongful Death* II, pp. 64–67.

69. Simmel, *Philosophy of Money,* p. 369.

70. Custodio v. Bauer, 251 C.A. 2d. 303, 59 Cal. Rpt. 463 (1967). Christensen v. Thornby 192 Minn. 123, 255 N.W. 620 (1934). There is some unusual historical precedent for making the birth of a child a profitable event. In the midst of an insurance mania in eighteenth-century England, some companies insured against the contingency of having children. Barry Supple, *The Royal Exchange Assurance* (London: Cambridge University Press, 1970), p. 9.

71. Terrell v. Garcia, 496 S.W.2d. 124, (Tex.Civ.App. 1973); 192 Minn. 123; 64 Wash. 2d. 247 (1964). See also Shaheen v. Knight, 11 Pa. D & C.2d. 41 (1957), where recovery was denied on public policy grounds. Some courts have ruled that the legal differentiation of children's economic costs vs. sentimental benefits creates an unacceptable form of surrogate parenthood as parents keep their child, but physicians pay for it. 83 ALR 3d. 48. In Coleman v. Garrison, 349 A.2d. 8 (Del. 1975), the measurement of a child's value was avoided by limiting damages to pregnancy-related expenses.

72. See 83 ALR 3d. 24; Alexander M. Capron, "Tort Liability in Genetic Counseling," 79 *Columbia Law Review* 618, at 632, fn. 52. There are three different "child life" actions: 1) in negligent sterilization cases, parents can sue for the birth of an "unwanted" healthy child; 2) recovery is allowed when failure to diagnose pregnancy in time for abortion results in the birth of a physically handicapped child; 3) the child itself sues for wrongfully being born. My analysis is limited to the "unwanted" healthy child.

73. Troppi v. Scarf, 31 Mich. App. 240, 187 N.W. 2d 511 (1971).

74. Gerald B. Robertson, "Civil Liability Arising from 'Wrongful Birth' Following

an Unsuccessful Sterilization Operation," 4 *American Journal of Law and Medicine* 156 (1978–79); Some courts justify wrongful birth suits by insisting that the child is "not to be thought of as unwanted or unloved but unplanned." Jackson v. Anderson, 230 So. 2d. 503 (1970).

75. Thomas J. Miller, "Redressing a Blessing: The Question of Damages for Negligently Performed Sterilization Operations," 33 *University of Pittsburgh Law Review* 886 (1972). See also Dierdre A. Burgman, "Wrongful Birth Damages: Mandate and Mishandling by Judicial Fiat," 13 *Valparaiso University Law Review* 127, at 153, fn. 173. In wrongful death cases, quantity of children reduces value. For instance, in Norton v. Argonaut Ins. Co., 144 So. 2d. 249 (1962), damages for a three-month-old girl were reduced as "parents had three other healthy children, and their inability to have additional children was not established."

76. Lynn G. Carey, "Wrongful Conception as a Cause of Action and Damages Recoverable," 44 *Missouri Law Review* 595.

Chapter 6

1. *New York Times*, Sept. 6, 1873, p. 4.

2. Mona Gardner, "Traffic in Babies," *Collier's* 104(Sept. 16, 1939):14.

3. Elizabeth Frazer, "We Have Done It!," *Saturday Evening Post* 202(June 21, 1930):59, 161.

4. On apprenticeship and indenture, see Homer Folks, *The Care of Destitute, Neglected and Delinquent Children* (New York: Macmillan, 1902), pp. 3,8; Grace Abbott, *The Child and the State* I (Chicago: University of Chicago Press, 1938), pp. 189–94; Robert H. Bremner, ed., *Children and Youth in America* I (Cambridge, MA: Harvard University Press, 1971), pp. 103–7, 262–63; Edmund S. Morgan, *The Puritan Family*, (New York: Harper & Row, 1966), pp. 75–77; Joseph F. Kett, *Rites of Passage*, (New York: Basic Books, 1977), pp. 17–18.

5. Folks, *The Care*, pp. 39, 64; David M. Schneider, *The History of Public Welfare in New York State, 1609–1866*, (Chicago: University of Chicago Press, 1938), p. 181; Susan Tiffin, *In Whose Best Interest?* (Westport, CN: Greenwood Press, 1982), pp. 70–71.

6. On the New York and other children's aid societies, see Hastings H. Hart, *Preventive Treatment of Neglected Children* (New York: Russell Sage Foundation, 1910), pp. 145–193; Miriam Z. Langsam, *Children West* (Madison, WI: State Historical Society of Wisconsin, 1964); Catherine J. Ross, "Society's Children: The Care of Indigent Youngsters in New York City, 1875–1903," Ph.D. diss. Yale University, 1977. On the British program of child-placing in Canada, see Joy Parr, *Labouring Children* (London: Croom Helm, 1980).

7. Cited in Henry W. Thurston, *The Dependent Child* (New York: Columbia University Press, 1930), p. 101.

8. Ross, "Society's Children," p. 130; Langsam, *Children West*, p. 25.

9. Bruce Bellingham, "Little Wanderers: A Socio-Historical Study of the Nineteenth Century Origins of Child Fostering and Adoption Reform, based on Early Records of the New York Children's Aid Society," Ph.D. diss., University of Pennsylvania, 1984, p. 119. This study provides an insightful revisionist interpretation of the New York Children's Aid Society.

10. See Peter Romanofsky, "Saving the Lives of City's Foundlings," *New York*

Historical Society Quarterly 61(Jan.-Apr. 1972): 49–68; Roger Lane, *Violent Death in the City* (Cambridge, MA: Harvard University Press, 1979), pp. 90–100; Paul A. Gilje, "Infant Abandonment in Early Nineteenth-Century New York City: Three Cases," *Signs* 8(Spring 1983): 580–90. On social class differentials in the use of abortion, James C. Mohr, *Abortion in America* (New York: Oxford University Press, 1978), pp. 93–98.

11. Mary Boyle O'Reilly, "The Daughters of Herod," *New England Quarterly* 43(Oct. 1910):143. This article, based on an investigation of New Hampshire baby farms, provides an unusual insight into the business. Although conducted in 1910, the report reflects the traditional practices of baby farmers.

12. "Baby-Farming Practices," *New York Times*, July 22, 1880, p. 5. Some baby farms also served as a lying-in hospital or maternity home for the unwed mother.

13. O'Reilly, "The Daughters of Herod," pp. 144–45.

14. New York Society For the Prevention of Cruelty to Children, 15th *Annual Report*, 1890, p. 32.

15. New York. State Board of Charities. Thirty-first Annual Report, 1897 (New York, 1898), quoted in Bremner, *Children and Youth in America* II, p. 316. Maybee defended the extra premium for illegitimate babies as a penalty to discourage immorality. For a fee, the New York branch of the Children's Home Society also took children from public and private agencies and placed them in foster homes.

16. *Children's Home Finder* 5(July 1897):29; Robert W. Hebberd, "Placing Out Children: Dangers of Careless Methods," *Proceedings of the 26th National Conference of Charities and Correction*, 1899, p. 176.

17. Homer Folks, "Family Life for Dependent Children," in Anna Garlin Spencer and Charles Wesley Birtwell, eds., *The Care of Dependent, Neglected and Wayward Children* (Baltimore, MD: Johns Hopkins Press, 1894), p. 76.

18. *Proceedings of a Conference on the Care of Dependent and Delinquent Children* (New York: State Charities Aid Association, 1893), p. 33.

19. William Pryor Letchworth, "Report on Pauper and Destitute Children," in *Homes of Homeless Children* (Albany, NY, 1876), p. 12.

20. *New York Times*, Sept. 6, 1873, p. 4. "Baby Butchery," the first *Times* editorial on baby farming, appeared on Aug. 29, 1872.

21. "Slaughter of the Innocents," *New York Times*, Aug. 6, 1874, p. 4.

22. New York Society for the Prevention of Cruelty to Children, 15th *Annual Report*, 1890, p. 31.

23. "Baby-Farming Practices," *New York Times*, July 22, 1880, p. 5. Day nurseries, established in the 1880s and 1890s, for the care of young children whose mothers worked, were not popular among working mothers. Sheila M. Rothman, *Woman's Proper Place* (New York: Basic Books, 1978), pp. 89–90.

24. Robert H. Bremner, "The Children with the Organ Man," *American Quarterly* 8(1956):277–82. See NYSPCC, 15th *Annual Report*, 1890, p. 31. For an excellent analysis of the campaign against baby farming in England, see George K. Behlmer, *Child Abuse and Moral Reform in England, 1870–1908*, (Stanford, CA: Stanford University Press, 1982), chapter 2.

25. *Proceedings of the 29th National Conference of Charities and Correction*, 1902, p. 404. Institutions, however, were difficult to displace. A 1923 U.S. Bureau of the Census report of child placing found that 64.2 percent of dependent and neglected children under care remained in asylums. On the turn-of-the-century debate between supporters of institutions and advocates of foster home care, see Martin Wolins and Irving Piliavin, *Institution or Foster Family—A Century of Debate* (New York: Child Welfare League of America, 1964).

26. *Children's Home Finder* 5(Apr.-May, 1897):21.

27. Rev. M.T. Lamb, *The Child and God*, (Philadelphia, PA: American Baptist Public Society, 1905), p. 66.

28. Ibid.

29. *Children's Home Finder* 10(Feb. 1902):7; *Delineator* 73(Mar. 1909):508.

30. Bellingham, "Little Wanderers," p. 68.

31. Cited in Abbot, *The Child and the State* II, p. 39.

32. Edward T. Hall, "Destitute and Neglected Children," *Proceedings of the 26th National Conference of Charities and Correction*, 1899, pp. 183–84.

33. Martha P. Falconer, *Proceedings of the Conference on the Care of Dependent Children* (Washington: U.S. Government Printing Office, 1909), p. 13. On the servant problem, see David M. Katzman, *Seven Days a Week* (New York: Oxford University Press, 1978), Chapter 6.

34. O'Reilly, "The Daughters of Herod," pp. 138, 146.

35. Albert S. White, "Reclamation of Children," *Proceedings of the 14th Annual Conference of Charities and Correction*, 1887, p. 237.

36. *Children's Home Finder* 11(Oct. 1903). See also N.Y. State Charities Aid Association, *Annual Report*, 1900, p. 17.

37. Lamb, *The Child and God*, pp. 84–85.

38. John N. Foster, "Ten Years of Child-Saving Work in Michigan," *Proceedings of the 11th National Conference of Charities and Correction*, 1884, p. 141.

39. Hart, *Preventive Treatment*, p. 244. As with regular child labor, farm work was usually categorized as "good" work.

40. *Children's Home Finder* 12(Feb. 1904):10.

41. Sophie Van Senden Theis and Constance Goodrich, *The Child in the Foster Home* (New York: New York School of Social Work, 1921), p. 83.

42. "Bound Out," *Survey* 56(Apr.-Sept. 1926):458. See *Children Indentured By The Wisconsin State Public School*, U.S. Children's Bureau Publication No. 150, 1925. The labor of foster children was difficult to regulate because it involved primarily domestic work and farm labor, two areas unprotected by child labor legislation.

43. Thurston, *The Dependent Child*, p. 136.

44. Homer Folks, "Why Should Dependent Children Be Reared in Families Rather Than In Institutions?" *Charities Review* 5(Jan. 1896):141.

45. Katherine P. Hewins, "The Child in the Foster Home," *Survey* 47(Mar. 18, 1922):964.

46. Theis and Goodrich, *The Child in the Foster Home*, p. 85. The possibility that spending money served as a crime deterrent for foster children was also introduced. *Child Welfare League of America Bulletin* 7(June 15, 1928):4.

47. *The A B C of Foster-Family Care for Children*, U.S. Children's Bureau Publication No. 216,1933 (first published 1929); Katharine P. Hewins and L. Josephine Webster, *The Work of Child-Placing Agencies* Bureau Publication No. 171,1927, p. 66–67.

48. *The Child in the Foster Home*, p.83; Ruth Berolzheimer and Florence Nesbitt, *Child Welfare in New Jersey*, U.S. Children's Bureau Publication No. 175,1927, pp. 58–59.

49. Miller v. Pelzer, 159 Minn. 375, 199 N.W. 97 (1924); 9 *Minnesota Law Review* 76(Dec. 1924); *Law Notes* (Jan. 1925), p. 193; 2 *New York Law Review* 480 (1924).

50. Fifth Annual Report of the Board of Charities of Massachusetts, January, 1869, quoted in Abbot, *The Child and the State* II, p. 39.

51. Folks, "Family Life for Dependent Children," p. 78.

52. Herbert W. Lewis, "Terms on Which Children Should Be Placed in Families,"

Proceedings of the 21st National Conference of Charities and Correction, 1894, pp. 141–42.

53. Edwin D. Solenberger, "Standards of Efficiency in Boarding-Out Children," *Proceedings of the National Conference on Charities and Correction* 1914, p. 182.

54. C. H. Pemberton, "The Boarding System for Neglected Children," *Proceedings of the 21st National Conference on Charities and Correction* 1894, pp. 138–39. Boarding homes also presented an alternative to institutionalization for parents forced to surrender their children temporarily, due to financial or health problems.

55. Lamb, *The Child and God*, pp. 50, 59.

56. Charles L. Brace, "'Placing Out' Plan for Homeless and Vagrant Children," Proceedings of the National Conference of Charities and Correction, 1876, p. 254.

57. Adelaide A. Calkings, "Boarding Out of Dependent Children in Massachusetts," cited in Bremner, *Children and Youth in America* II, p. 322.

58. Anne B. Richardson, "The Massachusetts System of Placing and Visiting Children," *Proceedings of the 7th Annual Conference of Charities and Correction*, 1880, p. 198.

59. Pemberton, "The Boarding System for Neglected Children," p. 137.

60. W. H. Slingerland, *Child Placing in Families* (New York: Russell Sage Foundation, 1919), p. 222.

61. C. C. Carstens, Annual Report, Child Welfare League of America Annual Report, 1922–1923, cited in *Foster Home Care for Dependent Children*, p. 11. Agencies also supported subsidized boarding because it gave them greater control in the selection and supervision of foster homes.

62. Anne O'Hagan, "The Biography of a Foundling," *Munsey's Magazine* 25(June 1901):313–34. The boarding-out of infants—devised as a solution to the high rates of infant mortality in institutions—pioneered the system of subsidized foster home care in the nineteenth century. In 1902, Henry Dwight Chapin, a noted children's specialist, instituted the Speedwell system, for the temporary care of needy babies in boarding homes closely supervised by physicians and nurses.

63. Jacob A. Riis, *How the Other Half Lives* (New York: Dover, 1971, first ed. 1890), p. 146.

64. Katharine Anthony, *Mothers Who Must Earn* (New York: Survey Associates, 1914), p. 160.

65. New York State Charities Aid Association, *Annual Report*, 1905, pp. 46–47.

66. Ibid., p. 48; Lillian D. Wald, *Boarded-Out Babies* (New York: State Charities Aid Association, 1907).

67. Mary E. Boretz, "The Child in the Boarding Home," in *Foster Home Care For Dependent Children*, pp. 58–59; *The A B C of Foster-Family Care for Dependent Children*, p. 11.

68. Massachusetts was an exception; the state not only pioneered the use of subsidized homes, but also relied on them extensively for both permanent and temporary care of dependent children.

69. *New York Times*, Feb. 5, 1921, p. 5. Apparently, tricking husbands into believing that an adopted child was really theirs was not uncommon. See, for example, Lillian Gaitlin, "Adopting a Baby," *Sunset* 46(Feb. 1921):83.

70. *New York Times*, Oct. 25, 1926, p. 18.

71. C. D. Gibson, "When a Child Adopts You," *Good Housekeeping* 85(July 1927): 133.

72. R. Shaffer, "Child Movie Stars Make Millions—For Others," *Chicago Sunday Tribune*, July 18, 1937. On file at the Performing Arts Research Center of the New

York Public Library. See also "Movie Star's Adoption," *Law Notes* (Nov. 1939), pp. 20–21.

73. Elizabeth Frazer, "The Baby Market," *Saturday Evening Post* 202 (Feb. 1, 1930), p. 88.

74. Robert Grant, "Domestic Relations and the Child," *Scribner's Magazine* 65(May 1919): 527. Legal adoption did not exist in common law. The first adoption statute in the United States was passed by Massachusetts in 1851 and it became the model for other states. See Jamil S. Zainaldin, "The Emergence of a Modern Adoption Law: Child Custody, Adoption and the Courts, 1796–1851," 73 *Northwestern University Law Review* 1038–89 (1979) and Stephen B. Presser, "The Historical Background of the American Law of Adoption," 11 *Journal of Family Law* 443–556 (1971).

75. *New York Times,* May 8, 1927, VII, p. 14. See "Moppets on the Market: The Problem of Unregulated Adoptions," 59 *Yale Law Journal* 716 (1950). The increase was not only in adoptions by unrelated persons but also in adoptions by relatives, particularly step-parents. By 1962, the 1923 statistics on the substitute care of dependent children were reversed; 69 percent of these children were in family care (adoptive and boarding homes), and only 31 percent in institutions. Wolins and Piliavin, *Institution or Foster Family,* pp. 36–37.

76. *New York Times,* Mar. 17, 1923, p. 9; Jan. 20, 1925, p.19; Dorothy Dunbar Bromley, "Demand for Babies Outruns the Supply," *New York Times Magazine,* Mar. 3, 1935, p. 9.

77. Ada Patterson, "Giving Babies Away," *Cosmopolitan* 39(Aug. 1905):411.

78. *New York Times,* July 7, 1925, p. 1; Aug. 5, 1925, p. 1; Aug. 10, 1925, p. 1.

79. Alice M. Leahy, "Some Characteristics of Adoptive Parents," *American Journal of Sociology* 38 (Jan. 1933): 561–62; Sophie Van Senden Theis, *How Foster Children Turn Out* (New York: State Charities Aid Association, 1924), pp. 60–63. On the increase of upper-class adoptive parents in England between the 1920s and 1940s, see Nigel Middleton, *When Family Failed* (London: Victor Gollancz, 1971), p.240.

80. Arno Dosch, "Not Enough Babies To Go Around," *Cosmopolitan* 49 (Sept. 1910):431.

81. Spence Alumnae Society, *Annual Report,* 1916, p. 37; Judd M. Lewis, "Dealing in Babies," *Good Housekeeping* 58 (Feb. 1914): 196; *New York Tribune,* cited in "Cradles Instead of Divorces," *Literary Digest* 77 (Apr. 14, 1923), p. 36; Vera Connolly, "Bargain-Counter Babies," *Pictorial Review* 38 (Mar. 1937), p. 17. The Spence Nursery, as well as the Alice Chapin Adoption Nursery, organized respectively in 1909 and 1910 in New York, became leading agencies for the placement of infants.

82. "Blue-Eyed Babies," *New York Times,* Jan. 17, 1909, VI, p. 7.

83. Mabel P. Daggett, "The Child Without a Home," *Delineator* 70(Oct. 1907): 510.

84. Dosch, "Not Enough Babies to Go Around," p. 434; Carolyn C. Van Blarcom, "Our Child-Helping Service," *Delineator* 95 (Nov. 1919):34; *New York Times,* Mar. 12, 1927, p. 3.

85. Hastings H. Hart, *Proceedings of the 29th National Conference of Charities and Correction,* 1902, p. 403.

86. Spence Alumnae Society, *Annual Report,* 1916, p. 38.

87. Frederick A. Given, "Bargains in Babies," *Canadian Magazine* 83(Apr. 1935): 30; Frazer, "The Baby Market," pp. 25, 86. For an analysis of daughter preference in adoption, see H. David Kirk, "Differential Sex Preference in Family Formation," *Canadian Review of Sociology and Anthropology* I(Feb. 1964):31–48, and Nancy E. Williamson, *Sons or Daughters,* (Beverly Hills, CA: Sage, 1976), pp. 111–15.

88. Josephine Baker, "Choosing a Child," *Ladies' Home Journal,* 41(Feb. 1924):36.

89. Grant, "Domestic Relations," p. 527. See Tiffin, *In Whose Best Interest?*, pp. 269–70.

90. Gatlin, "Adopting a Baby," p. 84; Ida Parker, *"Fit and Proper"? A Study of Legal Adoption in Massachusetts*, (Boston, MA: Church Home Society, 1927), p. 18. A more lenient view of illegitimate children was consequential, since most adoptable children were born out of wedlock.

91. Honore Willsie, "When Is a Child Adoptable?," *Delineator* 95(Dec. 1919):35; Honore Willsie, "Not a Boy, Please!," ibid., (July 1919):33.

92. Mary Buell Sayles, *Substitute Parents* (New York: Commonwealth Fund, 1936), p. 17.

93. *New York Times*, May 8, 1927, VII, p. 14.

94. George Walker, *The Traffic in Babies*, (Baltimore, MD: Norman Remington Co., 1918), p. 151.

95. Ibid., pp. 130, 136, 153. See also Carrington Howard, "Adoption by Advertisement," *Survey* (Dec. 11, 1915):285–86.

96. Dosch, "Not Enough Babies To Go Around," p. 435; W. Almont Gates, "Caring For Dependent Children in California," *Proceedings of the 40th National Conference of Charities and Correction*, 1913, p.309; Arthur Alden Guild, *Baby Farms in Chicago* (Chicago: Juvenile Protective Association, 1917), pp. 24–25.

97. See *New York Times*, Apr. 9, 1922, IX, p. 12; Apr. 16, 1922, II, p. 8; Mar. 11, 1923, VIII, p. 14, and NY State Charities Aid Association, *Annual Report*, 1922, p. 20.

98. Parker, *Fit and Proper*, p. 31. See also Arlien Johnson, *Public Policy and Private Charity* (Chicago: University of Chicago Press, 1931), p. 73.

99. See Ernest K. Coulter, "The Baby Farm and its Victims," *National Humane Review* 14(Jan. 1926):3–4; *New York Times*, May 8, 1925, p. 1; May 9, 1925, p. 1; May 21, 1925, p. 1; July 16, 1925, p. 21; July 23, 1925, p. 1.

100. Ibid., Apr. 9, 1922, IX, p. 12; Apr. 16, 1922, II, p. 8. For a good overview of the professionalization of child-placing, see Tiffin, *In Whose Best Interest?*, pp. 253–80.

101. *New York Times*, July 23, 1925, p. 1.

102. Parker, *Fit and Proper*, p. 29; Josephine Nelson, "Would You 'Bootleg' a Baby?," *Independent Woman* 15(Feb. 1936):43. On regulation of child-placing and adoption laws, see Abbott, *The Child and the State*, II, pp. 17–21; Emelyn Foster Peck, *Adoption Laws in the United States*, U.S. Children's Bureau Publication No. 148, 1925.

103. Connolly, "Bargain-Counter Babies," p. 96.

104. Francis Lockridge, *Adopting a Child* (New York: Greenberg, 1947), p. 7; "Moppets on the Market," p. 715, fn.2; *New York Times*, Jan. 2, 1945, p. 22.

105. Hearings before the Subcommittee to Investigate Juvenile Delinquency of the Committee on the Judiciary. United States Senate. 84th Congress. First Session, 1955, pp. 9, 153.

106. Paul Popenoe, *The Conservation of the Family* (Baltimore, MD: Williams & Wilkins, 1926), p. 95. Wilson H. Grabill, Clyde V. Kiser, and Pascal K. Whelpton, "A Long View," in Michael Gordon, ed., *The American Family in Social-Historical Perspective* (New York: St. Martin's Press, 1973), pp. 393–94, note a gradual increase in involuntary sterility after 1910. See also Nancy J. Davis, "Childless and Single-Childed Women in Early Twentieth-Century America," *Journal of Family Issues*, 3(Dec. 1982):431–58.

107. Henry F. and Katharine Pringle, "Babies for Sale," *Saturday Evening Post* 224 (Dec. 22, 1951); p. 11. The secrecy and speed of black-market sales also appealed to

the unmarried mothers. On the mothers' pension movement, see David M. Schneider and Albert Deutsch, *The History of Public Welfare in New York State, 1867–1940*, pp. 180–99. A new awareness of high infant mortality rates among illegitimate children further encouraged programs to prevent the separation of babies from their unwed mothers. See *The Welfare of Infants of Illegitimate Birth in Baltimore*, U.S. Children's Bureau Publication No.144,1925; A. Madorah Donahue, *Children of Illegitimate Birth Whose Mothers Have Kept Their Custody*, U.S. Children's Bureau Publication, No. 190, 1928.

108. Handicapped and minority children were also excluded from the adoption market. Only recently have agencies begun seriously considering adoptions for such children. Barbara Joe, *Public Policies Toward Adoption* (Washington, D.C.: Urban Institute, 1979), p. 6. See also David Fanshel, *Study in Negro Adoption* (New York: Child Welfare League of America, 1957).

109. Hearings before the Subcommittee on Children and Youth of the Committee On Labor and Public Welfare, 94th Congress, 1st Session (1975), pp. 142–45.

110. *New York Times*, Nov. 11, 1934, IV, p. 5.

111. Mona Gardner, "Traffic in Babies," *Collier's* 104 (Sept. 16, 1939): 43.

112. Elisabeth M. Landes and Richard A. Posner, "The Economics of the Baby Shortage," 7 *Journal of Legal Studies* 339 (June 1978). On the similarity of outcome between agency and independent adoptions, see Joe, *Public Policies Toward Adoption*, pp. 48–49; Daniel G. Grove, "Independent Adoption: The Case For the Gray Market," 13 *Villanova Law Review* 123–24 (1967).

113. Hearings Before the Subcommittee on Children and Youth (1975), pp. 2, 3, 580.

114. *See* Margaret V. Turano, "Black-Market Adoptions," 22 *Catholic Lawyer* 54–56 (1976); "Moppets on the Market," pp. 732–34.

115. Bernard Barber, "The Absolutization of the Market: Some Notes on How We Got From There to Here," in G. Dworkin, G. Bermant, and P. Brown, eds., *Markets and Morals* (Washington, D.C.: Hemisphere, 1977),p. 23.

116. Statement by Joseph H. Reid, Executive Director, Child Welfare League of America, in Hearings Before the Subcommittee on Children and Youth (1975), p. 19.

117. "Moppets on the Market," p. 715.

118. Hearings Before the Subcommittee on Children and Youth (1975), p. 4.

119. "Survey of New Jersey Adoption Law," 16 *Rutgers Law Review* 408 (1962) fn. 34; Grove, "Independent Adoption," p. 127. Independent, "gray-market" adoptions are justified as a necessary alternative to often highly bureaucratized and overworked agencies, Robert H. Mnookin, *Child, Family and State* (Boston: Little, Brown, 1978), pp. 621–22. The number of independent placements has significantly diminished. While in 1945 only about one-fourth of nonrelative adoptions were made by authorized child-placing agencies, in 1971, almost 80 percent of all nonrelative adoptions were arranged by agencies. Joseph L. Zarefsky, "Children Acquire New Parents," *The Child* 10(Mar. 1946):143.

120. Letter to the Editor, *Child Welfare League of America Bulletin* 20 (Dec. 1941):9.

121. Georg Simmel, *The Philosophy of Money* (London: Routledge & Kegan Paul, 1978), p. 373.

122. Dorothy Canfield, "Children Without Parents," *Woman's Home Companion* 66(May 1939): 48.

123. *Child Welfare League of America Bulletin* 20(Nov. 1941):9.

124. C. Rollin Zane, "Financial Practices of Children's Agencies," *Child Welfare League of America Bulletin* 25(Oct. 1946):5.

125. Sybil Foster, "Fees for Adoption Service," *Child Welfare League of America Bulletin* 26(May 1947):11.

126. See Michael Shapiro, *Fees in Adoption Practice* (New York: Child Welfare League of America, 1956), p. 12; Eilene F. Corsier, "Fees for Adoption Service," in I. Evelyn Smith, *Readings in Adoption* (New York: Philosophical Library, 1963), pp. 381–82. The average adoption fee charged by a public agency in 1975 was $200–400, and $450–900 for private agencies licensed by the state. Turano, "Black-Market Adoptions," p. 51, fn. 17.

127. See "Cost Plus Service," *Child Welfare League of America Bulletin* (Mar. 1945):12, and "Board Rates-Agency Payments for Foster Care," ibid. (Sept. 1945):12. On the increased use of boarding homes as a preferred alternative to working homes or free foster homes, see Helen Glenn Tyson, "Care of Dependent Children," American Academy of Political and Social Science, *Annals* 212(Nov. 1940):173; Alfred Kadushin, *Child Welfare Services* (New York: Macmillan, 1976), p. 425.

128. Lockridge, *Adopting a Child*, pp. 61–63.

129. Joseph Goldstein, Anna Freud, Albert J. Solnit, *Beyond the Best Interests of the Child* (New York: Free Press, 1979); Kadushin, *Child Welfare Services*, p. 419; Rosemarie Carbine, *Foster Parenting: An Updated Review of the Literature* (New York: Child Welfare League of America, 1980), pp. 2, 30–31; Mnookin, *Child, Family and State*, p. 536, fn. 40; Joe, *Public Policies Toward Adoption*, pp. 27–28. On the unusual blend of altruism and self-interest in foster care, see Richard M. Titmuss, *The Gift Relationship* (New York: Vintage, 1971), pp. 215–16.

130. Esther Glickman, *Child Placement Through Clinically Oriented Casework* (New York: Columbia University Press, 1957), p. 180. See also Dorothy Hutchinson, "Casework Implications in the Use of Money in Child Placing," in *Cherish the Child: Dilemmas of Placement* (Metuchen, NJ: Scarecrow Press, 1972), pp. 67–74; Kadushin, *Child Welfare Services*, p. 417; Alfred Kadushin, "Children in Foster Families and Institutions," in Henry J. Maas, ed., *Social Service Research: Review of Studies* (Washington, D.C.: National Association of Social Workers, 1978), p. 123. On the social class of foster parents, see Carbino, *Foster Parenting*, pp. 3–4. Most foster children come from low-income families.

131. Simmel, *The Philosophy of Money*, p. 405. Adoption subsidies, which since 1968 have provided financial assistance to adoptive parents of children with physical, emotional, or mental handicaps, children of minority groups, and older children, create a similar type of structured ambivalence.

132. Landes and Posner, "Economics of the Baby Shortage," p. 343.

133. Quoted in Lynne McTaggart, *The Baby Brokers* (New York: Dial Press, 1980), p. 318.

Chapter 7

1. E. S. Martin, "Old-Fashioned Children," *Harper's Monthly Magazine* 126(Jan. 1913):242.

2. Carl N. Degler, *At Odds: Women and the Family in America from the Revolution to the Present* (New York: Oxford University Press, 1980), p. 472.

3. Thomas Crump, *The Phenomenon of Money* (London: Routledge & Kegan Paul, 1981), p. 20.

4. Robert Coles, *Migrants, Sharecroppers, Mountaineers*, vol. 2 of *Children of the*

Crisis (Boston: Little, Brown, 1971), p. 63. Lois W. Hoffman and Jean D. Manis's study of the psychological satisfactions of having children in the United States found that 10 percent of the men in their sample and a smaller percentage of the women mentioned the economic-utilitarian advantage of children, "The Value of Children in the United States: A New Approach to the Study of Fertility," *Journal of Marriage and the Family* 41(Aug. 1979), p. 590.

5. Bennett M. Berger and Bruce M. Hackett, "On the Decline of Age Grading in Rural Hippie Communes," in *Family in Transition,* ed. by Arlene S. Skolnick and Jerome H. Skolnick (Boston: Little, Brown, 1977), pp. 427–41.

6. *New York Times,* Mar. 23, 1981, B15; Sheri Singer and Tom Alderman, "How To Get Your Child in TV Commercials," *Good Housekeeping* 197(July 1983):87. In their study of Oakland children, Elliot A. Medrich, Judith Roizen, Victor Rubin, and Stuart Buckley, *The Serious Business of Growing Up* (Berkeley, CA: University of California Press, 1982), found that only 15 percent of the sample held regular jobs; these were mostly paper routes or babysitting, pp. 236, 149. On class similarities in the occupational world of children, see ibid., p. 138. Bernard Goldstein and Jack Oldham, *Children and Work* (New Brunswick, NJ: Transaction, 1979), pp. 78, found only minor differences by socioeconomic status.

7. Vance Packard, *Our Endangered Children* (Boston: Little, Brown, 1983), Neil Postman, *The Disappearance of Childhood* (New York: Laurel Book, 1982); Marie Winn, *Children Without Childhood* (New York: Pantheon, 1983); Letty Cottin Pogrebin, "Do Americans Hate Children?" *Ms.* 12(Nov. 1983): 47–50, 126–27; Germaine Greer, *Sex and Destiny* (New York: Harper & Row, 1984), p. 2. See also David Elkind, *The Hurried Child* (Reading, PA: Addison-Wesley, 1981).

8. W. Norton Grubb and Marvin Lazerson, *Broken Promises* (New York: Basic Books, 1982), pp. 51–52, 85. For a different view of this issue, see Gilbert Y. Steiner, *The Children's Cause* (Washington, D.C.; Brookings Institution, 1976).

9. Pogrebin, "Do Americans Hate Children?," pp. 49–50.

10. Packard, *Our Endangered Children,* p. 23.

11. Winn, *Children Without Childhood,* pp. 5, 196. See also Postman, *The Disappearance of Childhood.*

12. Greer, *Sex and Destiny,* pp. 3–6,27.

13. Richard Farson, *Birthrights* (New York: Penguin, 1978), pp. 154, 162, 174.

14. Arlene Skolnick, *The Intimate Environment* (Boston: Little, Brown, 1978), p. 331.

15. Sarane Spence Boocock, "Children in Contemporary Society," in *Rethinking Childhood* (Boston: Little, Brown, 1976), ed. by Arlene Skolnick, p. 434; Sarane Spence Boocock, "The Social Context of Childhod," Proceedings of the American Philosophical Society, 119(Nov. 1975):428. See also William Stephens, *Our Children Should Be Working* (Springield, IL: Charles C Thomas, 1979); Elise Boulding, *Children's Rights and the Wheel of Life* (New Brunswick, NJ: Transaction, 1979); David Stern, Sandra Smith, and Fred Doolittle, "How Children Used to Work," 39 *Law and Contemporary Problems* 93–117 (1975); White House Conference on Children (Washington, D.C., Government Printing Office, 1970).

16. M. Engel, G. Marsden, and S. Woodaman, "Children Who Work and the Concept of Work Style," *Psychiatry* 30(Nov. 1967):392–404; and "Orientation to Work in Children," *American Journal of Orthopsychiatry* 38(Jan. 1968):137–43; Jerome Kagan, "The Child in the Family," *Daedalus* (Spring 1977):43.

17. Beatrice B. Whiting and John W. M. Whiting, *Children of Six Cultures* (Cambridge, MA: Harvard University Press, 1975), p. 106; Glen H. Elder, Jr., *Chil-*

dren of the Great Depression (Chicago: University of Chicago Press, 1974), pp. 71, 80, 291.

18. Alvin Toffler, *The Third Wave* (New York: Bantam, 1980), p. 220; Robert H. Mnookin, *Child, Family and State* (Boston: Little, Brown, 1978), p. 655. See also "Note: Child Labor Laws—Time To Grow Up," 59 *Minnesota Law Review* 575(1975); Peter Edelman, "Child Labor Revisited," *The Nation* 235(Aug. 21–28, 1982):136–38.

19. Unpublished data, Bureau of Labor Statistics, Mar. 1983; Sheila B. Kamerman and Cheryl D. Hayes, eds., *Families That Work* (Washington, D.C.: National Academy Press, 1982), p. 14; Sheila B. Kamerman and Alfred J. Kahn, *Child Care, Family Benefits, and Working Parents* (New York: Columbia University Press, 1981), p. 8.

20. Valerie Polakow Suransky, *The Erosion of Childhood* (Chicago: University of Chicago Press, 1982), p. 189; Winn, *Children Without Childhood*, p. 121; Postman, *The Disappearance of Childhood*, p. 151.

21. Degler, *At Odds*, p. 461. See Judith Blake, "Is Zero Preferred? American Attitudes Toward Childlessness in the 1970s," *Journal of Marriage and the Family* (May 1979):245–57.

22. Degler, *At Odds*, p. 471.

23. Eleanor Berman, *The Cooperating Family* (Englewood Cliffs, NJ: Prentice-Hall, 1977), pp. 13, 136.

24. Ibid., p. 31.

25. Philip Blumstein and Pepper Schwartz, *American Couples* (New York: William Morrow, 1983), p. 146. Some studies, however, suggest that there is a reduction of sex typing in the division of household work when the wife is employed, especially if she earns well. See Catherine E. Ross, John Mirowsky, Joan Huber, "Dividing Work, Sharing Work, and In-Between: Marriage Patterns and Depression," *American Sociological Review* 48(Dec. 1983):809–823 and Laura Lein, *Families Without Villains* (Lexington, MA: Lexington Books, 1984), p. 41.

26. See William H. Gauger and Kathryn E. Walker, *The Dollar Value of Household Work*, Information Bulletin 60 (Ithaca, NY: New York State College of Human Ecology, Cornell University, 1977). Medrich et al., in their valuable study of children's lives in Oakland, California, found that children of working mothers, especially daughters, increased somewhat their contributions to housework. But they found almost no difference in the level of children's chore responsibilities between one and two parent households, *The Serious Business of Growing Up*, pp. 142–44.

27. Sally Helgesen, "Do Your Parents Ask Too Much of You?," *Seventeen* (Apr. 1982):176–77; Barbara Delaniter, "Should You Pay Your Kids to Help?," *Working Mother* 2(May 1979):44–45.

28. Carrie Tuhy, "The Star Wars Generation Takes on Inflation," *Money* 10(July 1981):88.

29. Ibid., p. 92; Rosalie Radomsky, "Children's Allowances: What the Economists Pay," *New York Times*, Mar. 14, 1982; Medrich et al., *The Serious Business of Growing Up*, p. 149. Goldstein and Oldham found no significant differences by socioeconomic status in the size of children's allowances, *Children and Work*, p. 71.

30. "You *Can* Get a Job!," *Penny Power* 2(June–July 1982):8; Berman, *The Cooperating Family*, p. 98.

INDEX